ACTING LOCALLY

Local campaigns are the most persistent and ubiquit͏̲ ͏̲ ͏̲ ͏̲ environmental contention. National and transnational mobilisations come and go and the attention they receive from mass media ebbs and flows, but local campaigns persist. Indeed, in periods in which national environmental movements are in abeyance or, more often, are neglected by the media, it is local campaigns that serve as reminders that environmental issues have not been quietly absorbed by bureaucratic administration and representative democratic politics but remain as matters of more fundamental contention. The persistence or re-emergence of local campaigns is also a reminder that it remains possible to mobilise people around environmental issues, and they have often served as sources of innovation in and re-invigoration of national organisations that have allegedly been co-opted by the powerful and incorporated into the established political and administrative system.

But local environmental campaigns have been relatively neglected in the scientific literature. Drawing on examples from Britain, France, Greece, Ireland and Italy, this volume seeks to redress that neglect by examining the networks among actors and organisations that connect local mobilizations to the larger environmental movement and political systems, the ways in which local disputes are framed in order to connect with national and global issues, and the persistent impacts of the peculiarities of place upon environmental campaigns.

This book was previously published as a special issue of *Environmental Politics*

Christopher Rootes is Professor of Environmental Politics and Political Sociology and Director of the Centre for the Study of Social and Political Movements at the University of Kent, Canterbury.

ACTING LOCALLY

Local environmental mobilizations and campaigns

Edited by Christopher Rootes

Routledge
Taylor & Francis Group

LONDON AND NEW YORK

First published 2008 by Routledge
2 Park Square, Milton Park, Abingdon, Oxfordshire OX14 4RN

Simultaneously published in the USA and Canada by Routledge
711 Third Avenue, New York, NY 10017

First issued in paperback 2014

Routledge is an imprint of the Taylor & Francis Group, an informa business

© 2008 Edited by Christopher Rootes

Typeset in Times by KnowledgeWorks Global Limited, Chennai, India

British Library Cataloguing in Publication Data
A catalogue record for this book is available from the British Library

ISBN 978-0-415-45764-4 (hbk)
ISBN 978-0-415-76205-2 (pbk)

CONTENTS

Preface

This volume has been a long time gestating, and it owes its realisation to two estimable European institutions: the European Commission's Directorate General Research (EC DG-R) and the European Consortium for Political Research (ecpr).

My own interest in local environmental politics goes back a long way, but it was considerably stimulated by the EC-funded FP4 project on *Policy-making and Environmental Movements: The Case of Waste Management* (ENV4-CT96-0239), in which I collaborated with Enrique Laraña. The EC's generous funding of the *Transformation of Environmental Activism (TEA)* project (ENV4-CT97-0514) brought the opportunity to develop that interest and to situate it in some historical, organisational and political context, and, directly and indirectly, it first brought together in research collaboration several of the authors whose work is assembled here. That network was consolidated and extended by two workshops at the ecpr Joint Sessions, in Grenoble in 2001 and in Nicosia in 2006.

Institutions make things possible, but it is individuals who make them happen. I am enormously indebted to the contributors to this volume, to the other partners in our research projects, and to the many contributors to the workshops whose work is not represented here; I have learned from them all. I am, however, especially grateful to those people who have given advice and support during the process of selecting and editing the contents of this volume, especially John Barry, JoAnn Carmin, Mario Diani, Brian Doherty, Graeme Hayes, Clare Saunders and John Scott.

Christopher Rootes
Harbledown, Canterbury, Kent

Acting Locally: The Character, Contexts and Significance of Local Environmental Mobilisations

CHRISTOPHER ROOTES

Local campaigns are the most persistent and ubiquitous forms of environmental contention. National and transnational mobilisations come and go and the attention they receive from mass media ebbs and flows, but local campaigns are persistently recurrent. Indeed, in periods in which national environmental movements are in abeyance or, more often, are neglected by the media, it is local campaigns that serve as reminders that environmental issues have not been quietly absorbed by bureaucratic administration and representative democratic politics but remain as matters of fundamental contention. The recurrence of local campaigns is also a reminder that it remains possible to mobilise people around environmental issues, and they have often served as sources of innovation in and re-invigoration of national organisations that have allegedly been co-opted by the powerful and incorporated into established political and administrative systems.

Christopher Rootes is grateful to Clare Saunders for comments on an earlier draft.

Yet local environmental campaigns have been relatively neglected in the scientific literature. Drawing on examples from Britain, France, Greece, Ireland and Italy, this volume seeks to redress that neglect by examining the networks among actors and organisations that connect local mobilisations to the larger environmental movement and political systems, the complex and recursive relationships between place and contentious campaigns, and the ways in which local disputes are framed in order to create or connect with national and global issues.

The evidence presented and discussed here is derived by the employment of a variety of research methodologies, including ethnography, surveys, interviews and participant observation. Participant observation of protests and campaigns and interviews with participants are invaluable to the collection of data that records and makes comprehensible their rich particularity, but while many more or less systematic ethnographies of local environmental campaigns and/ or groups have been undertaken, few have found their way into the published monographic literature.[1]

One reason for this is that, whilst ethnographic methods provide the foundation for understanding local environmental campaigns, they do not by themselves enable us to generalise. In order to situate particular local campaigns within the bigger picture of contention over environmental issues, researchers have recourse to analysis of the public record of events, principally as it appears in 'quality' newspapers, but also in state archives and activist media.

Protest event analysis and ethnographic methods can provide the clues but not the answers to one question, crucial to our understanding of the character of local environmental campaigns and their place in the larger universe of contention over environmental issues: the relationship of local environmental organisations to other local groups, political actors and institutions, and to national, regional and supranational environmental organisations. It is here that network analyses of surveys that focus upon organisational linkages of various kinds and at various levels are invaluable.

Local Campaigns and Environmental Movements

The relationship between local environmental campaigns and national or transnational environmental movements is complicated. Most of the national environmental organisations that we have become accustomed to refer to collectively as the 'environmental movement' did not begin as local campaign organisations. Typically, they began as elite initiatives, inspired by an appreciation of the urgency of environmental issues generally ignored or neglected by governments and citizens alike, and often informed by leading edge scientific knowledge.

The emergence of WWF is a case in point. Worldwide Fund for Nature (WWF) was designed by its conservationist founders, with the aid of its royal patrons, to raise funds for scientific research on conservation, notably in support of the IUCN (International Union for the Conservation of Nature). True, when it was launched in 1961, it was by means of an appeal through the pages of a mass-market tabloid newspaper, and though it solicited donations from the general public, sought a mass 'membership', and aspired to generalise concern about vanishing iconic species and, by extension, diminishing biodiversity, it never pretended to be a grassroots organisation.

Even Friends of the Earth (FoE) did not grow from the grassroots. Founded in 1969 by David Brower after he failed to persuade the members of the Sierra Club, of which he was Director, to support his active, but autocratic, campaigning, FoE was conceived as an international franchise with head-quarters in the US. Brower personally recruited the founders of the initial European branches of FoE, and it was only after some persuasion that he agreed that they should be autonomous of their US parent (Lamb, 1996: 37–8). Even so, it was more by accident than design that FoE in England became a decentralised, grassroots-friendly organisation (Lamb, 1996: 97–9).[2]

The US is perhaps the extreme case in the extent to which its major environmental organisations are the products of elite initiatives. As Bosso (2005) observes, most national environmental organisations in the US were initiatives of foundations or government agencies, and were designed to fill gaps that those foundations or agencies perceived in the representation of environmental interests, principally in respect of the conservation of the natural environment. Dependent for funding upon foundations or government agencies, these national environmental organisations collectively constituted something closer to a public interest lobby or 'advocacy community' than anything that might sensibly be described as an environmental movement. The involvement of their supporters and 'membership' was something most national environmental organisations concerned themselves with only when US politics lurched to the right, and government and foundation funds for environmental conservation dried up as a consequence, under President Ronald Reagan. Even the Sierra Club, which had always been a membership organisation and had some semblance of internal democracy, became enmeshed in the Washington, DC lobby and appeared more interested in litigation than mobilisation (Dowie, 1995).

In reaction against the disconnection between conservationist and preserva-tionist national environmental organisations on the one hand and grassroots concerns with the human consequences of environmental degradation on the other, what has come to be called the environmental justice (EJ) movement developed in the US. Growing directly out of grassroots experience of struggle against industrial pollution, its key organisations have been designed to give aid, support and advice to other local campaigners, but they have not set out to build a new formal, centralised organisation, much less to join the Washington lobby circuit. Its organisational form is not the bureaucratic organisation but the network (Schlosberg, 1999).

But if this attests to the divisions between the established national environmental organisations and the grassroots in the US, there is other evidence that demonstrates a connection, albeit lagged, between them. Carmin (1999) found that in the years 1975–90, unconventional actions by voluntary organisations tended to be followed, after a lag of one or two years, by action on the same issues by professionalised environmental organisations. Thus local campaigners, by highlighting otherwise neglected issues, appear to perform a 'discovery' role for national organisations that are better placed to shape policy agendas and to affect policy outcomes. While the national organisations 'provide a foundation and offer stability to the movement', and so serve a crucial function, it is local groups that, by identifying and responding to emerging issues, establish the pace and tone of the movement (Carmin, 1999: 118).

If Carmin's account of local–national interactions in the US suggests that professionalised national environmental organisations tend to play a reactive rather than agenda-setting role, it is nevertheless apparent that the relationship between local campaigns and national organisations has been symbiotic rather than exclusive. Of course, what is true for the US in one period may not be the same at all times or in all other countries, and the relationship between local campaigns and national organisations therefore requires further and recurrent examination.

Clare Saunders' contribution to this volume examines relations between national organisations and local and regional environmental groups in two contrasting parts of the greater London area. Employing network analysis on data collected by administering questionnaires to organisations at each level, she found that national groups dealt mainly with other national organisations, and regional organisations mainly with national organisations. Thus it appears that the role regional organisations play in networking and coordinating among the various local groups is secondary to the role regional organisations play as intermediaries between the national and the local. Local organisations were, unsurprisingly, involved in asymmetric exchanges with national and regional organisations. But that is not to say that local groups were – or felt – unsupported by national organisations. On the contrary, some national organisations – most notably, FoE, Greenpeace and the Campaign to Protect Rural England – go to some lengths to recruit, train and encourage active supporters at the local level, albeit that they differ in the degrees of autonomy they concede to local groups, particularly in their choice of issues about which to campaign. FoE has been increasingly willing to encourage community involvement in local campaigns, even where no FoE group is involved, and, in recent years, no doubt influenced by a political climate in which there has been increasing discussion about the need to encourage the development of 'active citizenship', even Greenpeace has become more concerned to encourage local activists to initiate local campaigns. Nevertheless, more generally, Greenpeace has been rigorous, not only in the defence of its reputation, but also in restricting its active support to local campaigners working on issues squarely within the national organisation's campaigning priorities, and treating local active supporters as a pool of labour for its own campaigns.

Local groups affiliated to diverse national organisations collaborate in local campaign actions, irrespective of the issue specialisations of their national parent organisations, sometimes in defiance of advice from regional or national organisers to avoid contact with certain rival organisations or more radical direct action groups whose unconventional and sometimes confrontational forms of action might sully the reputations of the respectable and established. Nor do local groups confine themselves to information provided by their national organisations, instead seeking what they consider to be the most authoritative sources of information on any particular issue. In general, this has been increasingly characteristic of an environmental movement sector that has in Britain come to practise a specialised division of labour within a generally cooperative rather than competitive milieu.

Nevertheless, local organisations' interactions with other local organisations were significantly greater in northwest London, where there was, at the time of the research, an active campaign (against the proposed expansion of Heathrow airport) in which many were involved, than in southeast London where there was at the time no active campaign of broad common interest. However, we know from previous research (Rootes *et al.*, 2001) that, when in the recent past there were active campaigns in southeast London (against the proposed routing of the Channel Tunnel Rail Link through south London, and, especially, against the proposed commercial redevelopment of Crystal Palace; Saunders, 2007), interactions among local environmental organisations were frequent and intense. Thus it appears clear that it is the presence of active campaigns of wide local concern that encourages interaction among local environmental organisations and reduces their reliance on and interest in national organisations.

Suddenly imposed grievances might well stimulate action where previously there was none, but this is not to suggest that local environmental organisations are simply NIMBY campaigners[3] at times when there is a pressing local issue. It may simply be an ecological effect – intensity of local interactions leaving little energy for attending to national organisations – but it is likely also to reflect the construction of social capital that occurs in the course of direct interaction at the local level and that leads local coalitions to generate or attract their own resources and expertise and so to lean less on national organisations. It probably also reflects the fact that, as local campaigns develop, so local activists develop knowledge and expertise relevant to their specific issues that is more directly useful to their campaigning than is the more general and context-independent knowledge that national organisations are most likely able to provide.

Campaigns are shaped by the characteristics of localities, but they also shape the environmental identities of communities and local environmental networks. Major campaigns may, depending on the circumstances, summon into existence groups and organisations that may leave more or less durable legacies by reshaping local environmental identities and producing new organisations and relationships among them. The campaign against the

Channel Tunnel Rail Link was a turning point in the recovery of the identity of southeast London as an urban environment and a series of communities worth preserving, rather than simply a rundown area with concentrated social deprivation, the poor relation in London's renaissance. Indeed, the threat of their loss awakened an enhanced appreciation of the Georgian and Victorian streetscapes so characteristic of southeast London, and led to the extension of local conservation areas. As a result of that campaign, southeast London became home to a rich and diverse range of environmental amenity societies and groups.[4] This was reinforced by the later campaign over Crystal Palace, albeit that in the periods of abeyance that followed the success of these campaigns, the intensity of networking diminished and a number of groups disappeared (Saunders, 2007).

Environmental Networks and Others

Environmental movements are networks, and several contributions here illuminate the ways in which local organisations and campaigns are linked to and help to constitute geographically more extensive environmental movements. But even in their local actions, local environmental organisations do not operate in a vacuum. However, although some attention has been paid to the implications of local political structures for the outcomes of mobilisations, much less has been given to the broader organisational fields within which local groups act. Mario Diani and Elisa Rambaldo's contribution to this volume illuminates such local networks for two quite different British cities and one Italian city, and traces their distinct characteristics to locally distinctive structures of political opportunities.

The principal purpose of Diani and Rambaldo's contribution is, however, to illuminate the conditions under which networks of local organisations constitute a social movement. For it to be sensible to speak of the existence of a social movement, it is necessary not merely that organisations should be more or less closely linked in alliances and collaboration in collective action, but that they should share a sense of identity that enables organisations to feel part of the same enterprise even in the absence of action, and that lays the basis for possible future collective action. If, they suggest, mobilisations on environmental issues were conducted by organisations practising a clear division of labour, with few joint initiatives and little in the way of shared identity, the dynamics of their interaction would be merely organisational, and it would make little sense to speak of an environmental movement. As Saunders makes clear, that is scarcely the situation that exists in London, where there is *both* a division of labour among environmental organisations *and* a substantial number of joint ventures, as well as an overriding sense of common purpose that speaks to the existence of a shared identity. But what is true of (two areas of) London is not necessarily true of other cities.

Distinguishing between movement and organisational dynamics and classifying organisations accordingly, Diani and Rambaldo find that in Bristol and Verona movement relationships characterise and extend beyond those organisations whose primary identity is environmental. However, in Glasgow the strength of the competing agenda of a social movement dynamic focused upon social and economic justice is such that even organisations that, from the outside, might be expected to identify and act as part of the environmental movement do not reliably do so, but are instead implicated in dense networks among a more heterogeneous assortment of civic organisations that do not themselves identify as primarily environmental, even where they may be involved in action on environmental issues. Thus, while it makes sense to speak of local environmental movements in Bristol and Verona, it does not in Glasgow.

This is a salutary reminder that local organisational fields shape alliances, collective action and identities, and that relationships among organisations in one locality cannot simply be read off from knowledge of their namesakes' identity and relationships in another. Local contexts do not merely dictate the possibilities of local alliances; they shape the very identities of local activists and the organisations to which they belong.

Among the more potentially potent actors in local environmental campaigners' organisational fields are the members and representatives of national political parties. The extent to which they have been involved, or even interested, in matters of local environmental contention varies, but it has been supposed to be especially great in the recently democratised states of southern Europe where civil society was believed, as a result of years of authoritarian rule and rampant clientelism, to be underdeveloped, and where political parties were alleged to be dominant in all kinds of political participation. However, as Maria Kousis demonstrates in her contribution to this volume, it is apparent that the relationship between local environmental protests and national politics in Greece is more complicated than has often been supposed. The claim that Greece is a country in which civil society is weak and party politics is all-pervasive is contradicted by the fact that even of the local environmental protest reported in national media, only a minority of cases involved political parties, and that the proportion that did declined substantially with the normalisation of Greek democratic politics during and after the 1980s. Nor does the evidence unambiguously support the contention that environmental protests flourish when parties of the left are out of power and are subdued when they are in office.

If political parties only sometimes play a role in local environmental contention, our awareness of the extent to which they do so is shaped by the sources of data upon which we rely. Thus, comparing the character of local environmental protests in relatively highly politicised Heraklion County in Crete as it appears from reports in the national press with the more comprehensive picture constructed from the archival records of the various local state agencies reveals that only a small proportion of the cases of environmental contention recorded in official archives is ever exposed to the glare of the national media spotlight. Media attention is systematically biased toward contention in which representatives of political parties are involved, that are more long-running and confrontational, and that involve major issues of national or transnational contention. If the prevalence of environmental contention that does not involve political parties is any indicator, then civil society in Greece appears to be alive and well; the involvement of the parties, where it occurs, appears to be a mostly opportunistic attempt to keep in step with the larger popular mobilisations.

Local Contexts and Direct Action

If local environmental organisations are influenced by the organisational fields within which they operate, what of those environmental campaigners who abjure formal organisation as a matter of principle, and who are committed to a politics of (predominantly non-violent) direct action? Brian Doherty, Alex Plows and Derek Wall examine the hitherto neglected local dimension of environmental direct action (EDA) in Britain. Those who are committed to EDA are less interested in influencing public policy than in mobilising members of the public and creating a culture of resistance to corporate capitalism. Moreover, their anarchism entails a large measure of individualism and spontaneity, and so it is not surprising that they should not seek the attention of mass media or, indeed, be so organised that they might meet the needs of journalists. The result is that the great majority of their actions that are reported in the activist media go unremarked by the national press. Basing their account on an analysis of reports in activist newsletters, Doherty, Plows and Wall develop an unprecedentedly comprehensive account of EDA networks and their actions in three representative localities: Manchester, Oxford and North Wales.

Given their disdain for formal organisation, it is not surprising that local EDA networks should be disconnected from the organisations that form the core of the broad environmental movement. Even when they participated in local campaigns, in Manchester and Oxford they mostly acted alone. However, in North Wales, where the critical mass for EDA was smaller and the number of local targets was fewer, they were more inclined to enter campaign alliances with other, more conventional actors and organisations, albeit that such alliances do not appear to have inhibited EDA activists from militant action even where it jeopardised those alliances. In this, and in the greater propensity of the North Wales activists to participate in actions beyond their locality, the constraints and opportunities of differing local contexts are apparent. Yet the incidence of EDA over time does not appear to be explicable by changes in structures of political opportunities. Rather – and this is as much a reflection of the relatively small size of those networks as of their dispositions toward the wider world of politics – the pattern of EDA action appears to be better explained in terms of the dynamics of small groups: exhaustion following periods of intense campaigning, and interpersonal relations. The apparent decline of EDA after 2000 is similarly explicable. EDA was sustained by intense interpersonal bonds among people who had grown to political adulthood in activist milieu, and so, as ageing activists retired, it was difficult to recruit from successor generations whose experience was very different.

If EDA has been relatively disconnected from the broader environmental movement, it is partly because it does not conceive of itself as exclusively environmental. Indeed, EDA activists often refer to themselves as part of the 'direct action movement', a movement defined by the priority it gives to a form of political action and a lifestyle rather than by the themes of its actions (cf. Doherty, 2002). In this they constitute part of an activist subculture that has sustained protests across a broad range of issues, notably those otherwise associated with the anti-capitalist, anti-war and global justice movements.

Place and Protest

Similarly pluralistic in its movement affiliations is the succession of campaigns that have developed in and around the Larzac region of southern France. The Larzac has been a site of protest for more than three decades, since the earliest campaigns of resistance against the proposed expansion of the military encampment there during the 1970s, but as Gaël Franquemagne describes, it has also become a symbol of protest such that events and place have been effectively conjoined. Larzac has thus come to signify not merely a place with a particular topography, beauty and cultural significance but a spirit of resistance, most recently associated with the campaigns against globalisation and genetically modified organisms and in favour of sustainability, fair trade, a globalisation from below, and a way of life more in tune with natural rhythms than the hyper-mobility of globalising capitalism. Thus a region that was occupied by draft resisters and some of the 'back to the earth' enthusiasts of the counterculture that emerged in France from the ferment of 1968 became the site of an iconic struggle against militarism, capitalism, colonialism and globalisation, long before José Bové, who settled there in the 1970s, became the internationally celebrated spokesman for the *Confédération paysanne* and an iconic figure in the global justice movement. Particularly in the latter stages of its development, and in its identification with the complex phenomenon of the '*malbouffe*', the Larzac contention has come to represent a contention and a global worldview to which the relationship to nature is central. However, transcending 'the environment' as we have more usually and narrowly conceived it, it centrally embraces social concerns, celebrating community and criticising industrialism and technocracy.

In a strict and narrow sense, the Larzac case might, especially in its early stages, be considered to be only incidentally a local environmental campaign, but it is illustrative of the ways in which the conception of 'environment' may be enlarged so as to encompass not merely the physical space but the meanings attached to and the struggle associated with that space. Moreover, it highlights the ways in which places become invested with meaning and so justify their defence against threatened encroachment, as well as becoming resources for future mobilisation.

The case of Rossport, County Mayo, on the west coast of Ireland, which Mark Garavan discusses, may not yet have acquired iconic status comparable with that of the Larzac but it raises similar issues. There too 'the environment' is only one element, and not always the most important, in local campaigners' resistance against the construction of a gas refinery and pipeline that they fear will violate their sense of place, destroy their community and way of life, and present unacceptable risks to their health.

Inevitably, in some respects the Rossport case is peculiar. It occurs in a country in which environmental movement organisations have struggled to develop because the political culture remained dominated by nationalism, not least because Ireland has only very recently escaped from centuries of poverty and emigration to become home to one of the fastest growing and, in per capita terms, most affluent economies in Europe. Irish 'localism' was widely seen as a mark of the economic backwardness it shared with southern Europe. Most environmental protest is local but, as Garavan's analysis shows, in Ireland even nationally reported environmental protest is local in the level of mobilisation, the scope of the underlying issue and the level of the target of protest, to a greater extent than in any country but Greece among the seven other EU states for which systematic analyses of environmental protest have been conducted (Rootes, 2003).

Yet it is by no means the case that local environmental protest in Ireland is either ineffective or conservative in its implications simply because it is overwhelmingly local. In the 1970s, local resistance to the proposed siting of a nuclear power station was generalised into a successful campaign against the introduction of nuclear energy into Ireland, and more recently local campaigns against particular proposals for waste incinerators have engendered more widespread scepticism toward such purportedly 'modern' means of waste management. A single vigorous campaign may thus inspire wider resistance so that a facility that cannot be sited in the place first proposed for it may become impossible to site anywhere.

Moreover, fundamental issues about the nature of the 'good life' and about the costs of economic development and industrialised modernity are often implicit in local resistance to specific proposals, and in this Irish case they are made uncommonly explicit. It is this that encourages Garavan to believe that the Rossport case might become a rallying point for a more than merely local campaign of opposition to prevailing conceptions of 'progress' and 'development'.

Although their initial opposition to the development was instinctive, the Rossport community's framing of the issues changed as the dispute developed. It was not so much that the community mobilised to defend its longstanding interests as that the threat the development posed forced the community to reflect on its identity and its relationship to place. The sense of community and place thus was not primordial so much as it was realised in the course of mobilisation against the threat to its existence.

Building Identity through Local Action

This character of local resistance as at once reactive to threat and creative of community is familiar from accounts of local campaigns everywhere. It is clearly apparent in Donatella della Porta and Gianni Piazza's accounts of the struggles against the high speed railway line through the Val di Susa and the bridge across the Messina Straits. They, like Garavan, focus upon the ways in which identity, interests and discourses are formed in the course of and as a result of struggle.

Like Garavan, della Porta and Piazza challenge the accuracy of the characterisation of these local campaigns as essentially NIMBY protests. NIMBY, as Kate Burningham (2000) has argued, is not an analytical characterisation but a political label stuck by the impatient politician or policy-maker upon those whose resistance spoils the grand schemes of the planners and architects of policy. Defence of one's own habitat may be an instinctive reaction, but local people have good reasons for resisting schemes that would so change the local environment that their well-being and their livelihoods would be jeopardised. These protests would be vulnerable to the NIMBY charge if they ended with the defence of immediate habitat. But they did not. Not only did they develop identity and reflexively recover a sense of community in the course of struggle, but they also developed more profound understandings of the issues that were at stake. Challenging the subordination of environmental concerns to the imperatives of economic development that such projects entail, these people who would pay the price of particular developments were thus stimulated to question the costs of development in general. Challenging the pro-development lobbies' conception of the public interest and of progress, the protesters assert the necessity of prioritising use values over exchange values, well-being over economic development.

This goes to the heart of local resistance. For locals, the fundamental issue is their defence of their habitat, their identity rooted in a sense of place, and their refusal to become 'rootless cosmopolitans'. This is perhaps the central disjunction of our increasingly globalised age: we are governed by political, corporate and intellectual elites who celebrate their cosmopolitanism and who scorn all resistance to the imperatives of 'progress' by those who wish to conserve those things that give value and meaning to their lives and who either reject or cannot imagine the purported advantages of the hyper-mobility that is the lifestyle and vision of those elites. This resistance is not simply selfish conservatism, but it is instead informed by an appreciation of what it takes to live sustainably in an environmentally imperilled world. In the words of one of the Rossport Five, 'The whole point of community is not moving on: community is rooted and so builds up strategies and implementations for survival' (O'Seighin, quoted by Garavan, this volume).

The fundamental divide between use and exchange values, between levels and conceptions of identity and interests, provides motives for resistance. These are not made more intelligible or tractable by labelling them 'NIMBY'.

Indeed, they may not be tractable at all. Much has been written about the value of participatory mechanisms to efforts to resolve disputes and dilemmas over the siting of locally unwanted, 'bad neighbour' industrial and waste facilities, but it is striking that the most genuine of these efforts produced no resolution; after all the reasonable discussions and agreements in principle, the dilemmas remained, and those who were potentially adversely affected would not fall quietly on their swords (Renn *et al.*, 1998). The transient, exploitative culture, rooted in exchange values, of globalising capitalism and the culture of rooted, sustainable communities are simply irreconcilable, reflecting two radically opposed conceptions of being-in-the-world.

Environment and Democracy

Local struggles over environmental issues may be misunderstood if characterised as environmental struggles alone, for it is often the environmental issue that is the touchpaper for a much more far-reaching explosion of grievances. Indeed, it may often be almost accidental that the struggle becomes represented as 'environmental' at all; in many places in the global South, environmental issues are part and parcel of popular movements that only rarely take the form of 'environmental movements' (Haynes, 1999; cf. Doyle, 2005). If 'identity' is constructed in the course of struggle, so 'the environment' and the 'environmental' may be as well (Burningham & O'Brien, 1994). If there is a pattern, it is that popular local struggles emerge along the faultlines most prominent in a country at a particular time; in the global North the environmental faultline has become discursively salient, whilst in the global South it still competes with those of human rights and democracy.

On the evidence presented here by Garavan and by della Porta and Piazza, so it still does in Ireland and Italy. In both countries, local campaigners have articulated a critique of the shortcomings of a purportedly democratic system that has denied them voice. The complaint about the shortcomings of representative democracy in dealing with land-use planning issues is, however, almost universal. In national policy debates, conflicts of interest may be resolved, usually by appeals to a larger public interest, but arguments about national or transnational environmental policy necessarily have a somewhat abstract character, devoid from considerations of the peculiarities of place and the interests of the people who inhabit it. But the *implementation* of environmental policy is necessarily local; the local is where the rubber of policy meets the road of obdurate local circumstances.

Garavan argues that, in Ireland, local struggles may be only incidentally 'environmental', indeed that to label them 'environmental' may be to obscure the much wider constellation of interests and issues involved. In his discussion of the Rossport case, he shows how a sense of place and community is invoked in a discourse of resistance to 'outside' intrusion in which the rhetoric of 'the environment' finds no resonance. Local protests, he and other observers of Irish struggles argue, are a series of defences of place that have not (yet) been subsumed by a larger environmental movement or by a discourse of ecological resistance. Yet Garavan concludes by suggesting that such local instances of resistance may nevertheless be linked to others in 'reactive alliances' that might create a new 'global network of resistance corresponding to (and unintentionally created by) the contemporary global configuration of power'.

This latter argument is uncomfortably redolent of the utopian element of Marx's theory of the development of proletarian class consciousness; after all the evidence of the persistent particularisms of local protests, we are tantalised with the prospect that they might, somehow, be transmuted from a recognition by local people of their common interests, through their identification of a common enemy, to the realisation of a collective consciousness of the people/ class as a whole that transcends and subordinates their particular, local interests, perhaps even on a global scale. It is a matter of fine judgement whether that is possible, or whether the persistence of localism will continue to divide people and communities one from another even as they are severally oppressed, exploited and deracinated by globalising capital and its willing servants, the governments of nation states. The dilemma of the strength of a 'sense of place' and of community is that it may more assuredly inhibit the forging of the translocal links that are essential to the effectiveness of campaigns about environmental issues than foster them. It becomes a wager between optimism and pessimism.

Della Porta and Piazza present us with two Italian cases that do appear to encourage optimism, insofar as they have succeeded in developing translocal linkages and a connection with the putative global justice movement in a way that is, in the Irish case, only a gleam in the commentator's eye. What makes the Irish and Italian cases so different? How is it possible that in Italy local concerns have been effectively mobilised in an argument that has apparently successfully challenged ideas of the 'greater public good' inherent in large-scale development projects? One difference is in the respective communities' prior experience of unifying campaigns, icons and rhetoric. In the Val di Susa, campaigners were able to invoke the memory of the Resistance to Nazi occupation. In Ireland, nationalism and republicanism have been invoked, but both are also claimed by the proponents of development. Another striking difference is that whereas there is a rich and strong tradition of left politics in Italy, the left in Ireland, weakened by the competing political claims of republicanism and nationalism, is neither a potent ally nor a source of inspiration. National histories and 'political cultures' provide or withhold resources just as surely as political opportunity structures provide or foreclose opportunities to act and to realise objectives.

The Italian protesters are also able to deploy arguments about the waste of public money in projects that will be economically useless or worse, and to invoke suspicions of corruption, alleging that the beneficiaries will be construction companies or even the mafia. Against projects that they are able to represent as anachronistic, hangovers from an era of development by means of symbolic mega-projects fixated upon the speed of physical mobility, Italian campaigners are able to advance images of alternative futures that are not simply recapitulations of the pre-industrial past. Because it is private money that funds the County Mayo gas installations, such arguments are not available to the Irish protesters, and they have more difficulty in proposing alternatives that appear to be anything other than the preservation of things as they are. Both Italian and Irish cases represent the collision between a high industrial vision of modernity and a more sustainable alternative, but the Italians appear more successfully to have rebutted the charge that they are simply against development.

Transcending the Local, Universalising the Particular

The proposition that the universalisation of grievances and issues is a condition of success of local campaigns is well entrenched in the literature (see e.g. Walsh *et al.*, 1993, 1997; Gordon & Jasper, 1996). Yet, whether the employment of universalistic discourse is the result of instrumental, strategic choice or the developmental outcome of a learning process, the universalisation of claims and grievances does not necessarily lead to success. Indeed, the constraints of planning law very often mean that it is only particularlistic, localist arguments that are even admissible (cf. Burningham & O'Brien, 1994: 925–6; Rootes, 2006a). The outcomes of local contention are more often than not determined by non-local actors or events (Rootes, 1999a, 1999b, 2006a).

The challenge for local campaigners is, therefore, to frame their grievances in such a way that their universality makes them into a political issue that transcends the normal and routine decision-making processes, that turns the issue from a routine planning dispute into a high profile political issue. This, of course, is a high risk strategy because to do so invites the big battalions of non-local political actors into the fray, making it likely that the contention will become one between non-local actors and reducing local campaigners to the status of onlookers. Since most local issues are, taken singly, unlikely candidates for such a transformation, however uncertain its outcomes, it is scarcely surprising that most focus their limited energies upon fighting within the constraints of the land-use planning system.

The possibility remains, however, of linking several local disputes in order to coordinate a national or at least regional campaign capable of mounting an effective political challenge. Such networks are, however, difficult to establish and maintain, not least because the timetables of local cases rarely coincide and because other local circumstances are typically idiosyncratic to varying degrees (cf. Markham, 2005, on the travails of the German Federal Alliance of Citizens' Initiatives for Environmental Protection, BBU). Overcoming such obstacles requires resources that local campaigners are more likely to choose to invest in local action, and so it is non-local actors and, especially, organisations that are best placed to establish and to support networks (cf. Gould *et al.*, 1996: 182). It is here that the quality of the network links between local and national organisations becomes crucial, but their realisation requires a coincidence between the interests of local campaigners and the campaign priorities of national organisations that is by no means automatic.

The adoption of an issue by a national organisation may enhance its legitimacy simply because non-local organisations can more convincingly deploy universalising rhetoric (Gordon & Jasper, 1996: 175–8), but national and regional environmental organisations generally stake their claims to legitimacy upon their ability to ground their claims in scientific evidence, whereas local campaigners characteristically raise issues such as attachment to place and anxieties about possible rather than proven risks to health which may sit uneasily with the science-informed priorities of the national organisations. A substantially decentralised organisation, attentive to the concerns of its local groups (such as FoE is in England), may establish campaigns as a compromise between the science-based advice of its officers and the demands of local groups (Rootes, 2005:37), but others, less in thrall to principles of local accountability, simply turn their backs on local campaigns that do not fit with their own campaign priorities. The fate of the various efforts to set up a national network of anti-incineration campaigners in England is a case in point. The issue that most concerns local campaigners – the threat to air quality, and thence to health, posed by incinerator emissions – is not one well supported by the available scientific evidence, and although they received somewhat half-hearted support from FoE, and a brief if character- istically spectacular series of interventions by Greenpeace, anti-incineration campaigners have mostly been condemned to fight lonely battles whose outcomes depend upon factors quite other than the quality of their arguments (Rootes, 2006a).

It is noteworthy that the singular success of anti-toxics campaigners in the US is attributable not to the networking efforts of a national environmental organisation but to the energy and determination of a remarkable individual, Lois Gibbs, a veteran of the iconic struggle at Love Canal, who started the Citizens Clearinghouse for Hazardous Wastes to advise and support local campaigners across the US (Szasz, 1994). Anti-incineration campaigners in the US were able to draw inspiration and support from a network initially focused upon the unambiguously harmful impacts of ill-managed and discriminatorily sited hazardous waste facilities, with the result that, after the mid-1980s, incinerator sitings became so contested that few were built (Walsh *et al.*, 1997: 15, 244–5). In other words, it was a local campaigner whose initiative inspired and supported other successful campaigns; the national environmental organisations were otherwise engaged.[5]

National environmental organisations that neglect or fail to respond to local campaigns jeopardise the popular legitimacy they earn by their national campaigning, and pass up the opportunity to broaden their own mobilising capacity. It is, however, clear that they do not have the resources to respond to, much less to support, every local campaign that is brought to their attention. Confronted with the organisational dilemmas imposed by limited resources and the tensions between alternative strategies (Diani & Donati, 1999), and driven by their perception of the urgency of the issues on their own science-driven agendas, it is scarcely surprising that elite-dominated national organisations will often disappoint local campaigners and fail to realise the full potential of networking local mobilisations.

From the Local to the Global?

The prospect of a global movement may be intimated in local struggles, and one advantage of close ethnographic study of local campaigns is that the universal themes and interests soon emerge from beneath the embellishments of local, regional and national cultures. But recognition of common humanity and the universality of the predicament of local communities faced with the grand projects of others does not automatically build useful bridges. How realistic is it to expect local–global linkage to be achieved in practice?

Much encouragement has been taken from the spread of social forums operating at local, national, regional and global levels. The mere existence of these is encouraging, as is their evident capacity to learn from and not simply to repeat past errors, but their durability is in question. In Europe, local social forums were most prevalent in Italy, Spain and France; despite promising beginnings in such places as Sheffield and Manchester, they never became well implanted in Britain. Even in Italy, it proved difficult to maintain momentum once the initial wave of enthusiasm wore off. Nevertheless, the World Social Forum and some regional and local social forums continue, albeit that explicitly ecological organisations and agenda are not prominent in them.[6]

Discouraging examples are, however, legion. Thus far, the experience of the environmental movement in the relatively favourable circumstances of the European Union suggests that national peculiarities continue to divide environmental campaigners more than their common cause unites them (Rootes, 2003, 2004). The obstacles to the realisation of a genuinely global environmental movement remain formidable (Rootes, 1999a, 1999b), and although there are many laudable efforts to overcome them, the troubled history of Friends of the Earth International testifies to their persistence (Doherty, 2006).

Local environmental campaigns may achieve redress of local grievances, and they may even place more general issues on national agenda, but it would be a triumph of optimism over experience to suppose that they will always or even usually contribute directly to the achievement of global environmental justice. Whilst it is indeed the case that, as Pellow and Brulle observe (2005: 2), it is the poor who 'are the first to feel the adverse consequences of growing ecological degradation', it is by no means obvious that it is they who will campaign most effectively against the environmental ills that afflict them. Indeed, it is unlikely. The longstanding suspicion and sometimes outright hostility that socialists and social democrats in many countries harboured toward environmentalists was founded on the belief that environmentalism was the self-interested defence of the privileges of the rich against the interests of the poor, whose conditions of disadvantage could be overcome only through increased economic develop-ment, which would necessarily involve further encroachment upon the environments the relatively privileged sought to defend. The realities of the unequal distribution of wealth, power and access to means of communication are everywhere such that poor communities find it more difficult to campaign effectively than those that are resource-rich. So nearly does the struggle against environmental degradation resemble a zero-sum game that the successes of local campaigns very often have the effect not of permanently obstructing environmental degradation but of displacing it from the environments of the rich to those of the poor.

This, moreover, is not an effect containable by the boundaries of nation states. As Pellow and Brulle (2005: 11) observe, 'as the mainstream environmental movement and white communities are partly responsible for influencing the shift in waste dumping into communities of colour in the United States and abroad (through anti-toxics mobilisations and the passage of more stringent and costly environmental regulations), the EJ movement may contribute to the globalisation of environmental inequality in the same manner'. Thus just as environmental inequalities are exacerbated by the transnationalisation of the 'treadmill of production' (Gould *et al.*, 1996: ch. 1), so they may be sharpened by the successes of local campaigners in the global North.

Recognising a problem is, however, the necessary first step to overcoming it. We might draw inspiration from what the EJ movement has achieved. If, as Pellow and Brulle (2005: 13), contend, 'the EJ movement has succeeded in framing ... environmental concerns as civil rights, social justice, and human rights issues', it has already begun to bridge a cognitive gap between the experience of the global North and those countries of the global South where collective action on environmental issues does not take the form of distinctively environmental movements because environmental issues are so tightly bound up with issues of democracy, human rights and social and economic justice. This has been recognised and built upon by FoE International and, sometimes controversially, in the reorientation of the agenda of other Northern environmental organisations (Rootes, 2006b). If environmental organisations increasingly alert to the human dimensions of environmental change, and to the implications of social inequalities for human behaviour toward the natural environment, are increasingly challenging globalising capitalism, its institu-tions and its policies, they may yet be among the agents of a profound change in the global order.

Even if the stretch between local environmental campaigns and a global social movement capable of shaking the citadels of global capitalism appears an improbably long one, local campaigns may nevertheless serve several purposes. They provide bases for communal action that might positively address and attempt to remedy environmental ills. They provide the rudiments of an education in activism, and provide some at least with the skills, confidence and experience to embark upon an activist career. Local organisations may sometimes grow into or instigate the transformation of geographically more extensive ones; witness the 'rhizomic' growth of the environmental justice movement in the US (Schlosberg, 1999). And local campaigns may not only perform a discovery role for national organisations but furnish them with a pool from whom future national activists might be drawn. But perhaps most importantly, they keep alive the conviction that silent resignation is not the only possible response to the degradation of the environment.

Acting locally will not usually be enough to secure redress of environmental grievances, but, for most people, local campaigns offer the only accessible entry to the political struggle for ecological sustainability. For that reason, but certainly not for that reason alone, they are most unlikely to fade away.

Notes

1. Berglund (1998) is a salutary exception.
2. FoE International is a confederation of autonomous national organisations, many of which existed before they were accepted as FoEI affiliates. Thus the German affiliate, BUND (Bund für Umwelt und Naturschutz Deutschland), which dates from 1975, is itself based on pre-existing regional groups and comprises over 2,000 local groups.
3. NIMBY = Not In MY Back Yard.
4. The campaign against the Channel Tunnel Rail Link in Kent, at the other end of the line, did not, however, have any such durable effects. In Kent, although the campaign included *ad hoc* local action groups, it relied heavily upon the mobilisation of the established interest groups of the country-side lobby and, especially, upon the institutionalised political structures and influence of Conservative-dominated Kent County Council and local Conservative Members of Parliament. Southeast London, by contrast, lacked a single overarching local authority or a well-established and concerted interest lobby and so campaigners there, even though they had the support and sympathy of local borough Councils and their (mostly Labour) MPs, were obliged to forge new links and to rely more upon their own resources, including the expertise of resident professionals. The result in southeast London, but not in Kent, was the invigoration of local civil society (Rootes *et al.*, 2001: 41).
5. The networking roles of key individuals are generally understated in organisation-focused accounts. In England, John Stewart was instrumental in creating two very important single-issue networks: Alarm UK and Airport Watch, focused upon roads and airports, respectively, the ground for the latter being prepared by the success of the former. But, in contrast to the US experience, Stewart was successful in securing the active support of national organisations too, especially FoE. I am grateful to Clare Saunders for pointing this out.
6. Encouragement might also be found in the persistence of the Global Ecovillage Network (GEN), a global confederation whose aim is to support and encourage the evolution of sustainable settlements. The members of the network are extremely diverse, consisting mainly of intentional communities, educational and cohousing projects in the North, but including large networks of sustainable villages in Sri Lanka and Senegal. Claiming to be truly global, GEN was set up in 1995 with encouragement and seedcorn funding from the Denmark-based Gaia Trust. It was approved as an official UN NGO with Special Consultative Status by Ecosoc in 2000, and in 2001 GEN-Europe received a modest grant from the European Commission Directorate General of Environment (http://gen.ecovillage.org/about/index.html, accessed 20 August 2007).

References

Berglund, E. K. (1998) *Knowing Nature, Knowing Science: An Ethnography of Environmental Activism* (Cambridge: White Horse Press).

Bosso, C. J. (2005) *Environment, Inc.: From Grassroots to Beltway* (Lawrence: University Press of Kansas).

Burningham, K. (2000) 'Using the language of NIMBY: a topic for research, not an activity for researchers', *Local Environment* 5(1): 55–67.

Burningham, K. & O'Brien, M. (1994) 'Global environmental values and local contexts of action', *Sociology* 28(4): 913–32.

Carmin, J. (1999) 'Voluntary associations, professional organisations and the environmental movement in the United States', *Environmental Politics* 8(1): 101–21.

Diani, M. & Donati, P. (1999) 'Organisational change in Western European environmental groups: a framework for analysis', *Environmental Politics* 8(1): 13–34.

Doherty, B. (2002) *Ideas and Action in the Green Movement* (London: Routledge).

Doherty, B. (2006) 'Friends of the Earth International: negotiating a trans-national identity', *Environmental Politics* 15(5): 860–80.

Dowie, M. (1995) *Losing Ground: American Environmentalism at the Close of the Twentieth Century* (Cambridge, MA: MIT Press).

Doyle, T. (2005) *Environmental Movements in Majority and Minority Worlds: A Global Perspective* (New Brunswick, NJ and London: Rutgers University Press).

Gordon, C. & Jasper, J. (1996) 'Overcoming the "NIMBY" label: rhetorical and organizational links for local protestors', *Research in Social Movements, Conflict and Change* 19: 159–81.

Gould, K. A., Schnaiberg, A. & Weinberg, A. S. (eds.) (1996) *Local Environmental Struggles: Citizen Activism in the Treadmill of Production* (Cambridge: Cambridge University Press).

Haynes, J. (1999) 'Power, politics and environmental movements in the Third World', *Environmental Politics* 8(1): 222–42.

Lamb, R. (1996) *Promising the Earth* (London: Routledge).

Markham, W. T. (2005) 'Networking local environmental groups in Germany: the rise and fall of the Federal Alliance of Citizens' Initiatives for Environmental Protection (BBU)', *Environmental Politics* 14(5): 667–85.

Pellow, D. N. & Brulle, R. J. (2005) 'Power, justice, and the environment: toward critical environmental justice studies', in D. N. Pellow & R. J. Brulle (eds.), *Power, Justice, and the Environment: A Critical Appraisal of the Environmental Justice Movement*, pp. 1–19 (Cambridge, MA: MIT Press).

Renn, O., Webler, T. & Kastenholz, H. (1998) 'Procedural and substantive fairness in landfill siting: a Swiss case study', in R. Löfstedt & L. Frewer (eds.), *The Earthscan Reader in Risk and Modern Society*, pp. 253–70 (London: Earthscan).

Rootes, C. (1999a) 'Acting globally, thinking locally?', *Environmental Politics* 8(1): 290–310.

Rootes, C. (ed.) (1999b) *Environmental Movements: Local, National and Global* (London and Portland, OR: Frank Cass).

Rootes, C. (ed.) (2003) *Environmental Protest in Western Europe* (Oxford and New York: Oxford University Press).

Rootes, C. (2004) 'Is there a European environmental movement?', in J. Barry, B. Baxter & R. Dunphy (eds.), *Europe, Globalization, Sustainable Development*, pp. 47–72 (London and New York: Routledge).

Rootes, C. (2005) 'A limited transnationalization?: the British environmental movement', in D. della Porta & S. Tarrow (eds.), *Transnational Protest and Global Activism*, pp. 21–43 (Lanham, MD: Rowman and Littlefield).

Rootes, C. (2006a) 'Explaining the outcomes of campaigns against waste incinerators in England: community, ecology, political opportunities and policy contexts', *Research in Urban Policy* 10, special issue on 'Community and Ecology', A. McCright & T. N. Clark (eds.): 179–98.

Rootes, C. (2006b) 'Facing South? British environmental movement organisations and the challenge of globalisation', *Environmental Politics* 15(5): 768–86.

Rootes, C., Adams, D. & Saunders, C. (2001) 'Local environmental politics in England: environmental activism in South East London and East Kent compared', paper presented to the workshop on 'Local Environmental Politics' at the 29th Joint Sessions of the European Consortium for Political Research, Grenoble, 6–11 April (Canterbury: University of Kent Centre for the Study of Social and Political Movements Working Paper 1/2001).

Saunders, C. (2007) 'Comparing environmental movement networks in periods of latency and visibility', *Graduate Journal of Social Science* 4(1): 109–39.

Schlosberg, D. (1999) 'Networks and mobile arrangements: organisational innovation in the US environmental justice movement', in *Environmental Politics* 8(1): 122–48.

Szasz, A. (1994) *Eco-populism* (Minneapolis: University of Minnesota Press).

Walsh, E., Warland, R. & Clayton Smith, D. (1993) 'Backyard NIMBYS and incinerator sitings: implications for social movement theory', *Social Problems* 40(1): 25–38.

Walsh, E., Warland, R. & Clayton Smith, D. (1997) *Don't Burn it Here: Grassroots Challenges to Trash Incineration* (University Park, PA: Penn State University Press).

The National and the Local: Relationships among Environmental Movement Organisations in London

CLARE SAUNDERS

Resources, Strategic Imperatives and Relations between National and Local Environmental Movement Organisations (EMOs)

Resource mobilisation theory stresses the inevitability of movement organisations' obsession with organisational maintenance – especially their budgets and their public image (McCarthy & Zald, 1977: 1220–4). To survive, resources – whether in the form of money or active support – are crucial. Informally organised 'new social movement' groups tend to extract resources from members in the form of active participation, whereas 'protest-businesses'[1] (Jordan & Maloney, 1997) mobilise direct-mail subscriptions to raise finances. Concerns about resources influence EMOs' relations with local supporters and campaigns: some consider that they do not have sufficient resources to support all local campaigns; others – especially those financially reliant on direct-debit

This research is based on the author's PhD funded by the Economic and Social Research Council (Saunders, 2005).

supporters –seek to appease supporters rather than active local campaigners. It is important for EMOs that derive a large proportion of funds from 'supporters'[2] to maintain their loyalty, especially in the face of high levels of multiple memberships (in 1997, 66% of Friends of the Earth's paper membership also belonged to at least one other EMO; Jordan & Maloney, 1997: 82). Thus, national EMOs may choose to focus on issues or campaigning styles that maximise public sympathy and enhance, or at least protect, their budgets. This can become a vicious circle to the extent that maintaining a public image might, at least in theory, take priority over campaigning. Indeed, by the mid- to late-1990s commentators noted that large EMOs like Greenpeace and Friends of the Earth (FoE) appeared increasingly motivated by self-investment, that their activities were curtailed by increasingly cumbersome budgets, and that they were, in consequence, ignoring grassroots issues and local groups (Rawcliffe, 1998: 78).[3]

In the early 1990s, Andrew Lees, FoE's campaigns coordinator, contacted local groups asking them to refrain from contact with direct action groups, fearing it would spoil FoE's reputation and credibility.[4] FoE upset many grassroots direct activists when, in 1992, faced with an injunction unless it discontinued its Twyford Down protest camp, it withdrew from campaigning against the M3 motorway extension rather than risk organisational collapse (Lamb, 1996: 177). For direct action protesters, however, the sole objective was to prevent roads being built. Lush (quoted, Wall, 1999: 68) was, however, understanding:

> [Direct action protesters proclaimed] 'we're the best, FoE copped off and f*****d off'... yet when you look at it, they [FoE] really tried to help the Twyford Down Association. They set up this extremely bizarre 'we are the middle class, we are representative of middle England' and extremely media-obsessed camp. They were uncomfortable, but they were f**king there... after three days the police cut through this very easy to cut chain and they got slapped with an injunction... and as a company they have to make decisions... unless they wanted to cease to be Friends of the Earth.

Unfortunately for FoE, the majority of direct action protesters were unsympathetic to its need for organisational maintenance. The resulting chasm between them deepened when FoE claimed credit for the victory of the East London River Crossing road campaign, a victory more plausibly claimed by the Oxleas Alliance, a coalition including EF!, the Wildlife Trusts and local campaigners (Stewart interview, June 2001).[5] On the other hand, the conservative Twyford Down Association (TDA) did not believe FoE had let them down, accepting that all legal means had been exhausted and thanking FoE for continuing a tactical voting campaign after the injunction was served (Porritt, 1996). FoE's need to both survive and protect its organisational image, as resource mobilisation theorists would predict, was largely responsible for the rift.

FoE certainly takes its organisational image seriously, as its *Five Year Plan* (2003–8) indicates:

> There is a great deal of competition from other environmental campaigning organisations, other NGOs and the background noise of the consumer society in which we live, all of which want their messages and calls to action to be heard over the others. Friends of the Earth has to make its comparatively limited resources count, in every way possible, every time... we have to present ourselves consistently in a way that is appealing and acceptable to a large number of different stakeholders. A strong brand and positioning are vital to achieving this. (FoE, 2003: 35–6)

Part of FoE's strategic plan is to monitor public perceptions of the FoE brand and to undertake work to strengthen it accordingly (FoE, 2003, strategic aim 6).

Similar stories have been told of Greenpeace. By 1992, its ex-employees and ex-allies alleged that:

> time and again... Greenpeace had become mired in its own bureaucracy and had lost touch with the grassroots, that it had become a cumbersome sluggish organisation that decreased in effectiveness as it increased in size. (Dale, 1996: 5)[6]

Greenpeace works hard to control its public image, and seeks to keep its image distinct from other EMOs that the media can more easily ignore. 'Greenpeace today is run like a company... Its mission statements... read like corporate reports. The Greenpeace name is marketed as a brand' (Eden, 2004: 599).

Thus, in their quest to improve their bank balances and public reputation, EMOs carefully craft a favourable public image and focus upon popular and winnable issues. According to Weston (1989: 205), the two main factors shaping FoE's decisions on campaign issues were funding availability and winnability. Diani and Donati (1999: 23) report that established Italian EMOs support local mobilisations against high-risk plants 'to gain visibility for themselves [rather] than promoting the struggles in the first place'. In the US, Schlosberg (1999: 122) found local groups increasingly alienated from major EMOs because of the latter's oligarchic tendencies and preference for maintaining supporters over assisting local campaigns.[7] The result of such emphases on organisational maintenance might be that local campaigns are not always fully supported by national EMOs, leaving local campaigners dissatisfied (Hannigan, 1995; de Shalit, 2001).

Methodology

In order to ascertain whether local campaigns in London are marginalised by national organisations more concerned with self-promotion, a triangulated research strategy was employed. A questionnaire survey administered by mail sought network data, and interviews with key campaigners at national, regional (London-wide) and local (borough or below) levels provided qualitative material to help explain the network data. To provide further contextual information, the researcher participated in one conservation, one reformist and one radical EMO one day a week for three months. All known national and regional EMOs in London, and local EMOs in the areas surrounding Greenwich (southeast) and Heathrow Airport (northwest London)[8] were surveyed. Of the 440 questionnaires sent to EMOs, 32% were returned completed.[9] At the national level, campaigners from FoE, Greenpeace, Campaign to Protect Rural England (CPRE) and the Campaign Against Climate Change were interviewed. At the regional level, staff from London FoE and London Wildlife Trust, and campaigners from London Rising Tide were questioned. Local campaigners interviewed included local FoE and Greenpeace activists, Wildlife Trust volunteers and campaigners fighting the third runway at Heathrow. Three types of network relationships are considered. The 'collaboration network' consists of the respondent organisations and the organisations they listed in response to the request, asked in respect of each of local, regional and national:

> Please list the five most important environmental organisations with which your organisation has *collaborated* on a campaign or environmental activity in the last 12 months.

The 'information-provided network' is the result of a similar question asking for five organisations at each of local, regional and national levels to which respondent organisations had 'provided information and advice', and the 'information-received network' comes from questions asking for the same number and type of organisations from which organisations had 'received information or advice' – all within the last 12 months.

Findings

Network Ties among Local, Regional and National EMOs

A scan of the network data list (DL)[10] compiled for national EMOs shows that the national EMOs that responded to the survey have more links with other national groups than with regional and local groups. As each organisation was given the opportunity to list five organisations with which they have links at each spatial level, it might be expected that there be the same number of links at each level. However, national EMOs frequently named fewer than two local and regional EMOs.[11] Similarly, in the information received and provided, and collaboration networks, there are over 50 linked pairs of national organisations, but national group ties with regional and local groups number 17 pairs at most. This clearly shows a tendency for national groups to work together and share information with one another to a much greater extent than they do with their local and regional counterparts (Table 1).

Table 1. National groups' ties in the network data list (DL) by sphere of operation

Network	Number of pairs listed in national DL			
	Southeast	Northwest	Regional	National
Collaboration	12	8	11	62
Received-information	12	8	12	67
Provided-information	17	9	13	55

In the collaboration network, 170 organisations were in the main component[12] and had a known or easily ascribed sphere of operation, henceforth referred to as a 'block'. This included 37 southeast, 53 northwest, 27 regional and 53 national organisations. Of the 75 collaborative ties (roughly two ties per organisation) mentioned by southeast London groups, 36 (48%) were directed towards other southeast London groups, 14 (19%) towards regional groups and 25 (33%) towards national groups (50%). In support of the theory that national groups turn their backs upon local groups, it can be seen that collaborative ties between national groups amount to 54% of their collaborative ties (compared to 25% for local groups – 15% southeast, 10% northwest). This inbreeding (Skovertz, 1991) is common too amongst other blocks, each having most ties with others with the same geographical sphere of operation. The northwest block shows a high level of independence, with 73% of the collaborative ties of such groups being directed towards others in the northwest.

The high level of independence of the northwest block is probably a function of the well-developed and internally supportive networks between local EMOs there. Ealing Wildlife Network brings together a conglomeration of concerned conservationist interests, perhaps making it unnecessary to call upon national groups for assistance.[13] FoE too is very well networked in the northwest of London. Ealing and Hillingdon FoE are part of the well-organised West London FoE (classified here as a northwest rather than a regional one) that is both influential and well connected to London FoE, which in turn gets support from national FoE. Paul de Zylva, Head of England Regions at FoE (interview, January 2004), agrees that West London FoE 'reduces reliance on Friends of the Earth [nationally]' and that 'sub-regional networks like this should be encouraged because they aid communication and cooperation between local groups'. However, such autonomy of a local environmental movement may also be the outcome of the long and sustained campaigns against expansion of Heathrow Airport. The links between these organisations are also tight because of the brokerage role played by a particular key activist, Nic Ferriday of West London FoE, who suggests that:

> ...they are all very close because I am active in all of them...there would be a link anyway because...a lot of members of West London FoE are members of AEF [Aviation Environment Federation]...(Interview June 2003)

Ferriday works part-time for AEF and FoE on aviation issues, coordinates West London FoE, is an active member of Ealing FoE and helps coordinate the Wildlife Network. His extensive knowledge of aviation issues filters through the network at national, regional and local levels and helps bind the movement.

It is local campaigning groups that have most ties with other local groups, and this is more prominent when there is a contentious local issue at stake. A survey of local FoE groups in 1998 showed that 89% were involved in coalitions or forums, including most prominently Local Agenda 21 and Transport coalitions; 76% of them claimed to work with other community groups and over half of these collaborations were with local single-issue campaign groups (Richie, 1998).

Days of action called by coalitions consisting of national organisations that have branches increase the propensity for cooperation between local organisations. Stop Esso days of action, for example, have brought together a variety of local organisations. As Cat Dorey (Greenpeace Marine Campaigner and northwest London area networker) claimed (interview, January 2004):

> the last time we went out and did an action against Esso, we got people from four different Greenpeace groups, two FoE groups and a People and Planet group.

It is only regional groups that have a greater proportion of ties with groups at other spatial levels than with themselves, and they especially have strong collaborative ties with national organisations (Table 2). Local groups in both southeast and northwest have fewer top five important collaborative ties with regional groups than with national groups. If the problematic relationship between London Wildlife Trust (LWT) and one of its satellite organisations, Chiswick Wildlife Trust, is any guide to the type of relationships between regional and local organisations, this is an unsurprising finding. At Gunnersbury Triangle nature reserve there has been conflict between the regional body of LWT, the management committee for the site, and Chiswick Wildlife Trust that forms the steering committee. LWT's aim is to gain tighter control of its steering groups[14] and to manage the reserve centrally and thereby reduce the

Table 2. Collaboration network by sphere of operation

Initiators of ties	Receivers of ties (expressed as a percentage of ties from initiators)			
	Southeast	Northwest	Regional	National
Southeast	48	0	19	33
Northwest	0	73	14	14
Regional	14	17	35	34
National	15	10	21	54

power of local volunteers. Conflict has occurred because many volunteers have been committed to the site for at least 15 years and know the reserve intimately, whereas staff have less knowledge and experience and are therefore perceived as inept. This perception is strengthened by the fact that there is a relatively high turnover of staff at LWT (due to lapses in funding) and, to Chiswick Wildlife Trust, it seems different staff members are posted each year. According to one warden:

> Support from London Wildlife Trust has been limited and is on the whole disappointing. It may be that the staff are stretched, but there is a lack of expertise and management skill. An organisation offering low salaries is bound to recruit young staff with limited experience, often staying in post for a short time, which leads to a lack of continuity. (Rear interview, February 2004)

A paid member of LWT staff was posted at the Triangle throughout the summer months to manage the reserve. The paid warden came from a countryside management background, whereas the volunteer warden had an intimate knowledge of local ecology, having been a committed naturalist for the previous 25 years. At least twice, these differences in background and levels of experience created conflicts. The first related to what local volunteers perceived to be inappropriate strimming of brambles and the other to the use of a brush-clearing machine in an area of sensitive habitat. The management plan states a clear policy of leaving brambles uncut to allow them to produce more fruit to encourage birds, except where brambles become dangerous to volunteers and visitors. However, on orders of the summer warden, a volunteer cut a stretch of bramble down to the roots. The volunteer warden was unhappy about this infringement of policy. Second, at LWT's request, the summer warden used the brush-clearing machine to clear a pathway in an area very close to the usual nesting site of harriers. Unfortunately, he did so without checking the management plan, which states that the area near the nesting site should remain quiet, and allegedly frightened the potential breeders away.

London FoE may not be perceived as an important collaborator for local groups, including FoE groups, because it has a small budget, low manpower and a multitude of tasks. Its coordinator, Jennifer Bates, was working on a campaign against the Thames Gateway Bridge, attempting to set up regional networks of campaigners to input into regional government decisions, as well as ensuring that local groups within London were functioning as effectively as they ought, and promoting FoE's policies to the Greater London Authority. In interview, she compared London FoE to the Simon Wolfe Charitable Foundation, a small locally based organisation that has two full-time campaigners, and concluded that:

> ... even though it [Thames Gateway Bridge] is the main campaign that I am doing, the reality is that they have probably got more time and

money than I have, because in reality it is only me! You know, with a tiny budget and some local groups if I am lucky...(Bates interview, February 2001)

There are also some interesting patterns in the partitioned matrix for the information-provided network. The majority of ties towards which southeast, regional and national organisations provide information and resources are national groups. Local groups in the southeast are especially likely to filter their information toward national groups, showing that they are non-NIMBY, and possibly reflecting a general trend for them to see national EMOs as the most important players in the movement. Again, northwest EMOs show a strong tendency to work independently with 45% of their ties directed towards others like themselves (Table 3).

For local organisations in the southeast, a very similar proportion of the important ties from which information is received are regional (39%) and national (36%) (Table 4). Similarly, in the northwest organisations, the scales balance between regional and national organisations (31% each). This indicates that regional groups play an important role in providing information to local groups, and that local groups see this as a credible and important source. Regional groups, however, rate information received from local southeast groups as unimportant. The most important sources from which regional groups receive information are northwest and national organisations (38% of ties apiece). This, again, is likely to be a result of northwest groups' integration into regional networks via London FoE and a function of the

Table 3. Information-provided network by sphere of operation

Initiators of ties	Receivers of ties (expressed as a percentage of ties from initiators)			
	Southeast	Northwest	Regional	National
Southeast	34	0	25	40
Northwest	0	45	22	33
Regional	10	12	37	40
National	18	10	16	56

Table 4. Information-received network partitioned by sphere of operation

Initiators of ties	Receivers of ties (expressed as a percentage of ties from initiators)			
	Southeast	Northwest	Regional	National
Southeast	14	0	39	36
Northwest	0	39	31	31
Regional	5	38	19	36
National	7	11	15	67

campaigns around Heathrow, a regional issue. Again, northwest groups show a reasonable level of independence, with 39% of their most important sources of information being other northwest organisations. However, most national organisations are too fully stretched maintaining their own local networks to be of help to local branches of other organisations. As Ferriday (West London FoE) suggests:

> We mainly link up to FoE nationally or we link up to other groups locally rather than with their national groups, so there wouldn't be much of that [links between Ealing FoE and other national groups]. Other local groups would speak to their own national group. (interview, June 2003)

However, the story is somewhat different if we consider information sent by email because of the small amount of time and energy involved in contacting people in this manner. Local groups signed up to FoE's activist mailouts include branches of other organisations such as Mid Devon Green Party, North Dorset Green Party and other smaller interests like East London Gardening Centre and Totnes Genetics group.[15]

Many activists find FoE email alerts and websites useful sources of information. Thornhill (interview, June 2003) commented that email postings from FoE are crucial for keeping informed. Sobey (interview, February 2004) commented that although FoE's information is not usually new to him, its accessible style and the ease of accessing information from the internet are especially useful.

Over two-thirds of national organisations' most important sources of information are other national EMOs. Given that most national organisations are careful to source credible information, and that national organisations are much more likely to have the resources to employ professional staff, this is not surprising (Table 4). There is a higher tendency for national EMOs to be involved in the mutual exchange of information with other organisations; there are more than twice as many links (11 compared to a maximum of five) as in other blocks in the exchange of information between national organisations (Table 5). This is likely to be a result of a number of factors. National organisations have more full-time staff and greater financial resources which make it easier to maintain relations with other organisations. In regional

Table 5. Information exchange network partitioned by sphere of operation

Initiators of ties	Receivers of ties (expressed as number of ties from initiators)			
	Southeast	Northwest	Regional	National
Southeast	7	0	4	3
Northwest	0	2	3	5
Regional	4	3	1	4
National	3	5	4	11

organisations like LWT, staff posts are usually dependent upon the success of bids for funding. Where these are unsuccessful, staff may be made redundant resulting in high turnover, little campaigning continuity and broken links with other EMOs (Waugh interview, June 2003). As national organisations effectively spearhead the movement, it is important for them to keep in contact with other national organisations.

Inbreeding

Inbreeding scores were calculated for each block using Skvoretz and Agneessens' (2002) SPSS Syntax Inbreeding Programme. 'Inbreeding bias' is 'when people [or organisations] tend to associate (over and above chance expectations) with others like themselves on the dimensions [observed]' (Skvoretz, 1991: 275). The concept of inbreeding expands upon Blau's (1977) distributional theory of social structure. Blau argued that inbreeding occurs along social dimensions of interest. The absence of inbreeding is as important as its presence because it is associated with seizing the opportunity to associate with others outside immediate social groupings.

Southeast groups have a 39% bias towards engagement with another group in the southeast over and above groups elsewhere. For groups in northwest London, the figure is substantially higher at 69%. Regional and national groups have a notably lower 'inbreeding bias' (8% and 20%, respectively). The high figure for the northwest can be explained by the existence of a high profile local campaign – the Heathrow Airport issue – which dominates the local environmental movement. Local groups are most likely to cooperate with one another frequently when there is a current campaign and local campaigners are focusing upon the same issues (Table 6).

In the collaboration network, the 'inbreeding bias' for regional groups is low at just 8%. This may be explained by the fact that regional groups tend to be information providers or receivers rather than collaborative partners. Most of the top five information providers for local organisations in southeast London

Table 6. 'Inbreeding biases' according to sphere of operation of EMOs

	Collaboration network	Information-provided network	Information-received network	Information exchange network
Southeast	39	22	10	9
Northwest	69	38	27	0
Regional	8	17	0	0
National	20	11	44	51

Note: These scores are expressed as percentages that indicate the extent to which organisations network with others from the same sphere of operation. It is calculated under the assumption that subgroups generate and receive contacts in proportion to their number in the population.

are regional organisations. Although northwest groups provide much information to one another and appear mutually supportive, regional groups are just as important, whereas collaborative ties between regional and national levels are much lower and less significant. Where a single organisation with local and regional chapters exists, regional groups have a strong tendency to be intermediaries between local groups and their national counterparts. Hence Chiswick Wildlife Trust collaborates relatively frequently with LWT (although less frequently than volunteers would like), but not with the national body. In the same way, local FoE groups in northwest London (Ealing and Hillingdon FoE) are more likely to collaborate with West London FoE, a semi-regional body, or regional London FoE than they are with national FoE. Their joint role as information providers and go-betweens means that regional organisations have fewer resources left to filter into actual collaborative campaigns. With the exception of LWT, regional groups generally lack collaborative partnerships.

In the information-provided network, the 'inbreeding biases' are still highest for northwest groups, although at 38% the figure is considerably lower than the bias for collaboration. Local EMOs in northwest London share a smaller proportion of their ties in the provision of information with other northwest organisations than in the collaboration network. This is because they are more likely to collaborate with other local concerns but may wish to share information more widely. The same pattern is seen in southeast London groups for which the bias for the information-provided network is 22% versus 39% in the collaboration network.

For national groups, the 11% 'inbreeding bias' in information provision is the lowest bias for national groups. This indicates that national groups are more likely to provide information to lower-level (regional or local) groups than they are to receive information from them, be involved in an information exchange, or collaborate with them. National groups like FoE are very efficient at sending out information whilst receiving minimal input. For instance, local activists are signed up to a variety of email alert lists (as with renewables/energy, waste, pesticides/food and chemicals lists). As FoE is regarded by most activists as a credible source of information, many sign up to receive email updates. This flow of information is unlikely to work in reverse; FoE is less likely to sign up to local email discussion lists, because the groups are relatively small and have narrow remits, and because FoE campaigners are at pains to reduce information overload. As a source of information, FoE campaigners favour other credible and reputable national organisations with particular specialisms. Thus, an FoE campaigner, carrying out research on signatories to a pro-GM letter to the Prime Minister to ascertain their pecuniary interests in the biotechnology industry, recommended that the search be carried out through the website of the Genetics Engineering Network, a website she frequently turned to for information on GM foods. For aviation campaigning, AEF, which knows 'more about aviation than any other organisation on earth' (Stewart interview, January 2004), is such an important source of information that FoE has been spared the need to do the groundwork itself (de Zylva interview, January 2004). On the Baku Ceyhan Campaign, Cornerhouse was an invaluable source of information for FoE on international financial institutions (IFIs), and Platform provided a wealth of knowledge on oil issues.

Biases for receiving information and exchanging information amongst national groups are 44% and 50%, indicating that around half of these kinds of ties from national groups are directed towards other national groups. Other 'inbreeding biases' regarding sphere of operation in the information exchange network (for regional, northwest and southeast groups) are very low (regional is 9%), or missing. All types of groups except national ones exchange information across geographical spheres of operation, whereas national groups tend to exchange information among themselves.

National EMOs Make Efforts to Support Local EMOs

Although the network data indicate that national groups' most important network links are mainly with other national groups, we should not assume that organisations like Greenpeace and FoE simply turn their backs on local groups. Cudworth's (2003: 93) claim that Greenpeace fosters 'little if any local activism' is mistaken. Neither can Diani and Donati's (1999: 23) finding in relation to the Italian environmental movement – that national EMOs only support local initiatives to gain visibility – be fairly said of British national EMOs. Both FoE and Greenpeace make conscious efforts to involve grassroots supporters, and to make their kinds of activism accessible to local people and community groups. FoE Regional Campaigns Coordinators work to involve local FoE groups and other local community campaigning groups and offer them support and advice. Part of FoE's ethos is to encourage 'people participating actively as citizens and organising, mobilising and inspiring people to become active citizens' (FoE, 2003). Greenpeace, on the other hand, is more concerned with providing people with the know-how, experience and confidence to take what they learn from Greenpeace and apply it to other campaigns independently of Greenpeace. This was the aim of Greenpeace's Incinerator Busters campaign from summer 2001 to 2002. The Basingstoke incinerator action in 2002 was the first, and possibly only, time that the actions team worked with local non-Greenpeace groups. It was arranged by Mark Strutt (Toxics Campaigner) and Miranda Holmes (Temporary Incineration Campaigner) and consisted of three people from South East Action Group for the Environment (SAGE) and two or three people from other local anti-incinerator groups (personal communication, Phil Scott, SAGE Coordinator, 2003). However, Greenpeace will only support local campaigns like this when there is a very tight link with its national priority themes.

Torrance (then Greenpeace Networker) said his job was all about:

> coordinating and managing a network of volunteers who want to, or at
> least say to us that they want to actively participate in Greenpeace

campaigns. Perhaps we train them up in NVDA, we involve them in our direct actions... There are a whole range of activities out there... from people receiving a newsletter we produce each month called *Network*, to getting people letter-writing, to people participating in Greenpeace campaigns, and ultimately to feel that they themselves could set up a local opposition group to any incinerator plan or whatever. And I think that Greenpeace is one of those organisations out there, which is just a real conduit for people... a kind of wake up call. (Interview, July 2003)

Thus Dorey began her activist career as a Greenpeace local supporter and went on to become increasingly involved in local group work and Greenpeace direct actions. From there she developed the know-how and confidence to help set up London Rising Tide, and in 2003 was Greenpeace's North London Area Networker and Oceans Campaigner. North London Greenpeace activists also set up London Against Incineration, which was successful in stopping plans for expansion of incinerators in north London, 'and there are countless examples of that ...' (Torrance interview, July 2003). FoE had a similar impact on Phil Thornhill who, almost independently, runs the Campaign Against Climate Change:

my whole roots of campaigning are as a local FoE group person, so that is absolutely important yeah, if I hadn't have been in a local FoE group, I would never have been doing anything remotely like this. (Thornhill interview, June 2003)

For local group actions, both FoE and Greenpeace campaigns follow a DiY-pack model. Although FoE groups can also campaign on their own initiative, choosing their own issues and methods (so long as they do not bring the FoE name into disrepute), most FoE local groups are involved in rolling out the national campaigns at local level and, in a similar manner to Greenpeace local groups, receive posters, briefings and instructions for these campaigns from the national office.

FoE is also supportive of other community groups. One of FoE's strategic aims for 2003–8 is to 'support and develop non-Friends of the Earth community groups so that they can be effective in campaigns that support and reinforce our Strategic Aims and Objectives' (FoE, 2003). This is the ethos behind FoE's new Community Website, launched in June 2003. The result of consultation with local group members and piloting by 100 local activists, it provides briefings, resources, campaign ideas, postings and the facility for non-FoE local activists to share thoughts, ideas and plans of actions. The idea of the website is to make local groups increasingly independent, encourage networking among them (some have considerable expertise on specific issues), and stimulate community campaigning. The website has around 1,500 unique users per month, with an average engagement time of 20 minutes (compared to 10 minutes for FoE's main website). Enquiring non-FoE activists are informed about the resources available through 'Community', and also sent FoE's campaigning handbook, *How to Win* (Sartori interview, November 2003).

Because local FoE groups campaign on a range of issues, local *ad hoc* environmental campaigns often latch on to FoE, sometimes without ever considering seeking help from Greenpeace. FoE was very active nationally, locally and regionally in the campaigns against airport expansion, but Greenpeace was notably absent. Pearce, a campaigner from Longford Residents Association who was involved in the campaign against the Third Runway at Heathrow Airport, said, when asked:

> I: I don't suppose you ever thought to yourselves 'Where's Greenpeace'?
> RP: I think Greenpeace deal with worldwide issues and I think that groups can't do everything and you have to leave certain things to certain experts...I don't think that anybody thinks that because a big organisation like that weren't at the inquiry that they should be ...
> I: If Friends of the Earth hadn't been there...do you think you might have thought...'where are Friends of the Earth?'
> RP: Oh yes, but I would have been very shocked actually if they weren't there because it is such a major issue...(Pearce interview, January 2004)

FoE's support for community campaigning organisations has become so entrenched as part of its remit that it is now par for the course that there be a FoE presence on major local environmental campaigns. The same cannot be said of Greenpeace whose support for local initiatives, although expanding, remains tightly controlled. Whilst Pearce accepts that Greenpeace's remit is working on international high profile issues, some are less pleased with Greenpeace's apparent lack of support for grassroots initiatives. Coleman (London Rising Tide activist), for example, explained that he had received an email informing him that:

> 'Greenpeace as an organisation doesn't get involved in local issues' and I couldn't believe it...It was a local community who wanted some help and wrote to Greenpeace. Greenpeace...wrote back to them and said 'don't worry, we will pass it on to some local groups, maybe FoE', they said, and maybe some other local groups in London, but I just thought, that is not good. That isn't a good way to be moving forward. (Coleman interview, November 2003)

Although Greenpeace and FoE both use local support to bolster their organisations, FoE clearly has a much larger presence at the community level and to a greater extent regards the contribution of grassroots campaigners as crucial to achieving the kind of sustainable society it envisages.

Greenpeace does, however, at least consider the views of its local group members when planning actions (Dorey interview, January 2004):

> ...every action we do on the street they ask us to send back a feedback form...[there is] constant feedback with the Supporters Unit and they...meet with the campaigners to listen to the ideas they have got and then they say 'I don't think it's going to work, or we need to do this'.

Local activists form a pool of labour for high profile Greenpeace actions and play a more integral role than is often assumed.

Similarly, local FoE groups now contribute substantially to FoE's planning and policies. The waste team has a Waste Advisory Group consisting of four local experts (including Scott from SAGE) that meets bi-annually to discuss FoE's waste policy.[16]

Between 2004 and 2008, the 'Curb the Power of Supermarkets' campaign will involve local groups in: several days of action; fighting supermarket mergers; surveying supermarkets for data on food miles and local produce; encouraging MPs to demand a Code of Practice and a Retail Regulator; at least two training days; writing to MPs for support for the Planning Bill at report stage; and raising awareness of supermarket over-packaging and pushing for legislation. The aim was to create, by 2005, a wide alliance of national and local organisations (not just FoE groups) campaigning to reduce supermarkets' dominance and impact. By spring 2006 there were expected to be 200 local and national groups working on this issue, in addition to a list of 'DIY activists' willing to take action (FoE, 2003).

Like FoE, CPRE sees its local groups as a vital part of its campaigning, but also as a central part of its marketing strategy. In 1995, consultants brought in to advise CPRE on membership recruitment reported that prospective members were suspicious of national institutions and recommended that CPRE present itself as 'a local body which has strong national backup' (Conder interview, 2000, in Rootes, 2007: 51).

> CPRE comes very much from local groups as much as nationally, so the groups have always had a...profile in developing and influencing policy. Any agreements we get from local groups are on the basis of negotiation, and some compromise and hoping that good sense prevails...We don't have any sense of signed agreement on delivery of service or anything like that. (White interview, October 2003)

Much of CPRE's work involves writing guidance that local groups put into action (Schofield interview, October 2003).

National and Regional Groups' Choice of Issues

FoE, Greenpeace and CPRE try to encourage local community campaigning, inside and outside their own branches, and all three organisations have actively campaigned, or pledged to do so, on aviation.[17] However, they still have organisational constraints that make it impossible to support every campaign arising. As Weston (1989: 105) suggested, there is always some consideration of which campaigns are winnable in terms of policy break-throughs and winning the hearts and minds of potential supporters. FoE's *Five Year Plan* states that:

> we must choose the right number of campaigns that will increase our chances of having some significant 'victories' (this is not likely to be achieved by a large number of lightly-resourced campaigns). (FoE, 2003: 33)

According to Sartori (interview, November 2004), the decision whether to support an issue is based on:

> ... how winnable a campaign is [and] whether it could be ... taken up as a national thing [and] if it is fitting in with our five-year plan and our campaign.

London Rising Tide campaigners who attended the COP9 UNFCC (Conference of Parties, United National Framework Climate Convention) discussion in Milan in December 2003 may have been dismayed to see that FoE was not present. Its absence was a carefully considered strategic decision on practical and logistical grounds:

> One was how significant are the negotiations going to be? Are they going to be newsworthy? Is there anything that is going to happen that we can make a difference to? ... Had the Russians ratified, or declared that they were going to ratify before Milan ... there might have been some big decisions made at Milan, in which case we would have gone. Second reason ... was 'was there a strong local group that would have been able to have a handle on logistics?' and FoE Italy aren't very strong actually, although FoE Milan are quite strong. And thirdly it is quite a long way ... you have to get people over the Alps, and without elephants, we couldn't have got enough people over the Alps. (Rau interview, January 2004)

National FoE has also been reluctant to give much backing to the Campaign Against Climate Change. FoE's Senior Climate Campaigner, Higman, was loath to get too deeply involved because of concerns that the campaign may be misdirected, or that campaigning resources might be better placed elsewhere:

> PT: He just kept whimpering on about Twyford Down and how it wouldn't work and so on.
> I: How was this related to Twyford Down?

PT: It was the fact that it was something that FoE was involved in that didn't succeed ... it was a bad experience as a FoE campaign. (Thornhill interview, June 2003)

FoE's selectivity about which campaigns to support can make the organi-sation appear somewhat fickle to outside organisations. Alistair Hanton, an established transport campaigner for a variety of EMOs, noted that FoE:

... come in and out of the transport scene. They're rather maverick actually, and there's a lot of rivalry between them and other people because they're very keen on expanding Friends of the Earth. (Interview, April 2001)

However, some activists appreciate that it is impossible for FoE to support every campaign initiative. Whilst pleased with his relationship with FoE, Ferriday is 'not always pleased with the amount of help they can give', but appreciates that '... they just don't have the time to respond to the campaigns of every group in the country' (Ferriday interview, June 2003). London Rising Tide – direct activists against climate change – have a range of views of FoE, but are mostly sympathetic to the work it does. By and large, they are, like Norbert[18] (activist with London Rising Tide, personal correspondence, January 2004), 'glad they are there', suggesting that the rift between them and radical activists has reduced since the heyday of direct action protesting against roads. Indeed, Rising Tide were happy to work alongside FoE as part of the 'No New Oil' coalition. Although several London Rising Tide activists were critical of FoE's absence from the Milan COP conference, Norbert admitted that 'it is simply not possible for FoE to be everywhere we want them to be'. Similarly, but this time with reference to the Wildlife Trusts, although critical of the apparent lack of support received from LWT, local volunteers also appreciated that there is a limit to what one relatively resource-poor organisation can do.

Indeed, all 14 local campaigners interviewed were either pleased with the support they received from national EMOs, slightly dismayed by lack of national support but able to account for it (without prompting) by reference to organisational resource deficiencies, or indifferent to it. Plumstead Common Environment Group, for example, is a local conservation organisation that does not require support from national organisations because it works closely with Greenwich Borough Council.

With aviation, however, FoE had no doubt about the need to support local interests. Rau went so far as to suggest that the campaign exists 'purely because of demand from local groups', but it is also considered a winnable campaign ('we beat them on roads and we can win again' (Juniper, Director, FoE, 2004) and relates to FoE's broader concerns about over-development in London, road congestion and climate change. Perhaps, then, it is not surprising that aviation campaigners felt fully supported by

FoE, and by CPRE, in their 2002–3 campaign against the Third Runway at Heathrow.

As local campaigners accept, it is impossible for national and regional organisations to support all local campaign issues. When he was FoE London Groups Coordinator, de Zylva limited himself to supporting no more than three local campaigns at once, 'otherwise it is like trying to keep too many plates spinning' (interview, January 2004). Nor is FoE the only EMO to have devised strategies for working out the issue or campaigns most worthy of support.

For CPRE, choices of which local interests to pursue are calculated using a Gateway Test, which involves:

> the capacity to do it, whether there are other organisations that are better placed to do it than we are, whether or not we have the time or resources, and whether it is a CPRE priority based on our mission statement which is quite specifically to do with the English countryside. (Schofield interview, October 2003)

CPRE goes against NIMBY wishes of branches or members if the proposed siting of a LULU (locally unwanted land use) is seen to be the most acceptable option from a broad policy perspective (White interview, October 2003). Greenpeace tends not to get involved in local campaigns unless they are a part of a corporate campaigning package. For LWT, the issue is always dependent on:

> what the local impacts will be, although there aren't a huge number of planning applications on metropolitan sites...it will always be dependent on our funding and whether it is in our remit... but we will certainly try to support any other local groups that do want to put in their own planning objections against proposals in their own area. (Waugh interview, June 2003)

However, it appears that requests for help from national organisations are relatively infrequent. In 2003, FoE's Local Group Development Officer's telephone may have rung on average only four to six times a day, and not all those calls were from local group members seeking help.[19] The few local group calls she did receive were mostly from newly established groups still finding their feet, or from more established groups making requests for mailings to be sent to national group members in their locality (Sartori interview, November 2003). Similarly for CPRE '...the demands that come in for that kind of campaign support aren't that great. It is usually information specifically that people want' (Schofield interview, October 2003). CPRE routinely sends out planning guidance notes to local people but provides little additional support.

The hypothesis that national groups tend to turn their backs on local campaigns is probably best supported by the example of Greenpeace, which has tended to ignore local campaigns with the exception of its 2002–3 venture into local environmental politics with its Incinerator Busters campaign. Although Greenpeace may have a tendency to promote its brand image, to sideline local issues and focus instead on a small number of potentially winnable campaigns, it does not entirely ignore local activists. In fact, it provides avenues for popular involvement in the environmental movement. However, Greenpeace has carefully crafted its image so that local campaigners do not question its absence from their pet campaign issues to the extent that they might question FoE's absence.

Conclusion

National EMOs have a tendency to list other national organisations as their five most important collaborative links. Despite their limited resources and the expectation that that they might consequently make frequent requests for help from national organisations, local groups tend to list other *local* organisations as their most important collaborators. This is especially noticeable when there is a current campaign. Overall, it appears that local groups are relatively independent and seek help from national organisations much less frequently than expected. Where local groups are branches of a broader organisation, their first port of call for assistance is their own headquarters, and information or advice can then be passed through the grassroots network to other local groups, whether independent or branches of other national EMOs. This 'subterranean' networking would not have been noticed had the research focused only on national organisations. Regional groups appear to play brokerage roles between national and local groups in collaboration and information-based networks, but much more often feature as information providers than as collaborators.

The lack of top five important ties from national to local groups should not be read as an organisational maintenance strategy whereby national groups prioritise their own concerns above grassroots campaigns. To the contrary, there is evidence that Greenpeace, FoE and CPRE increasingly, directly and indirectly, support grassroots campaigners. Whilst local groups do provide information to national organisations (especially in the southeast), there is a tendency for national organisations to list other national organisations as their most *important* sources of information. This is probably part of a quest for credible information. Inevitably, there are constraints that make it impossible for a national organisation to lend support to every local initiative; it is more effective for them to invest heavily in a few key campaigns than devote scant resources to many. Thus, most national EMOs choose campaigns that closely fit their organisational aims and objectives, are within their resource capabilities, and have some chance of 'success'. Inevitably, local groups sometimes feel sidelined, but most local EMO interviewees were content with their relationship to national organisations, and fully aware of the implications of the resource constraints upon them.

Notes

1. A protest business is a campaigning organisation for which docile supporters who contribute financially are more important than active members. Policy is made in an oligarchic fashion, and supporters influence policy through their capacity for exit. Political action is taken by staff rather than supporters. Staff shape the perceptions of followers by providing them with partial information, and supporters tend to be interested in narrow issue areas (Jordan & Maloney, 1997: 22).
2. Rootes (2007: 60, note 3) notes that the word 'member' means different things to different EMOs; and that some include 'all donors and volunteers as members' whereas 'others restrict "membership" to formal subscribers'.
3. Rawcliffe shows how EMO budgets have increased, for example, FoE's budget rose from £306,285 in 1985 to £3,839,325 by 1995.
4. Barkan (1986) found reformists had similar complaints about radicals in the southern civil rights movement.
5. Similarly, in the 1980s, Greenpeace stole the limelight from FoE on whales, and the seal pelt issue from IFAW.
6. This statement cannot be made with such conviction in 2006, because Greenpeace has, since 2002, worked hard to reinvigorate its connection with the grassroots, and now has a busy 'active supporters unit' (Torrance interview, 2003).
7. Note, however, that most national environmental NGOs in the US never had grassroots membership (Bosso, 2005).
8. Two smaller areas were chosen to sample local groups because local EMOs are numerous in London. See Saunders (forthcoming) for details of sample selection.
9. A further 6% were returned unanswered, some with a message informing me that the organisation had folded, others claiming that the organisation was unknown at the address to which the questionnaire had been posted. This is to be expected given the nature of collective action. As Knoke (1990) suggests, the environmental movement, especially at the grassroots level, is known to experience periodic attrition and renewal as organisations fold when issues are resolved or activists 'burn out', and new ones form to cover new issues or take their place. Although it seems low, this response rate is not drastically lower than the expected average response rate of 50% for SMO surveys (Klandermans & Smith, 2002), and Ansell's (2003) response rate for a similar survey of US EMOs (40%). However, not all respondents provided data on their network links. In all, 114 listed their five most important links with other environmental organisations at each of the national, London-wide and local (borough) levels. Because the data are explored relationally, there is no danger of misrepresenting the structure of the network (see Saunders, forthcoming).
10. A DL is a text-based format for entering network data in UCINet. Essentially it is a list of organisations and the network links that they mention. For instance, if CPRE lists FoE, Greenpeace, Wildlife and Countryside Link and WWF as four out of five top links, the following partnerships would be listed: CPRE FoE, CPRE Greenpeace, CPRE WildlifeCountrysideLink, CPRE WWF. The same would be done for each organisation's elected choices. UCINet converts data inputted in this format into a socio-matrix (Borgatti *et al.*, 1999).
11. It may be that the lists of local collaborators or information providers/receivers are too numerous or too difficult to rank. Anheier (1987: 579), for example, warns of the bias that 'power and size differentials' are likely to yield as 'smaller organisations tend to be well aware of informal and cooperative relations with larger organisations, but not vice versa'.
12. The main component of a social network is the largest linked group of actors in a social network. A component analysis singles out isolated organisations and small groups of actors not linked to the main network. It is easily performed in UCInet.
13. Ealing Wildife Network consists of the Brent and River Canal Society, Ealing Allotments and Gardens Society, Ealing Wildlife Trust, Friends of Litten Local Nature Reserve, Ealing Badger

Group, London Bat Group, Hounslow and Ealing Conservation Volunteers, Northolt and Greenford Country Park Society, Ealing Watch Group, West London Organic Wildlife Gardeners Association and Ealing WWF.

14. According to Roberts and Robertshaw (interview, February 2004), London Wildlife Trust have been gesturing about bringing local groups under tighter control for years. Due to lack of people power, in practice there has been little change except for Chiswick Wildlife Trust's changed 'label' from a management committee to a steering group.

15. Part of my participant observation in FoE London office included organising a database of activists signed up to various campaign update lists. In the main these were local group members, but activists from a wide range of other (mostly reformist) organisations had also signed up. These links may not register among the top five most important links.

16. A small but vocal minority of participants in the Waste Advisory Group have objected to FoE's campaigning shift from incineration to 'Reduce Resource Use'. During January 2004, FoE had only one live incineration campaign to support. Watson sees that the debate within local councils and nationally has shifted to a recognition of the need to reduce the amount of waste produced at source. FoE will continue to support local incineration campaigns, but this will be done at a national rather than local level by waging arguments about how incineration should not receive subsidies and seeking ways of making recycling more economically attractive (Watson interview, January 2004).

17. John Stewart contacted Steven Tindale, Greenpeace Executive Director, and secured a pledge that Greenpeace would contribute its expertise in direct action to the campaign.

18. This is a pseudonym.

19. Sartori attributes this partly to the community website, where local groups can now download briefings, application forms for the local groups support fund and so on, rather than have to phone or email her and wait for a postal or email response. Apparently the phone used to ring much more frequently.

References

Anheier, H. K. (1987) 'Structural analysis and strategic research design: studying politicised interorganisational networks', *Sociological Forum* 2(3): 562–82.

Ansell, C. (2003) 'Community embededness and collaborative governance in the San Francisco Bay Area environmental movement', in M. Diani & D. McAdam (eds.), *Social Movements and Networks: Relational Approaches to Collective Action*, pp. 122–44 (Oxford: Oxford University Press).

Barkan, S. E. (1986) 'Interorganisational conflict in the southern civil rights movement', *Sociological Inquiry* 56(2): 190–209.

Blau, P. M. (1977) *Inequality and Heterogeneity* (New York: The Free Press).

Borgatti, S., Everett, M. & Freeman, L. (1999) *UCInet 6 for Windows* (Lexington, KY: Analytic Technologies).

Bosso, C. (2005) *Environment, Inc.* (Lawrence: Kansas University Press).

Cudworth, C. E. (2003) *Environment and Society* (London: Routledge).

Dale, S. (1996) *McLuhan's Children: The Greenpeace Message and the Media* (Toronto: Octopus Books).

De Shalit, A. (2001) 'Ten commandments of how to fail in an environmental campaign', *Environmental Politics* 10(1): 111–37.

Diani, M. & Donati, P. R. (1999) 'Organisational change in west European environmental groups: a framework for analysis', in C. Rootes (ed.), *Environmental Movements, Local, National and Global*, pp. 13–34 (London: Frank Cass).

Eden, S. (2004) 'Greenpeace', *New Political Economy* 9(4): 595–610.

Friends of the Earth (FoE) (2003) *Five Year Plan* (London: FoE).

Hannigan, J. A. (1995) *Environmental Sociology: A Social Constructionist Perspective* (London: Routledge).

Jordan, G. & Maloney, W. (1997) *The Protest Business* (Manchester: Manchester University Press).

Klandermans, B. & Smith, J. (2002) 'Survey research: a case for comparative designs', in B. Klandermans & S. Staggenborg (eds.), *Methods of Social Movement Research*, pp. 3–31 (Minneapolis: University of Minnesota Press).

Knoke, D. (1990) *Political Networks: The Structural Perspective* (Cambridge: Cambridge University Press).

Lamb, R. (1996) *Promising the Earth* (London: Routledge).

McCarthy, J. D. & Zald, M. N. (1977) 'Resource mobilization and social movements: a partial theory', *American Journal of Sociology* 82(6): 1212–41.

Porritt, J. (1996) 'The aftermath', in B. Bryant (ed.), *Twyford Down, Roads, Campaigning and Environmental Law*, pp. 297–309 (London: Spon).

Rawcliffe, P. (1998) *Environmental Pressure Groups in Transition* (Manchester: Manchester University Press).

Richie, D. (1998) *Vision 2000* (London: Friends of the Earth).

Rootes, C. (2007) 'Nature protection organizations in England', in C. S. A. van Koppen & W. Markham (eds.), *Protecting Nature: Organizations and Networks in Europe and the United States*, pp. 34–62 (Cheltenham and Northampton, MA: Edward Elgar).

Saunders, C. (2005) 'Collaboration, competition and conflict: social movement and interaction dynamics of London's environmental movement', PhD thesis, School of Social Policy, Sociology and Social Research, University of Kent at Canterbury.

Saunders, C. (forthcoming) 'Using social network analysis to explore social movements: a relational approach', *Social Movement Studies*.

Schlosberg, D. (1999) 'Networks and mobile arrangements: organisational innovation in the US environmental justice movement', in C. Rootes (ed.), *Environmental Movements, Local, National and Global*, pp. 122–48 (London: Frank Cass).

Skvoretz, J. (1991) 'Theoretical and methodological models of networks and relations', *Social Networks* 13: 275–300.

Skvoretz, J. & Agneessens, P. (2002) *SPSS Inbreeding Programme* (Columbia: SC: University of South Carolina).

Wall, D. (1999) *Earth First! and the Anti-roads Movement: Radical Environmentalism and Comparative Social Movements* (London: Routledge).

Weston, J. (1989) *The F.O.E Experience: The Development of an Environmental Pressure Group* (Oxford: Oxford Polytechnic School of Planning).

Interviews

Where interviewees names are followed with (*), this indicates that these interviews were carried out whilst I was working as a research assistant on the TEA Project.

Bates, Jennifer, Coordinator London FoE and Greenwich FoE, 31 October 2003 and 6 November 2003.

Coleman, Matthew, Eco Activist, EDAG, 8 November 2003.

Cowdell, Julia, Chair, PCEG, 20 September 2003.

de Zylva, Paul, Head of England Team, FoE, 16 January 2004.

Dorey, Cat, Greenpeace Marine Campaigner and North West London Area Networker, 17 January 2004.

Ferriday, Nic, Coordinator West London FoE, 10 June 2003.

Hanton, Alisdair (*), Committee Member South Circular ALERT (1992), Vice Chair of Pedestrians Association, Committee Member of Transport 2000, London Transport Activist's Round Table attendee, 26 April 2001.

Juniper, Tony (*), Campaigns and Policy Director (now Director), FoE, interview with Ben Seel, 2000.

Pearce, Rita, Longford Residents Association, 30 January 2004.

Rau, Nic, Climate/Corporates Campaigner, FoE, 19 January 2004.
Rear, David, Voluntary Warden, Chiswick Wildlife Trust, 15 January 2004.
Roberts, Karen, Voluntary Warden, Chiswick Wildlife Trust, 17 February 2004.
Robertshaw, Emma, Voluntary Warden, Chiswick Wildlife Trust, 17 February 2004.
Sartori, Claudia, Local Groups Development Officer, FoE, 24 November 2003.
Schofield, Richard, Head of Regions, CPRE, 20 October 2003.
Sobey, Bryan, NoTRAG, Harmondsworth and Sipson Residents Association, 7 February 2004.
Stewart, John, HACAN, Airport Watch, 31 January 2004.
Sweeting, Susan, Coordinator Hillingdon FoE, 20 February 2004.
Thornhill, Phil, Coordinator Campaign Against Climate Change, 18 June 2003.
Torrance, Jason, Greenpeace Network Coordinator, 1 July 2003.
Watson, Anna, Waste Campaigner, FoE, 19 January 2004.
Waugh, Miranda, Volunteer Coordinator, London Wildlife Trust, 10 June 2003.
White, Rosy, Senior Development Officer, CPRE, 20 October 2003.

Still the Time of Environmental Movements? A Local Perspective

MARIO DIANI & ELISA RAMBALDO

Introduction

Since the 1990s, the question has been repeatedly posed whether environmentalism should still be conceived as a grassroots, participatory social movement. Some have argued that it should not, as environmental organisations have long acted mostly as scientific and policy innovators in a number of institutionalised settings and milieus, in the political as well as in the cultural, in the academic as

This work originates from a project on 'Networks of civic organisations in Britain', which Mario Diani conducted with Isobel Lindsay (University of Strathclyde in Glasgow) and Derrick Purdue (University of West of England, Bristol) from June 2000 to September 2003, and from Elisa Rambaldo's research for her Master dissertation, discussed at the Faculty of Sociology of the University of Trento in March 2004. The British study was part of the Democracy and Participation Programme, funded by the Economic and Social Research Council (contract L215 25 2006). We are grateful to programme director Paul Whiteley for his constant support, to Manousos Marangoudakis, organizer of the conference 'Nature, Science, and Social Movements' (Mytilene, June 2004), where a draft of this paper was presented, and to Christopher Rootes for his critical guidance.

well as in the industrial sphere. Accordingly, the tools of mainstream collective action theories would not be appropriate to capture recent developments, as environmentalists would engage primarily in cultural production rather than in political representation (e.g. Jamison, 2001). The association between environmental movements and grassroots politics has also been challenged, from a very different angle, by political analysts who have stressed the institutionalisation of those actors as interest groups (e.g. Jordan & Maloney, 1997).

However, others have countered that despite the obvious trends towards the professionalisation of the best known environmental organisations of the 1980s and 1990s, recurring waves of protest activity have also developed around environmental issues, involving both moderate citizens' organisations and newly formed radical, grassroots groups (e.g. Rootes, 2003). Most if not all of these instances of revamped environmental collective action have taken place in local communities, from the British anti-roads protests of the 1990s (Rootes, 2000) to the most recent Italian protests against high speed railway lines in Piedmont (della Porta & Andretta, 2002; Bobbio, 2006). Albeit from different angles, arguments about the end of environmentalism as a social movement stressed the role of actors operating at the national level – be they scientific communities, public intellectuals, or national environmental lobbies – while those emphasising the persistent vitality of local environmental campaigns have pointed to their role as a potential source of reinvigoration of environmental action also at the national or possibly supra-national level (see e.g. Carmin, 1999).

As we know, social movements have always developed in a creative tension between the local and the national (now also increasingly the transnational) sphere. On the one hand, the modern social movement has been famously characterised as the successful attempt to shift collective action repertoires and events from dispersed, unconnected local sites to national political arenas (Tilly, 1984, 1994, 2004). At the same time, it is not only environmental movements that have been strongly associated with locality. Specific territorial areas have long been analysed as distinctive sources of resources for action, as well as the context in which expanding or contracting political opportunities are more neatly perceived and exploited by grassroots organisers (Eisinger, 1973; Healey, 2002).

Here we contribute to this ongoing debate from a peculiar perspective. Instead of asking whether environmental activism should be currently located mostly at the local or the national level, or whether the traits of the actors mobilising on environmental issues render them closer to social movements rather than to interest groups, we shall investigate some instances of local collective action to advance a broader theoretical argument about the distinctiveness of social movements. We shall suggest a rethinking of the peculiarity of social movements *vis-à-vis* other forms of collective action, and the association of environmental movements (as well as social movements in general) with a particular social process, namely, a specific network dynamic (Diani, 1992; Diani & Bison, 2004).

If social movements are a network process, then social movement actors are no longer sets of individual actors sharing certain individual characteristics (such as the usual suspects conventionally described as loosely organised, prone to protest activity, poorly connected to institutions) but the actors involved in certain network patterns. It follows that in order to trace 'environmental movement processes' we have to look at a broader range of civic organisations than those normally associated with environmentalism because of certain traits. More specifically, we have to check to what extent and how public environmental identities, interests in environmental issues, and specific network dynamics intersect in concrete local settings. As we shall see, similar levels of interest in environmental issues correspond to different social processes in different local contexts, raising the question of the mechanisms through which local context shapes network patterns.

Our argument develops in three steps. First, we introduce Diani and Bison's (2004) typology of collective action processes, based on Diani's (1992) view of social movements as social networks. This provides us with the analytical tools for identifying different logics of action among organisations sharing similar levels of interest in environmental issues. Second, we offer a brief profile of the cities in which our empirical analysis is located, and of the organisations acting on environmental issues in each, stressing in particular the variable relationship between interest in the issues and environmental identity (the two, as we shall see, only partially coincide). This enables us to define the boundaries of the 'environmental organisational fields' in the three cities. Finally, we conduct a network analysis of organisational fields in the three cities. By identifying two structural positions in each city, we are able to show how organisations with relatively similar profiles get involved in different logics of collective action, and to relate those differences to some traits of local political contexts.

Organisational, Coalitional, and Social Movement Processes

The existence of organisations sharing an interest in environmental issues does not imply the presence of environmental movements – or more precisely, of social movement processes in which actors, associated with environmental conflicts, are involved. Social movements cannot be reduced to the sum of the organisations sharing distinctive traits, or simply the interest in certain issues (Andrews & Edwards, 2005). Their specificity lies at the intersection of three elements: dense networks of informal exchanges between individuals and/or organisations; shared collective identities; and conflictual interactions with opponents (Diani, 1992, 2003; Diani & Bison, 2004). Different combinations of these elements define different collective action dynamics.

When collective action on environmental issues is mainly conducted within the boundaries of specific organisations, it is difficult to speak of environmental movements. If organisations broadly interested in the same themes are not involved in dense collaborations, nor share any specific identity, some of the most visible and distinctive traits of the social movement experience are missing. In such cases, *organisational* processes will prevail, as organisations focus on the strengthening of both their structure and their identity and secure control of specific issues or subsets of issues. Collaborations with other groups will be relatively rare and, most importantly, scattered across a broad range of different organisations.

Another possible pattern is that other organisations, similarly interested in environmental issues, may be involved in dense collaborative exchanges with groups with similar concerns, but those linkages may not correspond to identity bonds between the organisations involved. Groups may join forces to push forward a certain agenda without feeling linked to each other by a shared identity, once the specific actions and campaigns are over. In other words, alliances and collaborations may be mostly driven by an instrumental logic. Specific events may not be linked by actors into more encompassing narratives that might assign them a broader meaning and make them part of a sustained series of collective actions. Under those circumstances, collective action will be most effectively conceptualised as a *coalitional* process.

Finally, although coalitions are clearly an important component of social movement activity, the one cannot be reduced to the other. In a *social movement* process there will be more than networks of alliances and collaborations. Of course, organisations involved in a movement dynamic will share both material and symbolic resources in order to promote more effective campaigns, and will be fairly closely linked to one another. But, most important, they will also identify one another as part of a broader collective actor whose goals and existence cannot be constrained within the boundaries of any specific protest event or campaign. The existence of collective identity linking organisations to one another will enable them to feel part of the same collective effort even when specific actions may be over, and to develop further joint actions on that basis at a later stage.

Going back to our original question about the persistence or disappearance of environmental movements, the more mobilisations on environmental issues were conducted by organisations with a clear division of labour between them and very little in terms of joint initiatives and shared identities, the less would it make sense to speak of environmental movements, even in the presence of active participation by their members. Actors interested in those issues would actually resemble a set of independent, disconnected organisations, rather than a cohesive network. Organisational rather than social movement logics of action would prevail, as each organisation would tend to strengthen its own niche and pursue its own agenda without committing too much time or energy to alliance-building, nor to the development of broader, encompassing identities. Likewise, if alliances on environmental issues limited themselves to fighting specific battles, with little identity and solidarity between the organisations involved, and no attempts to connect to broader frameworks, there would be little analytical gain from labelling as a 'social movement' what would ultimately be little more than sets of organisations, instrumentally pooling resources in temporary, single-issue coalitions.[1] We can only talk of environmental movements if dense inter-organisational networks and shared collective identity may actually be found among organisations mobilising on environmental issues.

Environmental Organisational Fields in Glasgow, Bristol and Verona

The present work originates from a broader study of networks of organisations mobilising on environmental, ethnic and minority, community, and social exclusion issues in Glasgow and Bristol (Diani & Bison, 2004; Purdue *et al.*, 2004). These organisations provide a particularly interesting unit for the analysis of coalition-building and inter-organisational networking, for they are distinct enough to work independently, yet have enough potential areas of convergence to render cross-sector alliances a feasible option (e.g. on issues such as North–South relations, peace, refugees, urban decay, racism). Between 2001 and 2002, face-to-face interviews, based on a structured questionnaire,[2] were conducted with representatives of 124 organisations in Glasgow and 134 in Bristol. They differed substantially in length of existence (from the early 2000s back to late 1800s), main territorial focus (from neighbourhood to global), size of formal membership (from none to several thousands), yearly budget (from hardly any to six figure sums), and level of formalisation (from the totally informal to the highly bureaucratic (for details, see Baldassarri & Diani, 2007).

We looked in particular at participatory organisations promoting advocacy and interest representation on a broad range of public issues. Although we excluded from our sample organisations focusing exclusively on service delivery, we included organisations whose main focus was in that area as long as they would engage at least in some type of political pressure. In our selection we started from the directories of organisations generated by the umbrella organisations operating as service providers to the voluntary and community sector in the two cities, GCVS (Glasgow Council for the Voluntary Sector) and Voscur (Bristol's Voluntary Organisations Standing Conference on Urban Regeneration); we also relied on a limited number of informants: prominent figures in the voluntary and community sector, or academics familiar with the local scene.

We included all the organisations that according to our informants played a significant role at least at the city level (for an example of case selection based on reputation, see Laumann & Knoke, 1987). As for community organisations, rather than taking a small sample from across the city, efforts were concentrated on two areas, both relatively deprived. These were the Southside in Glasgow, historically associated with strong working-class presence, and more specifically neighbourhoods such as Govan, Govanhill, Gorbals and Pollokshields; and the neighbourhoods of Easton, Knowles, Withywood and Hartcliffe in Bristol, featuring a strong presence of ethnic minorities (Bull & Jones, 2006). If during the interviews other organisations, not included in our original list, were named as important allies by our respondents, they were noted, and interviewed after at least three references had been made.[3] Only one interview was refused, by a Bristol group that was central in the ethnic and migrants network but was going through a serious – if temporary – organisational crisis.

Respondents were asked to 'Please list up to five groups/organisations with which you collaborate most intensely'. While they were not presented with any predetermined list as a stimulus, later in the interview they were also asked whether, in addition to the five partners already mentioned, they had any connection to organisations in any of the following types: environmental groups, ethnic minority and migrants organisations, community organisations, unions and other economic interest groups, religious organisations, political parties, other political organisations, other voluntary associations, any other organisation. Participation in a formally constituted organisation, coordinating a number of different groups on a specific campaign, was recorded as an inter-organisational tie, similarly to an alliance between any two other formally independent organisations.

The resulting data on alliances should not be treated as a list of the groups with which our respondents exchanged most frequently or most intensely in objective terms, but of those they perceived as their most important allies at the time of the interview. Accordingly, the matrix of alliances, which represents the basis of our analysis, is best interpreted as an indicator of perceptions of closeness rather than objective intensity of exchange. It reflects, in other terms, how organisations perceive their social space and identify their most relevant contacts within it. In our analysis, we differentiate between two main types of networks. In particular, we contrast the network consisting of all alliance ties, as defined above, to the network restricted only to those ties that imply some longer-term and deeper connection between two organisations, such as the sharing of core members, or the presence of activists with strong personal ties to one another. In the latter network, the exchange of resources for action, typical of alliance ties, overlaps with deeper 'social bonds', created by shared core members or sustained involvement in joint campaigns.

When looking at the features of collective action in Glasgow, one must take into account: the strength of the 'Red Clyde' tradition of left-wing politics and the strong working-class presence; the role of ethnic minorities – especially Pakistanis – in the Labour political machine; and, more recently, the impact of devolution and the reshaping of centre–periphery relations this has prompted. Coupled with a struggling industrial economy, and despite a fairly successful conversion of the city towards a more diversified and service-driven economy, these traits have created a context which, by theoretical standards, appears particularly conducive to the persistence of collective action addressing social inequality, including action from a specific class perspective. In particular, given the difficult relationship between working-class socialism and environmentalism in Britain (Dryzek *et al.*, 2003), the persistent strength of working-class culture in Glasgow might result in many local environmental issues being treated as issues of inequality rather than as environmental issues (this, despite the recent spread of 'environmental justice' frames in both Scotland and Britain as a whole – e.g. Agyeman, 2002; Agyeman & Evans, 2004; Rootes, 2006). One should also take into account the persisting impact of religious sectarianism, in particular its contribution to an explicitly confrontational political style.

Although its city politics have also been dominated by Labour in recent decades (at least until the May 2003 local elections), the overall profile of Bristol is very different (Bull & Jones, 2006). Historically, the city has switched between Labour and Tory control, yet in a context of political moderation. Since the closure of the docks in the late 1960s–early 1970s, working-class presence in the city has declined. While areas of relative deprivation undoubtedly exist – and some are included in this study – Bristol is a very affluent city with a strong presence of professional bourgeoisie and highly qualified white collar workers. Its main employers are high-tech firms like those in the aeronautical industry, firms in the service sector, especially the financial sector, and big public employers such as the Ministry of Defence. Unemployment rates are extremely low (around 2.5–3%), in stark contrast to Glasgow where social deprivation still represents a major issue. The ethnic scene is larger – with some neighbourhoods having approaching 20% minority residents – and more diversified than in Glasgow, with a substantial presence of Indian, Pakistani, Asian, and Afro-Caribbean communities and a legacy of minority activism which at times even took radical forms, most notably in the St. Paul's riots of 1981. Bristol has also been one of the main centres of cultural innovation, with a flourishing milieu of youth subcultures and alternative lifestyles addressing issues of health, alternative food, and body care. This has corresponded to – if not necessarily overlapped with – a lively presence of environmental organisations and activism, including environmental direct action (Purdue *et al.*, 1997; Anderson, 2004).

In 2002–3, we replicated a part of this study by looking at the environmental organisational field in Verona and neighbouring towns. Located in the prosperous region of Veneto, in northeast Italy, Verona was politically characterised by the dominance of the centre–right Christian Democratic party until its collapse in the early 1990s. Since then, the city has been administered by both centre–right and centre–left coalitions. Overall, the Veronese social and political system offers a mixed political opportunity for forms of collective action close to the model of the so-called 'new social movements'. With its extended and wealthy small industry infrastructure and the strength of the tradition of participation in voluntary associations, the province provides a favourable setting for the development of middle-class politics. Although this has often meant radical right-wing politics (Verona was one of the strongholds of Italian neo-fascism in the 1970s and 1980s, and to an extent still is), it has also meant a lively scene of voluntary organisations mobilising on North–South relations, community issues, migrants' rights, and of course environmental issues. On the other hand, one should take into account the historically dominant presence of the Catholic church; many of the associations in the progressive voluntary and community sector have a Catholic background and strong ties to the Church. Even though changes have occurred in a Catholic culture that was traditionally regarded as anthropocentric and un-conducive to environmentalism, this tradition may not facilitate the spread of specific environmental cultures and identities across the local population.

All in all, the three cities offer quite different settings for the development of organisational fields dealing with environmental issues. By 'organisational fields' we mean 'sets of interacting organizations that together constitute either an institutionalized domain (e.g. health, higher education, aircraft industry) or a sector of substantive analytic interests (e.g. all voluntary organizations in Indianapolis ..., all health-related organizations in Philadelphia)' (Di Maggio, 1986: 337). In the first instance, 'local environmental organizational fields' may be associated with the set of environmental organisations acting in a given locality.

But what are 'environmental organisations'? There are several ways to identify them. One is based on their public image, i.e. in the association observers – including researchers – make between certain organisations and a specific area of collective action. This may be reflected in their names, or in the issues in which they invest most of their time and resources, as well as in all the traits that are likely to attract observers' attention to an organisation. But in the last analysis it depends on external perceptions, that is, on a hetero-definition of organisational identity. This is, incidentally, the conventional way by which organisational populations are selected in most studies. By this criterion, we identified 20 environmental organisations within the Glasgow sample, 35 in Bristol, and 27 in Verona.

Another way to identify environmental organisations consists of looking at their self-representations, and contrasting them with our classification, consistent with the principle that identity-building processes rest on some balance in the tense relationship between hetero- and self-definitions (Melucci, 1982). We then asked our respondents whether they regarded themselves as environmental organisations, but also whether they felt part of the environmental movement. Interestingly, we got very different replies in the three cities. In Glasgow, of the 20 organisations we had classified as environmental, only 13 identified as environmentalist, and only six claimed to feel part of the environmental movement. Likewise, in Verona, only 19 organisations out of 27 claimed an environmental identity. In both cities, hetero-definitions of actors as environmentalist by external observers well exceeded their self-perceptions. By contrast, environmental identification was much stronger in Bristol. Not only did 32 out of 35 organisations classified by the research team as environmentalist consider themselves to be so, but the overall number of organisations claiming some environmental identity exceeded our own classification, with 17 organisations identifying as environmentalist, and a further 26 as environmental movement actors (see Table 1 for details).

This account of identity is consistent with consolidated views of politics in the two areas: the difficult relations with environmentalist culture experienced

Table 1. Self- and hetero-definitions of environmental identity in Glasgow, Bristol and Verona

Organisations' self-definition as environmentalist	Hetero-definition by researchers			
	Environmentalist	Ethnic and migrants	Social exclusion and community	Total
Glasgow				
No identity	7	34	69	110
Environmental organisation	7			7
Part of environmental movement	6		1	7
Total	20	34	70	124
Bristol				
No identity	3	23	65	91
Environmental organisation	13		4	17
Part of environmental movement	19	1	6	26
Total	35	24	75	134
Verona				
No identity	8			
Environmental organisation	14			
Part of environmental movement	5			
Total	27			

in the past by the old left culture (in Glasgow) and the Catholic culture (in Verona) may explain why in the two cities there were more organisations substantively interested in environmental issues than those acknowledging an environmentalist identity; the (new) middle-class cultures and, to a smaller extent, the lifestyle politics orientation in Bristol (Purdue *et al.*, 1997; Anderson, 2004) may account for the opposite outcome in that city. We can take a broader view, however, and simply consider as part of the environmental field all organisations with more than a passing interest in environmental issues, regardless of whether their major sources of identification lie elsewhere.

To this purpose, in Glasgow and Bristol we submitted to principal component analysis expressions of interest in 49 different types of issues. Environmental problems emerged as a distinct factor, along with four other sets of issues (social exclusion, housing, ethnicity and migration, and globalisation; Diani, 2005). In Verona, we limited ourselves to environmental and peace and globalisation issues, and found them to be correlated along those two dimensions. We regarded organisations with interests in more than one environmental issue to be part of the environmental organisational field. This meant 68 organisations in Glasgow, 72 in Bristol, and 26 in Verona. With three exceptions in Bristol, all organisations that claimed an environmentalist identity also expressed an interest in at least two environmental issues.

Searching for Social Movement Dynamics within the Environmental Organisational Field

Let us now explore the extent to which alliance ties among organisations interested in the environment reflect organisational, coalitional, or social movement logics in our three cities. The density of the alliance network is fairly comparable across localities. In Glasgow, 2.9% of possible ties between the 68 organisations included in the field are activated, with an average of 1.96 ties per organisation; in Bristol, it is 2.6%, corresponding to 1.86 ties. In Verona, the density of the network is much higher (9% of ties activated) but this is largely due to the smaller size of the network. The average number of ties per organisation is still higher than in Glasgow or Bristol, but far less markedly so (2.3 ties per organisation).

Of course, it matters not only how much organisations interact, but also how ties are distributed across a specific network. In order to explore this, we first tried to identify organisations with similar structural positions in the alliance networks, i.e. that are structurally equivalent as they are linked to the same actors, or at least share some allies (Scott, 1992: 142–5). In particular, we used Concor, a procedure developed by Breiger et al. (1975).[4] Concor partitions a network into a number of blocks, the incumbents of which have similar, if not strictly identical, patterns of ties to the rest of the network. In practical terms, the original matrix is first split into two blocks, which may in turn be the object of further partition, as long as the structurally equivalent positions identified are substantively meaningful to the analyst (Scott, 1992: 134–40). The next step consists of identifying a blockmodel, summarising the ties between the different structural positions of the network. To this purpose, the density of ties between and across blocks is computed, and a binary *image matrix* is constructed, where cells have value 1 if the density of ties between incumbents of a certain position/block, or between them and the incumbents of other blocks, exceeds a certain threshold, 0 otherwise. The threshold value to decide whether two blocks should be regarded as connected or not is usually the density of the original matrix, although this can be changed according to substantive considerations.

If we apply this approach to our networks and split them into two blocks, we find that some organisations are densely connected to one another while others are far less so. For example, in Bristol, organisations in Block 1 are involved in a dense web of resource exchanges; those in Block 2 often adopt mainly an organisational style of collective action (i.e. as the high number of isolates [located on the left of the graph] shows, they are connected only to few or to no other organisations in the same position). The same pattern may be found in Glasgow and Verona (Figures 2–3).

Who are the incumbents of these different structural positions? And can we associate different types of involvement in environmental networks with specific organisational traits? Different localities provide different answers to this question. In Verona, the distinction between classic environmentalism and civic organisations, mobilising on specific environmental issues, often from a reactive perspective and on an *ad hoc* basis, is very neat (Table 2). In one position (Block 1) are all the major Italian environmental organisations, including animal rights organisations. In contrast, in Block 2 are mostly local groups and action committees, whose link to environmentalism varies in strength, depending on the availability of alternative ways of channelling their interest.

In Glasgow, the best known environmental organisations seem equally distributed in the two blocks. In both cases they occupy the same structural space with organisations with a broader range of interests in social exclusion and ethnic issues, both from a moderate and a radical perspective. Organisations with a clear environmental profile do not seem to be associated with any specific structural position.

In Bristol, again the divide is not as clear-cut as in Verona, as both structural positions see the presence of some established environmental organisations.

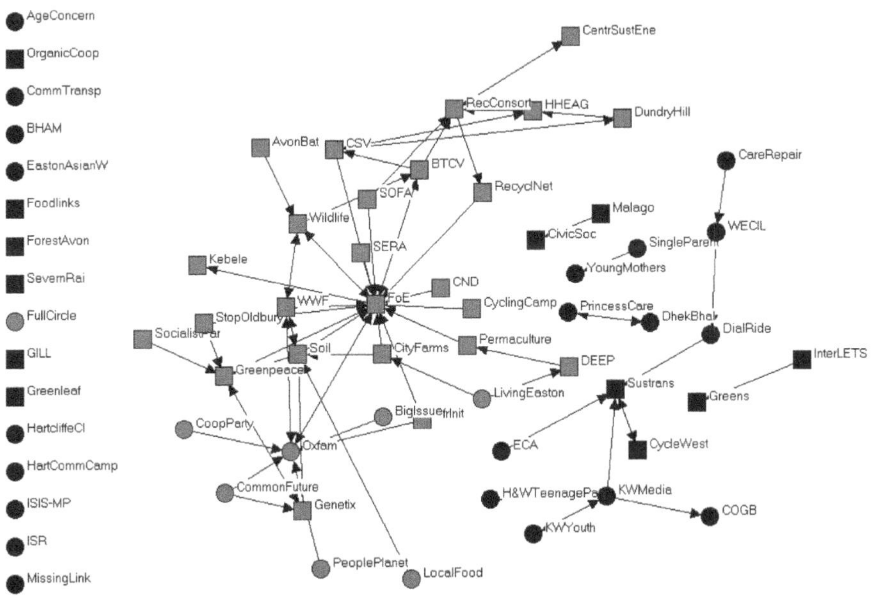

Figure 1. Bristol alliance network (ties within blocks only; black nodes identify Block 2 incumbents; square boxes indicate organisations with environmental identity).

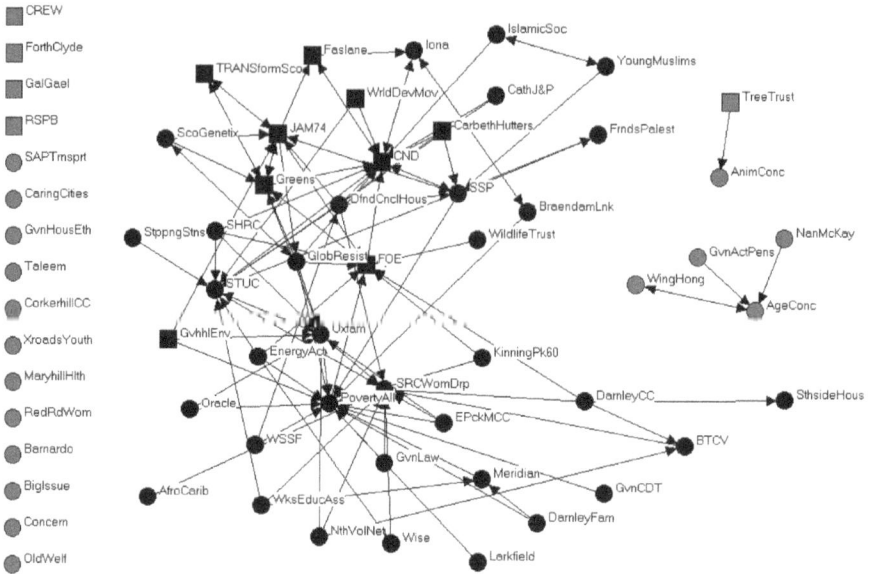

Figure 2. Glasgow alliance network (ties within blocks only; black nodes identify Block 1 incumbents; square boxes indicate organisations with environmental identity).

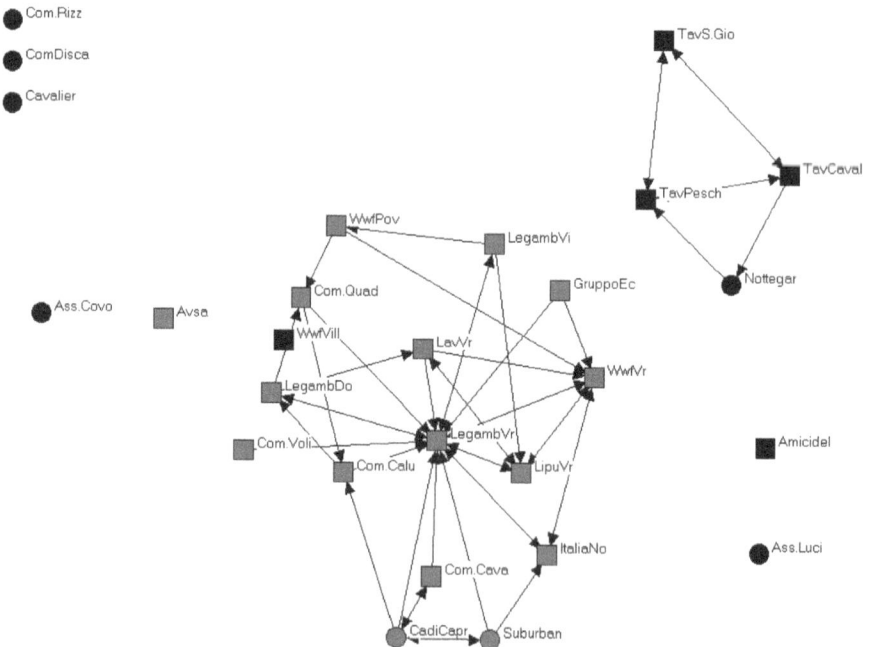

Figure 3. Verona alliance network (ties within blocks only; black nodes identify Block 2 incumbents; square boxes indicate organisations with environmental identity).

Despite the presence of organisations such as WWF, the Soil Association, or Sustrans in Block 2, however, it is Block 1 that most closely resembles an environmentalist profile, while many organisations in Block 2 seem closer to neighbourhood associations with a broader agenda than that of a classic environmental group.

Of course, ties also occur between organisations in different blocks, and we have to take this into account when trying to decipher the structure of environmental fields. Table 3 illustrates the overall structure of alliances in the three cities, with 1s and -1s indicating links within or across blocks that are significantly different (positively or negatively) from a random distribution of ties in that network. Table 3 shows that although differences in network patterns between the two blocks are stronger in Glasgow than in Verona, the two areas show a basically similar structure, that of a 'caucus model' with a single clique with an autonomous profile (see Bearman, 1993: 75). As for Bristol, the structural model differentiates between a passive and an active block, as organisations in Block 1 are both significantly exchanging among themselves and with the rest of the network.

Table 2. Main actors occupying structurally equivalent positions in the three cities

	Block 1	Block 2
Verona	Legambiente, WWF, Italia Nostra, LIPU (birds protection), LAV (anti-vivisection)	Local cultural associations, local conservation groups, anti-high speed trains action groups
Glasgow	British Conservation Trust, CND, Faslane, Oxfam, FoE, JAM74, Scottish Wildlife Trust, Barnardo's, Scottish Churches, housing associations and campaigns	SSP, Greens, Animal Concern, RSSPB, STUC, Globalise Resistance, Poverty Alliance, Age Concern
Bristol	Avon Wildlife, Cycling Campaign, BTCV, FoE, Cycle West, Malago Valley Conservation, Socialist Party	CND, Easton Community Association, Greens, North South Forum, Oxfam, Soil Association, Sustrans, WWF

Table 3. Distribution of alliances among organisations with environmental interests

	Bristol		Glasgow		Verona	
	Block 1	Block 2	Block 1	Block 2	Block 1	Block 2
Block 1	1	1	1	−1	1	0
Block 2	0	0	−1	−1	0	0

If we look at how social bonds (i.e. ties based on shared core members and past participation in collective action events) are distributed across the two structural positions we have just identified in reference to the exchange network, we find a striking similarity to the previous pattern (see Table 4 below). In both Glasgow and Verona we can then identify a social movement process at work in Block 1, as alliances that are significantly denser than the average are matched by identity bonds which are similarly dense (Diani & Bison, 2004). In contrast, organisations in Block 2 in the two cities act mainly 'as organisations', i.e. they do not engage in dense networks of alliances with other groups and act mainly on their own. The same can be said of Bristol, with the additional qualification that in terms of social bonds a centre–periphery structure emerges, with organisations in Block 2 tied to those in Block 1 by reciprocated ties. Incidentally, this finding confirms the stronger relevance of environmental identities in the Bristol area.

We can then observe substantive differences in network dynamics in the three cities. But how many actually reflect conflictual collective action? And how many are, instead, expressions of consensual action, oriented perhaps much more to voluntary work and single-issue pressure than to social or political conflict? Verona displays a particularly conflictual culture, with all organisations identifying specific public agencies or institutions as adversaries (yet in a context where collaboration with institutions is also extremely widespread, to suggest a 'critical collaboration' pattern), and almost all identifying specific private actors – mostly business (Table 5). In

Table 4. Distribution of social bonds among organisations, structurally equivalent in the alliance networks

	Bristol		Glasgow		Verona	
	Block 1	Block 2	Block 1	Block 2	Block 1	Block 2
Block 1	1	1	1	−1	1[a]	0
Block 2	1	0	−1	−1	0	0

[a]Sig. < 0.06.

Table 5. Percentage of organisations in different structural positions, identifying social or political opponents

	Bristol Block 1	Bristol Block 2	Sig.	Glasgow Block 1	Glasgow Block 2	Sig.	Verona Block 1	Verona Block 2	Sig.
Political opponents	41%	26%	n.s.	37%	4%	**	100%	100%	n.s.
Social opponents	21%	11%	n.s.	21%	4*	*	81%	91%	n.s.

*Difference significant at 0.05 level (Fisher's exact test).
**Difference significant at 0.001 level (Fisher's exact test).

Glasgow and Bristol, levels of political opposition in Block 1 exceed not only those of the other block, but, most importantly, the average of civic organisations we studied (in both cities about 25% overall identified political opponents). Consistent with what we found in that context, organisations in Block 1 in Glasgow also identify specific social targets (Diani, 2004).

Finally, it is also worth noting that relational measures of identity (social bonds) match subjective measures (actors' self-representations as environmentalist) in Bristol and Verona but not in Glasgow. In Glasgow, organisations that regard themselves as environmentalist are modestly represented in both structural positions in the network. Figures 1–3, with organisations claiming an environmental identity indicated by a square box, and those not doing so by a circle, illustrate this pattern (see also Table 6 below). For all the differences, Verona shares with Bristol a moderate political culture where the left–right cleavage is not as salient as in Glasgow, and this may be supposed to have created more room for organisations with a specific environmental identity to develop. In Glasgow, organisations mobilising on environmental issues are often included in a broader collective action sector, whose interest in environmental issues is part of a more differentiated agenda and is not sufficiently salient to shape their primary identities.

If we take relational and subjective properties into account, we can identify the following collective action dynamics in the three cities (Table 7).

In Bristol, environmental movement dynamics clearly operate in Block 1, as opposed to organisational dynamics with a dominant consensual orientation in Block 2. The latter are conducted by organisations with interest in environmental issues but a less pronounced environmental identity.

Table 6. Percentage of organisations in different structural positions, claiming an environmental identity

	Bristol**	N	Glasgow	N	Verona*	N
Block 1	76%	26	21%	9	87%	14
Block 2	37%	14	20%	5	45%	5

*Difference significant at 0.05 level (Fisher's exact test).
**Difference significant at 0.001 level (Fisher's exact test).

Table 7. Collective action processes in different structural positions

	Block 1	Block 2
Bristol	Environmental movement process	Consensual organisational process
Glasgow	Social movement process with low environmental identity	Consensual organisational process with low environmental identity
Verona	Environmental movement process	Conflictual organisational process with some environmental identity

In Verona, we also find environmental movement dynamics in Block 1, as opposed to organisational dynamics in Block 2. However, this time we have similar levels of environmental identity in the two blocks; conflictual, rather than consensual, dynamics are also prevalent in both structural positions.

In Glasgow, as in Bristol, social movement dynamics are at work in Block 1, as opposed to organisational dynamics with a dominant consensual orientation in Block 2. However, here environmental identities are not relevant among incumbents of either block. Rather, environmental issues are represented in the context of collective dynamics with a different main focus. While the appeal of environmental issues is undoubtedly broad, indeed comparable to that in Bristol, it is difficult to speak of environmental movements as a major force in Glasgow.

It is worth noting that the traits of the organisations involved in movement processes do not necessarily fit the stereotypical views of movements as we thought we knew them: protest-oriented; anti-institutional; suspicious of, if not hostile to, bureaucratic structures and organisational formalisation. It is certainly true that the environment as a political issue can hardly be detached from grassroots, participatory politics, either as a basis for specific social movement dynamics, or as a major issue for movements whose main focus lies elsewhere. However, this does not mean that arguments about the growing institutionalisation of environmentalism should be easily dismissed. As Table 8 below suggests, organisations in social movement processes in the three cities only partially differ from other, presumably more established, organisations, and when they do, this is not entirely according to expectations.

No differences in levels of organisational formalisation (measured on indicators such as presence or absence of a formally constituted board, secretary, treasurer, a constitution, etc.) can be detected between 'movement' organisations and others. Nor could we find differences in the quality of relationships between civic organisations and city councils, despite assumptions about the anti-institutional nature of social movements. In contrast, organisations involved in movement processes show a significant propensity to use a broader protest repertoire than other organisations (although not in Verona). However, they also show a similarly significant inclination to use a broader range of traditional pressure repertoires. This finding suggests the real divide might run between views of collective action oriented towards politics, spanning protest and pressure repertoires, and views of action emphasising voluntary work and community service. Indeed, in both Bristol and Glasgow there are significant differences between organisations involved in movement processes and the rest, in their propensity to regard themselves as charities (lower than the average) and political organisations (higher than average).

Still the Time of Environmental Movements?

We have here followed an approach to social movement analysis that parts company in significant ways from the mainstream. In particular, we have disregarded the conventional starting point for many analysts, namely, the

Table 8. Traits of environmental organisations involved in social movement processes, compared with the overall profile of civic organisations (only organisations with environmental interests in Verona)

	Bristol social movement	Bristol total	Sig.	Glasgow social movement	Glasgow total	Sig.	Verona social movement	Verona total	Sig.
Formalisation[a]	4.7	5.4	n.s.	4.5	5	n.s.	4.2	4.3	n.s.
Protest propensity[b] (0–100 scale)	45	26	**	41	32	*	51	44	n.s.
Pressure propensity[b] (0–100 scale)	82	70	*	86	76	*	78	70	*
Collaborative ties with city council out of all ties	50%	57%	n.s.	48%	49%	n.s.	75%	67%	n.s.
Identify as charity	27%	40%	*	33%	45%	*	–	–	
Identify as political organisation	47%	25%	*	37%	27%	*	–	–	

[a] Additive scale of nine indicators of organisational formalisation.
[b] See Diani (2004) for details on scale construction.

identification of environmental organisations on the basis of some specific traits or identities, and of the environmental movement as the set of those very same organisations, regardless of the presence or absence of social bonds between them. Instead, we have considered the possibility that organisations, defining themselves and/or identified by external observers as environmental, might act independently, without getting involved in the dense webs of alliances that we regard as a distinctive feature of social movements. Conversely, we have also considered the possibility that organisations, whose most obvious identity would not normally be associated with the environment but which are nonetheless interested in environmental issues, might be involved in what we have defined 'social movement processes'.

In order to take these different possible options into account, we have started with the concept of organisational field, which we have broadly defined to include all the organisations interested in more than just one environmental issue. We have then looked for social movement processes within those networks, with the assistance of blockmodelling network tools. Abandoning a view of movements as aggregates of discrete actors and adopting a process-oriented, relational approach has enabled us to address properly our starting question, but also to qualify it, as the impact and distinctiveness of environmental movements has turned out to vary significantly in different locations. In all the cities we looked at, we have detected distinctive collective action processes, involving organisations with strong interest in the environment, and with the properties of a social movement. But only in two of them, Bristol and Verona, can we confidently associate the social movement process to a significant presence of organisations with a specific environmental identity. In Glasgow, many civic organisations interested in environmental issues are linked to one another in dense alliance networks, and also share deeper bonds, but only a minority share a self-representation as environmentalist.

This points at the role of local political contexts in shaping patterns of collective action. While in general this is far from a new finding, our analysis expands the domain of application of 'political opportunity theory' (Kriesi, 2004) by looking at the impact of the local context on network structures. Normally, opportunities are taken as explanations of actors' behaviour: e.g. its radicalisation following systemic repression (della Porta, 1988), or of the overall frequency and intensity of collective action, as in the Italian protest cycle analysed by Tarrow (1989). Here, by contrast, we look at how local opportunities affect the ways actors interested in a certain cause relate to one another and create broader network patterns. The Glasgow case is particularly revealing in that regard. In Glasgow, collective action on environmental issues does not take the form of a distinctively environmental movement because environmental issues are often so tightly bound up with issues of economic justice and other political concerns as to make the emergence of a distinctive relational field difficult. This pattern makes Glasgow more similar to economically deprived communities of the global South, that also feature strong left-wing mobilisations, than to cities such as Bristol or Verona, where politics appears to be dominated by middle-class actors and concerns, whether on the progressive or the conservative side (Bull & Jones, 2006).

To sum up: yes, it is still the time of environmental movements. But it is not a spaceless time, as local political settings affect the role of environmental organisations in collective action processes, and their overall features. Moreover, actors involved in social movement processes nowadays hardly fit conventional accounts of social movements. Whether this reflects changes in the empirical features of contemporary collective action, or the sharpening of our analytical tools, remains to be seen.

Notes

1. Of course, nothing prevents a coalitional dynamic from evolving into a social movement one, but it is still important to recognise the analytical difference between the two processes (Diani *et al.*, forthcoming).
2. Questionnaire available from the authors.
3. We have strong reasons to believe that, with the exception of one ethnic organisation in Bristol, all the most central organisations in the two cities were contacted: while many organisations were mentioned by respondents (over 500 in both cities), none received more than three nominations.
4. Many have pointed out the ambiguous nature of the computation through which Concor generates its partition of a network, most forcefully Wassermann and Faust (1994: 380–1). However, it has also been remarked that it tends to generate substantively interpretable results (Knoke & Kuklinski, 1982: 74), and that its results are most problematic in the case of graphs consisting of different components (Scott, 1992: 140), which is not the case here.

References

Agyeman, J. (2002) 'Constructing environmental (in)justice: transatlantic tales', *Environmental Politics* 11: 31–53.
Agyeman, J. & Evans, B. (2004) '"Just sustainability": the emerging discourse of environmental justice in Britain?', *The Geographical Journal* 170: 155–64.
Anderson, J. (2004) 'Spatial politics in practice: the style and substance of environmental direct action', *Antipodes* 36: 106–25.
Andrews, K. T. & Edwards, B. (2005) 'The organizational structure of local environmentalism', *Mobilization* 10: 213–34.
Baldassarri, D. & Diani, M. (2007) 'The integrative power of civic networks', *American Journal of Sociology*, 113 (in press).
Bearman, P. (1993) *Relations into Rhetorics* (New Brusnwick, NJ: Rutgers University Press).
Bobbio, L. (2006) 'Discutibile e indiscussa: L'Alta Velocità alla prova della democrazia', *Il Mulino* 55: 124–32.
Breiger, R. L., Boorman, S. A. & Arabie, P. (1975) 'An algorithm for clustering relational data with application to social network analysis and comparison with multidimensional scaling', *Journal of Mathematical Psychology* 12: 328–83.
Bull, A. C. & Jones, B. (2006) 'Governance and social capital in urban regeneration: a comparison between Bristol and Naples', *Urban Studies* 43: 767–86.
Carmin, J. A. (1999) 'Voluntary associations, professional organizations, and the environmental movement in the United States', *Environmental Politics* 8: 101–21.
della Porta, D. (1988) 'Recruitment processes in clandestine political organizations: Italian left-wing terrorism', *International Social Movement Research* 1: 155–72.

della Porta, D. & Andretta, M. (2002) 'Changing forms of environmentalism in Italy: the protest campaign on the high speed railway system', *Mobilization* 7: 59–78.

Di Maggio, P. (1986) 'Structural analysis of interorganizational fields', *Research in Organizational Behavior* 8: 335–70.

Diani, M. (1992) 'The concept of social movement', *Sociological Review* 40: 1–25.

Diani, M. (2003) 'Networks and social movements: a research program', in M. Diani & D. McAdam (eds.), *Social Movements and Networks: Relational Approaches to Collective Action*, pp. 299–319 (Oxford and New York: Oxford University Press).

Diani, M. (2004) 'Do we still need SMOs? Organizations in civic networks', paper presented at the ECPR Joint Sessions of Workshops, Uppsala, 13–18 April.

Diani, M. (2005) 'Cities in the world: local civil society and transnational issues in Britain', in D. della Porta & S. Tarrow (eds.), *Transnational Activism between the Local and the Global*, pp. 45–67 (Lanham, MD: Rowman and Littlefield).

Diani, M. & Bison, I. (2004) 'Organizations, coalitions, and movements', *Theory and Society* 33: 281–309.

Diani, M., Lindsay, I. & Purdue, D. (forthcoming) 'Sustained interactions? Social movements and coalitions in local settings', in N. Van Dyke & H. J. McCammon (eds.), *Social Movement Coalitions*.

Dryzek, J., Downes, D., Schlosberg, D., Hernes, H.-K. & Hunold, C. (2003) *Green States and Social Movements* (Oxford: Oxford University Press).

Eisinger, P. K. (1973) 'The conditions of protest behavior in American cities', *American Political Science Review* 67: 11–28.

Healey, P. (2002) 'On creating the "city" as a collective resource', *Urban Studies* 39: 1777–92.

Jamison, A. (2001) *The Making of Green Knowledge: Environmental Politics and Cultural Transformation* (Cambridge: Cambridge University Press).

Jordan, G. & Maloney, W. (1997) *The Protest Business* (Manchester: Manchester University Press).

Knoke, D. & Kuklinski, J. H. (1982) *Network Analysis* (London and Newbury Park, CA: Sage).

Kriesi, H. (2004) 'Political context and opportunity', in D. A. Snow, S. H. Soule & H. Kriesi (eds.), *The Blackwell Companion to Social Movements*, pp. 67–90 (Oxford: Blackwell).

Laumann, E. O. & Knoke, D. (1987) *The Organizational State. Social Choice in National Policy Domains* (Madison, WI: University of Wisconsin Press).

Melucci, A. (1982) *L'invenzione del presente* (Bologna: il Mulino).

Purdue, D., Dürrschmidt, J., Jowers, P. & O'Doherty, R. (1997) 'DIY culture and extended milieux: LETS, veggie boxes and festivals', *Sociological Review* 45: 645–67.

Purdue, D., Diani, M. & Lindsay, I. (2004) 'Civic networks in Bristol and Glasgow', *Community Development Journal* 39: 277–88.

Rootes, C. (2000) 'Environmental protest in Britain 1988–1997', in B. Seel, M. Paterson & B. Doherty (eds.), *Direct Action in British Environmentalism*, pp. 26–61 (London: Routledge).

Rootes, C. (ed.) (2003) *Environmental Protest in Western Europe* (Oxford: Oxford University Press).

Rootes, C. (2006) 'Facing South? British environmental movement organisations and the challenge of globalisation', *Environmental Politics* 15: 768–86.

Scott, J. (1992) *Social Network Analysis: A Handbook*, 2nd edn (London and Newbury Park, CA: Sage).

Tarrow, S. (1989) *Democracy and Disorder* (Oxford: Clarendon Press).

Tilly, C. (1984) 'Social movements and national politics', in C. Bright & S. Harding (eds.), *State-Making and Social Movement*, pp. 297–317 (Ann Arbor: University of Michigan Press).

Tilly, C. (1994) 'Social movements as historically specific clusters of political performances', *Berkeley Journal of Sociology* 38: 1–30.

Tilly, C. (2004) *Social Movements 1768–2004* (Boulder, CO: Paradigm).

Wassermann, S. & Faust, K. (1994) *Social Network Analysis* (New York: Cambridge University Press).

Local Environmental Protest in Greece, 1974–94: Exploring the Political Dimension

MARIA KOUSIS

The relationship between political parties and the environmental movement has been studied since the 1990s (e.g. Jamison *et al.*, 1993; Diani, 1995; Kriesi *et al.*, 1995; Rucht, 1995) but, thus far, no systematic empirical work addresses the relationship between political parties and community-based environmental activism. Recent studies focus on the relationship between environmental organisations and political parties (van der Heijden, 2002; Dalton *et al.*, 2003), or on specific cases of grassroots activism (Rootes, 1995, 2006; Stearns & Almeida, 1998).

The author wishes to thank Mario Diani for his critical comments on the coding instrument which made this work possible as well as an anonymous referee and Minas Samatas for their constructive comments on earlier drafts. The helpful comments, generous editing and patience of Chris Rootes are gratefully acknowledged. Any remaining shortcomings are her own. The data derive from the 'Grassroots Environmental Action and Sustainable Development in Southern Europe' (GEA) and 'Transformation of Environmental Activism' (TEA) projects (DGXII, EC contract nos EV5V-CT94-0393 and ENV4-CT97-0514).

Political Opportunities and Constraints in Environmental Protest

Systematic empirical studies of political opportunities and local environmental activism at the community level are rare. Focusing on local campaigns against waste incinerators in England, Rootes (2006) finds that campaigners' discourse matters less than political opportunities as reflected in the structure of local political systems, and other aspects of the local and national policy context. Examining the Minamata mercury victims' grassroots movement, Stearns and Almeida (1998) show how changes in political opportunities affected the responses of challenged groups to victims' claims. They systematically examine two clusters of political opportunity variables: *external allies* (political allies and mass media bringing organisational, financial, and ideological support) and *elite instability* (elections, intra-governmental conflicts and symbolic government gestures). Political allies include political parties (especially opposition parties – Castells, 1983; Stearns & Almeida, 1998), students, organised labour, intellectuals and scientists.

Studies of political opportunities, political processes (Tilly, 1978, 2004) and new social movements in northern Europe show that changes in the structure of *political opportunities and constraints* impacted directly on the emergence and rise of the environmental movement (Kriesi *et al.*, 1995; van der Heijden *et al.*, 1999). Movement mobilisation is closely linked to conventional politics in the parliamentary as well as non-parliamentary national arenas, and political opportunity structure is seen as composed of national cleavage structures, prevailing strategies, and alliance structures. The political context influences environmental movements' organisational structure, action repertoire, hegemonic discourse and chances of success (van der Heijden, 1999).

Of particular interest are the alliance structures which Kriesi *et al.* (1995) identify as the less stable elements of political opportunities and constraints. Influenced by Tarrow (1990), they concentrate on two aspects of the changing political context for new social movements (NSMs): the configuration of power on the left, and the presence or absence of the left in government. They find that although facilitation of NSMs by established political actors, especially from the left, is omnipresent, its magnitude varies depending on the character of the configuration of the old and the new left and on whether the left is in or out of government. They conclude that 'in a polity with a pacified old left, NSMs strengthen the new left ...' (Kriesi *et al.*, 1995: 81). However, in a polity where the old left has not yet been pacified, NSMs do not have such an effect, but are transformed by a left that exploits them for its own political purposes, as in France.

In Greece, Spain and Portugal, where democracies were consolidated in the 1980s, changes in the political context, including their late EU membership, have influenced environmental movement potential (Jiménez, 1999, 2001; Kousis, 1999a, 2004; Barcena & Ibarra, 2001; Gil Nave, 2001). Alliance structures, especially with established parties of the left, and periods of political fluidity, such as elections, appear to affect the peaks of reported environmental protest waves (Kousis, 1999b; Kousis & Eder, 2001).

From the late 1970s, an informal relationship developed in Greece between political parties of the left and activists, especially those involved in environmental organisations. This was particularly visible in the early 1990s – the beginning of PASOK's[1] three consecutive terms in government (1993–2004) – with its novel commitment to environmental protection, its attempted co-optation of members of professional environmental NGOs and the Federation of Ecologists Alternatives (FEA), as well as in collaborations between the FEA and SYN[2] (the leftist coalition party), a collaboration contributing to SYN's new name: the Coalition of the Left, Movements and Ecology (Karamichas, 2002).

Qualitative studies have pointed out the importance of political parties in local environmental activism (Louloudis, 1987; Botetzagias, 2001). According to Alexandropoulos and Sertedakis (2000: 12), 'the state-led corporatist mode of interest intermediation and partyness [i.e. *party-dominated politics*] absorbed the participatory potential of Greek citizens...environmentalism could find access to a wider public only through its political formation, i.e. partyness'.

Comparative works on southern European community-based protest pay minimal attention to this relationship (Aguilar-Fernandez *et al.*, 1995; Kousis *et al.*, 1996; Jiménez, 1999; Kousis, 1999a, 1999b) when describing the basic features of post-dictatorial environmental activism. Greece, Spain and Portugal show similar tendencies: for the three countries as a whole, local representatives of political parties were more noticeable in about a quarter (23.4%) of environmental protest event cases lasting over a year than in those of shorter duration (8.4%). Residents/citizens/neighbours were most often participants in environmental protest (80.2% and 67.2%, respectively), followed by local environmental groups (32.3% and 24.9%) (Kousis, 1999a: 185).

Using the same data, Kousis found that in contrast to their rural counterparts, urban participants tended more frequently to include resource-rich groups such as environmentalists and political party representatives. Rural protesters were more likely affiliated to ruling socialist parties; urban protesters or coalitions of rural and urban protesters tended to be affiliated with combinations of leftist, green and other party representatives (Kousis, 1999b: 231).

A study of environmental protest events in Greece during 1987–98 (Kousis, 2003) offers only partial support to the political opportunities thesis that NSM protest is stimulated under right-wing governments, but depressed under those of the left. The pattern of these environmental protests shows both highest and lowest levels taking place under PASOK governments, while moderate levels occurred under the New Democracy (ND) government. Thus, the political identity of the governing party is not expected to be the major factor influencing the pattern of environmental protest in Greece.

Local Environmental Contention and the Political Dimension

Who are local environmental activists? The international literature has called them community, eco-populist, or grassroots groups (Szasz, 1994; Stearns & Almeida, 1998), local citizen-worker movements (Gould *et al.*, 1996), working-class activists (Cable & Cable, 1995), and new middle-class movements (Eder, 1996). Among the more prevalent are residents, and/or their committees, local government, local environmental groups, labour and trade unions, and local activity clubs (Kousis, 1999a). Community-based environmental mobilisers have been especially important within a given geographical area and seem to be increasing, especially since the 1980s. Unlike professionally organised mobilisations, these are simultaneously more temporary and richer (Tilly, 1994) and are not usually supported by larger environmental organisations (Szasz, 1994; Kousis *et al.*, 1996; Kousis, 1999b).

Studies of community as well as national level environmental activism note the strengths and weaknesses of protest event analysis (PEA). They mainly focus on the selectivity of the sources used (chances of being reported) and the systematicity of description biases (changes in rationale of media selection) (Franzosi, 1987; Rucht *et al.*, 1998; Barranco & Wisler, 1999; Fillieule & Jiménez, 2003; Ortiz *et al.*, 2005). PEA based on the national daily press covers only a small proportion of events (estimated at less than 10%) related to their size, novelty of actions, violence, and spatial distribution (Fillieule & Jiménez, 2003).

National media reports are still considered an adequate proxy for protest activity in view of the lack of other sources offering comparable data. In order to address the gaps, however, the few systematic PEAs of environmental protest suggest the use of additional data to supplement national daily press data (Kriesi *et al.*, 1995; Rootes, 2003; Ortiz *et al.*, 2005: 414).

Here we develop a systematic analysis of the participation of political parties in local environmental protest in Greece, from 1974 to 1994, and, through a comparative account based on national daily press and public agency archives, show how the use of different data sources influences the visibility of political party participation in local environmental protest.

Greece

From the 1970s through the 1990s, studies of the relationship between political parties and social mobilisations in Greece, like those of other post-dictatorial southern Europe regions (Diamandouros & Gunther, 2001), focused on civil society groups rather than social movements and activism, emphasising political clientilism, party-dominated politics, and populism (e.g. Lyrintzis, 1983; Mouzelis, 1989), a 'hyper-', but in essence a 'hypo-', politicisation (Tsoukalas, 1977; Spourdalakis, 1988) described as an intense illusionary and pragmatic adherence to the state which is seen as a locus of private gains of security, resources, privileges and status (Demertzis, 1990). Especially up to the late 1980s, party-dominated politics witnessed intense competition with political parties seeking to integrate organised groups and trade unions under party control (Mouzelis & Pagoulatos, 2002).

Bipartism, a feature of the pre-dictatorial period, was established in Greece with the 1981 elections (Mavris, 2004: 120–4) and climaxed with those of November 1989. An intense and enduring political competition took place between the two ruling parties, New Democracy (ND) of the 'right' and PASOK of the 'anti-right'.

While anti-dictatorial mobilisations dominated in the early 1970s, mobilisations of the 1975–85 period took place when PASOK's domination was increasing. Since 1974, and especially with PASOK's entry in government, in 1982–4, new voluntary associations such as cultural associations, sports clubs, internal migrant clubs, students' and parents' associations, were established. This trend reversed from the mid 1980s, when the number of newly founded voluntary associations began declining (Sotiropoulos, 1996). Although acknowledging that to a large extent, interest representation in Greece is dominated by state corporatism, Sotiropoulos argues that the consolidation of Greek democracy allowed for the emergence of multiple single-issue movements, such as ecological, feminist, health, cultural and consumer.

The high interest in politics during the 1974–81 period (Lyrintsis, 1983; Featherstone & Katsoudas, 1987) subsided by the late 1980s as PASOK was tarnished by scandals, and political cynicism and alienation rose (Kafetzis, 1994). Nevertheless, even since the late 1980s, parties continued to strive for control of newly founded NGOs. By the 1990s partitocracy lost ground to public cynicism, political de-ideologicalisation, and increasing professional opportunities in the private sector.

Based on research on public participation, volunteering and environmental activism, recent works on collective action of the post-dictatorial period tend to suggest reconsideration of the thesis that Greece has a weak civil society, dominated by party politics (Close, 1999; Kousis, 1999a, 1999b, 2003; Panagiotopoulou, 2003; Afouxenidis, 2004; Sotiropoulos, 2004), but systematic empirical work on political party representation in local environmental movements is nonexistent.

Political Facets of Community-Based Environmental Protest

The protest event and protest case analyses which follow explore the presence of political party participation or support in local environmental protest in Greece during the first two decades of the post-authoritarian period. Since previous analysis of national press reports of protest actions suggests that they represent only the tip of the iceberg, a key concern here is to enhance the image by offering a comparative account based on two types of data sources. National media reports during 1974–94 are supplemented by public agency archives to examine the case of Heraklion, the most populous county of Crete.

Protest Case Analysis Based on National Press: Greece

Protest case analysis, a variant of PEA (Kousis, 1999b),[3] focuses on protest cases, not events, and allows the tracking of measurable characteristics of community-based contentious activism over longer time periods, without losing a comprehensive view of the conflict, while saving time and resources. Protest case analysis combines elements from both qualitative and quantitative approaches to environmental activism, centring on the case of contention itself as the (meso) unit of analysis.

The data derive from articles located by reading every issue of the major national newspaper *Eleftherotypia*, an independent centre–left newspaper which appeared after the end of the dictatorship, ranking usually among the top three or four national dailies between 1974 and 1981. As well as covering the environmental movement well, it also provides the best coverage of domestic news (Komninou, 1996: 231–42).

The ecology magazines *Oikologia* and *Perivallon, Nea Oikologia* were used as supplementary sources. About 80% of the mentions come from *Eleftherotypia*, all sections of whose main editions and supplements were read. All mentions of local environmental activism were collated into cases. Thus 1,322 cases were reconstructed (Kousis, 1999b). The analysis uses the 1,282 of these that expressed pro-environment claims.

Two decades of political party participation and political opportunities and constraints. The overall presence of political party participation or support in local environmental protest appears minor. Only 12% of environmental protest cases involve participation of local representatives of political parties, or/and participation or support of non-local representatives of political parties.

The majority of political party representatives involved in local environmental protest cases (62%) are local representatives of political parties participating in, but not initiating protests, followed by a solid minority (28%) of non-local representatives of political parties participating in or supporting protests. Local and non-local politicians opposing their party's views constitute a noticeable minority (21%) in these cases.

The political affiliation of these politicians reflects not only the contribution of left parties to local environmental activism, but the eagerness of political parties of different political colours to 'participate' in protest initiated at the community level. A mix of left, right, centre and green party representatives were present in 32% of cases, a combination of socialist, communist, or other left, representatives in another 32% of cases (18% socialist, 12% communist, 2% other left) and a mix of left and green party[4] representatives in 19%. A similar pattern is evident for non-local political party representatives (31% mixed, 38% left, and 17% left–green, respectively).

Thus, it appears that political parties of various complexions compete, probably opportunistically, to become allies of local environmental activists. The facilitation of NSMs by established political actors of the left is also apparent.

The Greek political milieu has exerted an influence on local environmental protest and the involvement of political parties. As shown in Figure 1, the pattern of 'soft' and 'hard'[5] protest waves for the minority of cases with political party participation reflects the prevailing political opportunities and constraints.[6]

Of the four cycles of waves depicted, the highest waves involve soft actions in cases without political party participation. Election years, as periods of fluidity, exert a more noticeable influence on soft protest actions. Furthermore, it is before election years and especially under ND governments that such softer actions without political party participation flourish. Overall, whereas during 1974–9, the political opportunities of the end of authoritarian rule appear to have produced a spectacular rise in these protests, PASOK's hegemonic politics of the late 1970s and 1980s appear to have acted as constraints on them. With fewer hard actions, the second cycle of waves for cases not involving political party representatives depicts a much reduced effect of election years with a different pattern of peaks, the highest of which takes place during the late 1980s, when PASOK was in government.

Political party participation in local environmental protest, as depicted in the two lowest protest cycles, peaked in 1975–81, during the first two terms of right-wing (ND) rule. These cycles follow the same patterns, not reflecting the election-year effect shown for protest cases without political party representatives. This mobilising force consists of coalitions of left (PASOK, KKE [Communist], KKE-internal, or SYN) party participation in environmental protest, with peaks prior to election years. Before its first two election victories (1981 and 1985), PASOK's challenge was to unite all those voters who did not belong to the electoral public of the right. They included veterans of the Resistance movement against Nazi Germany, citizens independent of any party identity, and those who fought against the junta (Nikolakopoulos, 1990). During the first post-dictatorial years, the convergence of KKE and KKE-internal under PASOK's anti-right pole was facilitated by their common ideological positions, which included their: radical opposition to the seven-year dictatorship, viewed as the concentration of the post-civil war state of the right; intense anti-Americanism; and rejection of organisations seen to represent monopoly capitalism (Nikolakopoulos, 1990: 210). Environmental activists were very likely to be among them during this period (Louloudis, 1986; Kousis, 2004).

The drastic decline in soft and hard actions involving political party participation under the first PASOK government is as expected. Environmental protest facilitated by the opposition of the left appears pacified between 1981 and 1985. Even though of limited scale, this low point in both soft and hard actions involving political party participation reflects the political constraints imposed on community-based environmental activism by its alliances with the established political parties of the left. This continues even in the late 1980s, when PASOK's wide cross-class alliances were breaking down (Nikolakopoulos, 1990: 220–9).

A series of scandals between 1985 and 1989 led to PASOK's political isolation, erosion of the close relations within the anti-right pole, and a

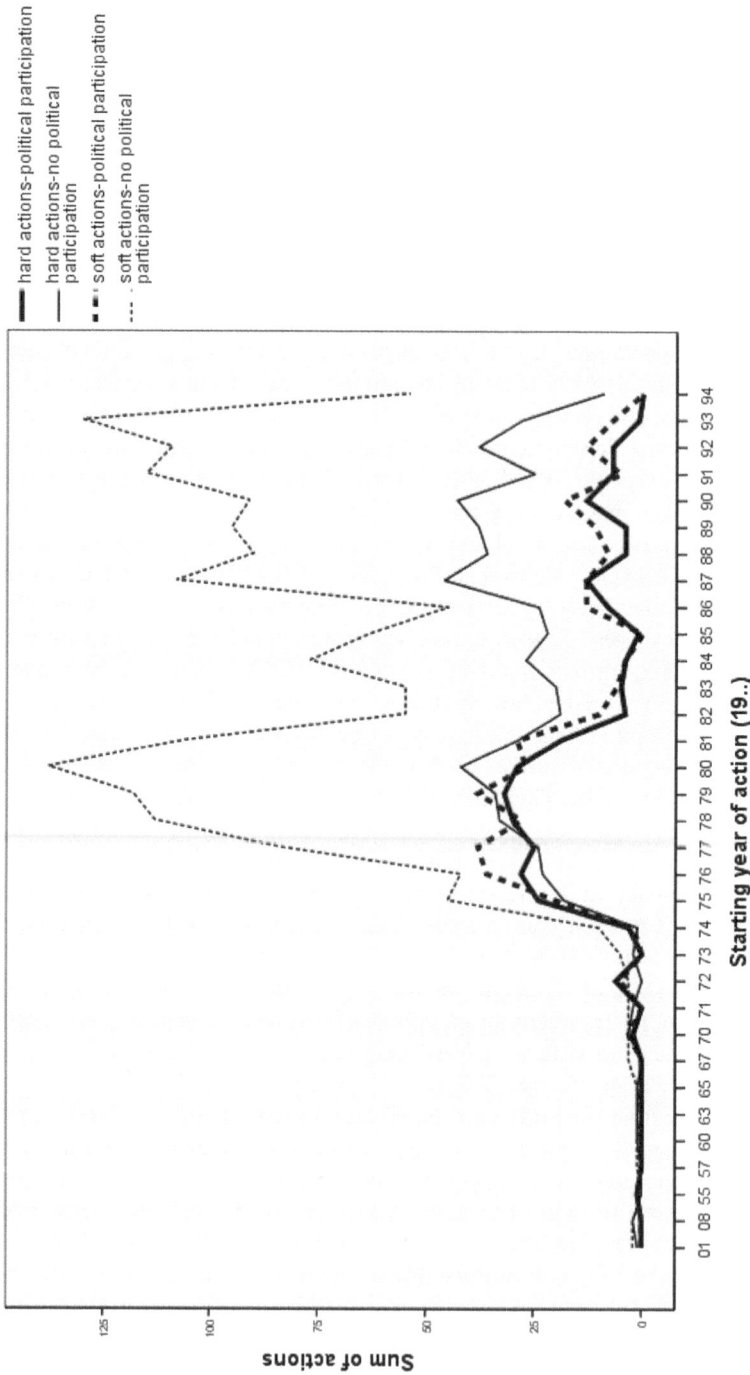

Figure 1. Environmental protest cases in Greece by type of action, political party participation and starting year of protest (*note*: national election years for Greece: 1974, 1978, 1981, 1985, 1989, 1990, 1993).

weakening of the 'right'–'anti-right' cleavage. The result was a tripolar system in which KKE and ND redefined their ideological positions (Nikolakopoulos, 1990: 211–2). These conditions functioned as political opportunities, leading to considerable increases even prior to election years for both soft and hard environmental actions not involving political party representatives (Figure 1).

With the return of ND to government in 1990, similar waves of political party involvement appear in soft and hard environmental actions, as in the 1970s when ND was also in government, with one major exception: the incidence of actions carried out with the participation of political party representatives dropped to about half of that before PASOK's first victory.

The data presented here offer new evidence on environmental contentious cases, which differentiates actions on the basis of political party involvement reported in national press, and illuminates the effects of political opportunities and constraints on local environmental activism.

Political party dimensions and characteristics of community-based environmental protest cases. Community-based environmental protest cases are led primarily by residents' groups, and secondarily by local government at the community or municipality level, both more prevalent when political party representatives are present (Table 1). This reflects the political ties and alliances between PASOK local governments of the 1970s and 1980s and protest activists.

Table 1. Participating groups by political party representation in local environmental protest cases

	Political party representation (%)*		
	Not present	Present	Total
Type of local participating group			
Residents/citizens	73.7	91.8	76.0
Local government	32.3	72.2	37.2
Labor and trade unions	10.9	36.7	14.1
Cooperatives	1.2	8.2	2.0
Employers	0.6	4.4	1.1
Cultural activities clubs	18.2	50.6	22.2
Environmental groups	15.5	20.9	16.1
Type of non-local supporting group			
Citizens from adjacent communities	1.2	7.6	2.0
Local government	2.2	29.1	5.5
Labor and trade unions	0.7	7.6	1.6
Environmental groups	3.8	13.9	5.1
Total	(1,124)	(158)	(1,282)

Source: GEA.
*Percentages were calculated for political party representation in local environmental protest cases which, for each category, was coded as a dichotomous yes/no variable; thus percentages do not add to 100.

Community and municipality level administrations (OTAs – First Degree) are an old institution, financially dependent on central government, with expanding power over local environmental issues – including construction and management of water and sewage projects, sites of recreation, physical planning and land management (Fousekis & Lekakis, 1997: 143–5).[7] Both municipalities and prefectural administrations are under the supervision of state-appointed heads of Regions (Periferiarhes).

The great increase in local government participation when political parties are present may be explained by the political environment of the period. State-dependent local self-administration organisations kept close ties to the ruling political parties, their channels of access to state resources. Municipal administrations tied to opposition parties challenged PASOK state policies, while OTAs with ties to PASOK functioned as dominant party outposts. During the 1980s, state subsidies, grants and transfers to local governments increased under PASOK governments, for political purposes. Although PASOK introduced legislation aiming to make the prefects accountable to judicial authority, critics argued that this led to considerable increases in control over the distribution of economic resources to municipalities and communities (Kioukias, 1997: 316–29).

Table 1 also reveals that local environmental protest cases involving political party representatives show notably higher involvement of unions, cooperatives, and cultural clubs. Greek unions are financially dependent on the state, their singular and non-competitive hierarchical structure imposed on them by law. Since the 1980s, the state has unofficially intervened in unions to regulate leadership and representation. In addition to its repression under the dictatorship, the labour movement's organisational weaknesses kept it from playing a major role in the 1970s and 1980s (Zambarloukou, 1996). The two major political parties infiltrated and dominated trade and labour unions. Increasingly dependent on state funds, farmers' cooperatives (Panhellenic Confederation of Unions of Agricultural Cooperatives, PASEGES) were similarly party-dominated.

These conditions served to induce political party participation in local environmental protest. This is also visible in protest cases involving non-local supporting groups which are markedly different when political parties are present: citizens from adjacent communities, unions, cooperatives, environmental groups, and especially local government are all more frequently involved.

Cultural associations showed dramatic increases in their numbers given the opportunity for freedom of expression in the first post-authoritarian period (1978–85), and boomed again in 1986–7. Since many were founded by local governments (Sotiropoulos, 2004), their participation in local environmental protest cases is directly or indirectly tied to the political opportunities and alliances raised by the left in the 1970s and 1980s. At the same time however, it is also an indication of the need to respond to local problems from a cultural (and not only political or economic) perspective.

Maintaining their focus on local environmental problems, local environmental groups are only modestly influenced by the presence of political parties. Non-local environmental groups appear more swayed, probably under the influence of their non-local political alliances.

Party representatives also participate in more demonstrations, confrontational and violent actions, as seen in Table 2. This is mostly a product of the political opportunities during the first post-authoritarian decade, including the alliances with political parties of the left.

In addition to being involved in more contentious actions, political party representatives participate in actions with higher numbers of participants, especially those involving thousands of participants (19% of the 158 cases involving party participation compared to 1.6% of all 1124 cases), apparent probably because political parties seek opportunities to engage with and influence larger numbers of citizens for their own political interests.

Local environmental protest claims reflect concerns related to domestic waste, manufacturing activities, wildlife, construction and transportation (Table 3).[8] Political party representatives were at least twice as likely to participate in protest concerning military installations and activities, toxic/hazardous waste, energy and manufacturing activities, which were also likely to involve harder forms of action.

Thus, although present in only a minority of environmental protest cases, political parties seize the opportunities of engaging with grassroots environmental activists who initiate struggles involving high numbers of participants and a specific set of issues. The presence of political parties increases significantly when it comes to marine, fresh water, and air pollution. They are also more prevalent when claims focus on life itself being threatened, on health and on the economy.

Table 2. Action forms by political party representation in local environmental protest cases

	Political party representation (%)*		
Action forms	Not present	Present	Total
Appeal	91.3	93.0	91.5
Demonstrative	30.2	82.3	36.6
Confrontational	14.3	37.3	17.2
Violent	3.2	10.1	4.1
Total	(1,124)	(158)	(1,282)

Source: GEA.
*Percentages were calculated for political party representation in local environmental protest cases which, for each action form type, was coded as a dichotomous yes/no variable; thus percentages do not add to 100.

Table 3. Source of environmental claims by political party representation in local environmental protest cases

	Political party representation (%)*		
	Not present	Present	Total
Sources of environmental damage			
Wildlife related activities	17.4	12.0	16.8
Agric/animal husbandry/fishing	6.9	5.1	6.6
Resource extraction	6.2	8.2	6.4
Manufacturing activities	17.5	35.4	19.7
Military installations & activities	3.2	9.5	4.0
Transportation	8.2	9.5	8.4
Toxic/hazardous waste	5.0	16.5	6.6
Domestic waste	21.7	25.3	22.1
Energy	3.3	8.2	3.9
Lack of environmental policy	3.2	5.1	3.5
Failure of environmental policy	9.4	13.9	10.0
Identified offenses			
Noise pollution	9.7	12.0	10.0
Atmospheric pollution	31.1	43.6	32.7
Fresh water pollution	19.1	27.8	20.2
Marine pollution	11.7	27.2	13.7
Land pollution	7.7	8.2	7.8
Other ecosystem damages	67.8	63.3	67.2
Identified impacts			
Health	34.3	51.3	35.5
Economy	19.4	29.1	20.5
Ecosystem	88.0	91.8	88.5
Life itself	11.2	25.9	13.0
Total	(1,124)	(158)	(1,282)

Source: GEA.

*Percentages were calculated for political party representation in local environmental protest cases which, for each action type, was coded as a dichotomous yes/no variable; thus percentages do not add to 100.

Interesting patterns emerge when the bodies approached for assistance and the groups challenged by political party participation are examined (Tables 4 and 5). Overall, the state is approached most frequently in cases with and without political party support. More importantly, the data reflect the powerful resources available to party-supported protest. When party representatives are present, aid is four times as likely to be requested from large environmental organisations, scientists, EU agencies, and twice as likely from regional courts and the Supreme Court. At the same time, however, their political networks constrain them from approaching politically affiliated sub-state agencies. During the 1970s and 1980s, these sub-state agencies, prefectural administrations, were central government representatives and appointees.

An alternative explanation of these patterns is that party representatives become involved in the higher profile cases *after* they have begun their climb to

Table 4. Bodies approached by political party representation in local environmental protest cases

	Political party representation (%)*		
Bodies approached	Not present	Present	Total
State	28.3	36.1	29.3
EU	1.7	7.6	2.3
Sub-state	7.3	2.5	6.7
Regional courts	4.4	11.4	5.3
Supreme courts	3.5	7.6	4.0
Large environmental organisations	0.8	3.8	1.2
Scientists	1.9	10.1	2.9
Police	3.0	4.4	3.2
Total	(1,124)	(158)	(1,282)

Source: GEA.
*Percentages were calculated for political party representation in local environmental protest cases which, for each action type, was coded as a dichotomous yes/no variable; thus percentages do not add to 100.

Table 5. Groups challenged by political party representation in local environmental protest cases

	Political party representation (%)*		
Group challenged	Not present	Present	Total
State	39.0	71.5	43.0
Central state reps at local level	14.9	10.1	14.4
Local government	15.4	15.2	15.4
State producers	8.5	13.3	9.1
Private producers	34.2	44.3	35.4
Pol. parties of the opposition	0.4	2.5	0.7
Total	(1,124)	(158)	(1,282)

Source: GEA.
*Percentages were calculated for political party representation in local environmental protest cases which, for each action type, was coded as a dichotomous yes/no variable; thus percentages do not add to 100.

public attention, leading to a spiral effect. The cases that remain at sub-state level are likely to be those raised by locals with few resources or limited knowledge that parties think too unimportant to take up.[9]

Local Environmental Protest: Profiles Based on Local Archives and National Media

The comparative accounts which follow are based on national daily press and public agency archives for Heraklion, to show how the use of different data sources impacts upon the visibility of political party participation in local environmental protest.

Comparing national press and archive-based local environmental protest cases: Heraklion County, Crete[10]. The protest case analysis here rests on two data sets. From *Eleftherotypia* and *Nea Oikologia*, 15 cases of environmental grassroots mobilisations were identified for the county of Heraklion between 1974 and 1994. The archival data contain information supplied by almost all relevant agencies located in Heraklion, including Periferia Kritis (Region of Crete), Nomarhia (Prefecture), Dimarhio (City Hall) and Technikon Epimelitirion Anatolikis Kritis (Technical Chamber of Eastern Crete, TEAK). The data were organised into 234 protest cases covering the period 1987–94.[11] About 80% of the documents were objections/complaints – the majority (57%) filed with the county's Department of Public Health. For 80% of protest cases, the Public Health Department was receiver of claims directly or indirectly, followed by the police department (28%), Department for Physical Planning, Public Works, and the Environment (16%), local government (14%) and the county office itself (14%).

According to both data sources, 50% of protesting groups originate from urban areas, and about 40% from rural areas, reflecting the spatial distribution of the county's population. The cases reported in *Eleftherotypia* are longer in duration than those found in the public agency archives (33% compared with 13%), possibly a result of the shorter period of the latter's coverage. Nevertheless, it suggests that the national newspaper picks up more significant and enduring cases. Protest cases in the public agency archives involve fewer participants (usually five to 25), almost exclusively from one community, whereas media-reported cases involve more participants and are more likely to have been organised from more than one community.

Political party representatives and non-local supporting groups are strikingly absent from both data sets; residents predominate (80% and 54%, respectively), local government maintains second place (33% and 32%) and environmental organisations are almost wholly absent. In almost one-tenth of the public archive cases but not in the media reports, employers appear as a participating group.

Appeals, the most common action form in both data sets, are present in almost all cases. By contrast, demonstrational, confrontational and violent actions are involved in about one-third of media-reported cases, but in less than 2% of those constructed from public archives. Waste related claims appear considerably more often in the archival data set (39% compared to 27%), followed by sewage and agriculture or animal husbandry problems, while wildlife intruding activities, manufacturing and energy installations are more important in media cases.

Challenged groups also differ. In cases reported in the media, the predominant challenged group is the state (40%), followed by local government, and economic actors. By contrast, in public archives, the most frequently challenged groups are economic actors/producers (63%), followed by other communities or citizens (15%) and the state.[12]

Conclusion

From this exploratory study, three major conclusions can be drawn concerning political opportunities, the tracing of local environmental activism and the implications for Greek politics.

The data first show how changes in elite instability during election years and political party alliances have influenced the amount and peaks of community-based environmental activism, lending support to Almeida and Stearns (1998). The differentiation of actions on the basis of political party involvement has shed light on the effects of political opportunities and constraints on local environmental activism, and improves our understanding of the impacts which elections or alliances with the left exert on community-based activism in a new southern European democracy.

The incidence and character of local environmental protest in Greece was influenced by the consolidation of democracy in the 1970s, PASOK's dynamic entry into the political arena of the 1970s, the strengthening of leftist and green parties in the 1970s and 1980s, as well as by the alliances of local environmental activists with political parties, especially opposition political parties, organised labour, scientists, and other social actors.

We have also provided evidence showing limited support of local environmental activism by established political actors especially from the left. Here too, the magnitude of facilitation varies depending on whether the left is in or out of government, as well as on the fluidity and political scandals of the period.

The evidence at hand offers only partial support to the political opportunities thesis (Kriesi *et al.*, 1995) that new social movement protest is stimulated under right-wing governments, but depressed under those of the left (cf. Kousis, 2003). The protest cycle of hard actions which did not involve political party representatives depicts similar waves under both right-wing and socialist governments. At the same time, the protest cycles of both hard and soft actions with political party participants peak during two right-wing governments of the 1970s, but subside under the right-wing government of the early 1990s. Yet, when looking at the 20-year period as a whole, the waves of the soft protest cycles without political party participation peak during right-wing governments.

Second, the data do not support studies pointing to an enduring dominance in Greece of party politics over all forms of new social movements, including the environmental movement. It is time to move on to examine data on specific forms of activism. The comparative evidence documents that community-based environmental activism stretches beyond clientelism, party loyalties and public cynicism since, even in media reports, political party participation does not appear to be the critical factor in the majority of local environmental protests.

The evidence presented here supports reconsideration of the contention that post-dictatorial Greece is characterised by the 'weakness of civil society', dominated by party politics (cf. Close, 1999; Kousis, 1999a; Sotiropoulos, 2004). By doing so, it does not so much imply that a strong civil society now exists in Greece as it highlights the need to shift attention away from the 'weakness of civil society' and top–down approaches, and toward political processes and systematic empirical analyses of contention at the grassroots.

Third, the analysis shows that those who are involved in environmental contention include a wide array of local social, economic, cultural and political groups whose relative prominence appears to vary depending on the source of the data. National media reports not only represent a small proportion of the local environmental protest identifiable from local sources, but they offer a very partial picture of the character and political salience of that community-based protest, insofar as it tends to report the largest and most contentious protests and those in which politicians are most involved. National media reports may give a clearer picture of the pattern of political party involvement, but public agency archives and the local activist press reveal a plethora of local, grassroots environmental contention which engages a radically different set of networks, issues and action forms than those reported by national media and involving political parties. The evidence presented confirms the persistence of concerned but also affected communities, making public claims and taking actions beyond party mechanisms.

Notes

1. Panhellenic Socialist Movement led by Andreas Papandreou
2. Synaspismos (Coalition of the Left and Progress), initially founded before the 1989 elections by bringing together the Greek Communist Party (KKE) and the Hellenic Left (EA), stemming from the EuroCommnist KKE-internal.
3. It provides more detailed coding for a wider unit of analysis (see Kousis, 1999b).
4. The green party, the Federation of Ecologist-Alternatives, was founded in October 1989 (see Karamichas, 2002; Karamichas & Botetzagias, 2003).
5. Soft actions include: demanding/general claiming, complaints to authority, press conference, signature. Hard actions include: *demonstrational*: court route, public referendum, demonstration/public protest, hunger strike; *confrontational*: occupation of public buildings, strikes and closing of shops, activity/source blockage, road blockades/sit-ins; *violent*: threat to use arms, damage to property, throwing things at responsibles, unintended injuries, intended injuries, deaths.
6. National election years for Greece were: 1974, 1978, 1981, 1985, 1989, 1990, 1993.
7. Until the mid 1990s there were more than 6,000 OTAs in Greece, many with populations below 500. Prefectural self-administrations, Second Degree, a new institution introduced by law in 1994, replaced the central government-appointed prefects, who often came into conflict with mayors and OTA administrators (Fousekis & Lekakis, 1997: 143–5).
8. The source/(in)activity, which according to the mobilisers caused ecosystem disturbance, was coded using a scheme of 84 dichotomous variables.
9. The alternative explanation of the patterns in these tables was pointed out by Chris Rootes.
10. This section draws from Kousis (1997).
11. Access to older archives was not possible due to technical reasons.

12. In addition, for Chanea, the second most populous county in Crete and the one with the oldest and most developed ecological tradition, we compared reports in the national daily *Eleftherotypia* with those in *Fourogatos*, the local newspaper, established in 1989, of the Ecological Initiative of Chanea, the major environmental activist group in the county (see Kousis *et al.*, 2001). The data for Chanea cover only the period 1994–7, and so cannot be directly compared with data for Greece and Heraklion covering the period 1974–94, but they nevertheless highlight the differences between the coverage by the national media and local activist press. Sampling 50% of the issues of *Eleftherotypia* yielded 11 protest events compared with 273 in all issues of *Fourogatos*. (As part of the TEA project, we also read *Chaniotika Nea*, a local daily comparable to *Eleftherotypia* in terms of the types of issues covered and its orientation; this yielded approximately 1,100 reports of environmental protest occurring in the county of Chanea during 1988–97.) In protests reported in *Eleftherotypia*, residents were the most prominent category of participants (73%) whereas in *Fourogatos*, environmental groups (52%) predominated. Mentions of environmental groups, almost nil in *Eleftherotypia* but abundant in *Fourogatos*, include not only local, but national and international NGOs. The role of local government is limited in both (18% in *Eleftherotypia* and 15% in *Fourogatos*). Political groups are absent from the national daily and almost so from the activist press. Whereas the major action form in the activist press is appeals (96%), these are reported in only one-third of events reported in national media. In both, demonstrations constitute one-quarter of actions, but harder (confrontational) action looms larger in *Eleftherotypia*. The kinds of claims also vary considerably: domestic waste is the issue in eight of 11 events reported in *Eleftherotypia*, yet domestic waste ranks only fifth in *Fourogatos*, which attends more to issues specific to the local ecosystem, including resource extraction, chemical agriculture, military installations and energy. National media coverage evidently selects cases of international and national importance such as that of Kouroupitos, which by mid 1989 led to the first EC warning to the Greek government and, in 1990, its first conviction for breach of environmental directives.

References

Afouxenidis, A. (2004) 'Social capital and non governmental organizations in Greece', *Koinonia Politon* 10: 60–5 (in Greek).

Aguilar-Fernandez, S., Fidelis-Nogueira, T. & Kousis, M. (1995) 'Encounters between social movements and the state: examples from waste facility siting in Greece, Portugal and Spain', Proceedings of the international conference Alternative Futures and Popular Protest, Manchester Metropolitan University, 4–6 April.

Alexandropoulos, S. & Sertedakis, N. (2000) 'Greek environmentalism: from the status Nascendi of a movement to its integration', paper presented at the ECPR joint sessions (Environmental movements in Comparative Perspective), Copenhagen, 14–19 April.

Barcena, I. & Ibarra, P. (2001) 'The Basque ecologist movement: from nationalism to localism', in K. Eder & M. Kousis (eds.), *Environmental Politics in Southern Europe: Actors, Institutions and Discourses in a Europeanizing Society* (Dordrecht: Kluwer).

Barranco, J. & Wisler, D. (1999) 'Validity and systematicity of newspaper data in event analysis', *European Review of Sociology* 15(3): 301–22.

Botetzagias, I. (2001) 'The environmental movement in Greece, 1973 to the present: an illusory social movement in a semi-peripheral country', unpublished PhD thesis, Department of Politics, Keele University.

Cable, S. & Cable, C. (1995) *Environmental Problems, Grassroots Solutions: The Politics of Grassroots Environmental Conflict* (New York: St. Martin's Press).

Castells, M. (1983) *The City and the Grassroots: A Cross-cultural Theory of Urban Social Movements* (London: Edward Arnold).

Close, D. H. (1999) 'Environmental crisis in Greece and recent challenges to centralized state authority', *Journal of Modern Greek Studies* 17(2): 325–52.

Dalton, R. J., Reccia, S. & Rohrschneider, R. (2003) 'The environmental movement and the modes of political action', *Comparative Political Studies* 36(7): 1–29.

Demertzis, N. (1990) 'The Greek political culture in the decade of the 80s', in G. Voulgaris *et al.* (eds.), *Elections and Parties in the Decade of the 80s: Developments and Prospects of the Political System* (Athens: Themelio) (in Greek).

Diamandouros, N. P. & Gunther, R. (2001) 'Introduction', in N. P. Diamandouros & R. Gunther (eds.), *Parties, Politics and Democracy in the New Southern Europe* (Baltimore: Johns Hopkins University Press).

Diani, M. (1995) *Green Networks: A Structural Analysis of the Italian Environmental Movement* (Edinburgh: Edinburgh University Press).

Eder, K. (1996) 'The institutionalization of environmentalism: ecological discourse and the second transformation of the public sphere', in B. Lash, D. Szerszynski & B. Wynne (eds.), *Risk, Environment and Modernity* (London: Sage).

Featherstone, K. & Katsoudas, D. (eds.) (1987) *Political Change in Greece, Before and After the Colonels* (London: Routledge).

Filieule, O. & Jiménez, M. (2003) 'The methodology of protest event analysis and the media politics of reporting environmental protest events', in C. Rootes (ed.), *Environmental Protest in Western Europe* (Oxford: Oxford University Press).

Fousekis, P. & Lekakis, J. N. (1997) 'Greece's institutional response to sustainable development', *Environmental Politics* 6(1): 131–52.

Franzosi, R. (1987) 'The press as a source of socio-historical data', *Historical Methods* 20: 12–24.

Gil Nave, J. (2001) 'Environmental politics in Portugal', in K. Eder & M. Kousis (eds.), *Environmental Politics in Southern Europe: Actors, Institutions and Discourses in a Europeanizing Society* (Dordrecht: Kluwer).

Gould, K. A., Schnaiberg, A. & Weinberg, A. S. (1996) *Local Environmental Struggles: Citizen Activism in the Treadmill of Production* (Cambridge: Cambridge University Press).

Jamison, A., Eyerman, R. & Cramer, J. (1993) *The Making of the New Environmental Consciousness: A Comparative Study of the Environmental Movements in Sweden, Denmark, and the Netherlands* (New York: Columbia University Press).

Jiménez, M. (1999) 'Consolidation through institutionalization? Dilemmas of the Spanish environmental movement in the 1990s', *Environmental Politics* 8(1): 149–71.

Jiménez, M. (2001) 'Sustainable development and the participation of environmental NGOs in Spanish environmental policy', in K. Eder & M. Kousis (eds.), *Environmental Politics in Southern Europe: Actors, Institutions and Discourses in a Europeanizing Society* (Dordrecht: Kluwer).

Kafetzis, P. (1994) 'Political crisis and political culture. Political alienation and interference in politics: an inharmonious relationship?' in N. Demertzis (ed.), *Greek Political Culture Today* (Athens: Odysseas) (in Greek).

Karamichas, J. (2002) 'Political ecology in Greece: ideology, political opportunities and contingency in the transition from movement politics to green party formation', paper presented at the Alternative Futures and Popular Protest Conference, Manchester Metropolitan University, 2–4 April.

Karamichas, J. & Botetzagias, I. (2003) 'Green party factionalism. The case of the Federation of Ecologists-Alternatives (FEA) of Greece', *Southern European Society and Politics* 8(3): 64–92.

Komninou, M. (1996) 'The role of MME in the third democracy: 1974–1994', in C. Lyrintsis, I. Nikolakopoulos & D. Sotiropoulos (eds.), *Society and Politics: Facets of the Third Hellenic Democracy* (Athens: Themelio) (in Greek).

Koukias, D. (1997) 'Interest representation and modernization policies in Greece: lessons learned from the study of labor and farmers', *Journal of Modern Greek Studies* 15(2): 325–48.

Kousis, M. (1997) 'Unravelling environmental claim making at the roots: evidence from a southern European country', *Humanity and Society*, 21(3): 257–83.

Kousis, M. (1999a) 'Sustaining local environmental mobilizations: groups, actions and claims in southern Europe', *Environmental Politics* 8(1): 172–98.

Kousis, M. (1999b) 'Environmental protest cases: the city, the countryside and the grassroots in southern Europe', *Mobilization* 4(2): 223–38.

Kousis, M. (2003) 'Greece', in C. Rootes (ed.), *Environmental Protest in Europe* (Oxford: Oxford University Press).

Kousis, M. (2004) 'Economic opportunities and threats in contentious environmental politics: a view from the European South', *Theory and Society* 33: 393–415.

Kousis, M. & Eder, K. (2001) 'EU policy making, local action and the emergence of institutions of collective action: a theoretical perspective on southern Europe', in K. Eder & M. Kousis (eds.), *Environmental Politics in Southern Europe: Actors, Institutions and Discourses in a Europeanizing Society* (Dordrecht: Kluwer).

Kousis, M., Aguilar Fernández, S. & Fidélis, T. (1996) *Grassroots Environmental Action and Sustainable Development in Southern European Union*, Final Report, European Commission, DG XII, Contract No. EV5V-CT94-0393.

Kousis, M., Petropoulou, E. & Dimopoulou, E. (2001) 'Local environmental politics in urban and rural Greece: a study of north-eastern Athens and the county of Chanea', paper prepared for the 29th ECPR joint sessions (Local Environmental Politics), Grenoble, 6–11 April.

Kriesi, H., Koopmans, R., Dyvendak, J. W. & Giugni, M. G. (1995) *New Social Movements in Western Europe: A Comparative Analysis* (Minneapolis: University of Minnesota Press).

Louloudis, L. (1986) *Polit-ecology* (Athens: Stohastis) (in Greek).

Louloudis, L. (1987) 'Social demands: from environmental protection to political ecology', in C. Orfanidis (ed.), *The Ecological Movement in Greece* (Athens: After the Rain Publications) (in Greek).

Lyrintzis, C. (1983) 'Between socialism and populism: the rise of the Panhellenic Socialist Movement', PhD thesis, University of London.

Mavris, Y. (2004) 'Party system and electoral competitions in Greece. Greek bipartism of the 1994–2004 decade', in Ch. Vernardakis, I. Georgantas, D. Gravaris & D. Kotroyiannos (eds.), *Thirty Years of Democracy: The Political System of the Third Hellenic Democracy, 1974–2004* (Athens: Department of Political Science, University of Crete & Kritiki) (in Greek).

Mouzelis, N. (1989) 'Populism: a new way of incorporating the masses', in N. Mouzelis, Th. Lipovatz & M. Spourdalakis (eds.), *Populism and Politics* (Athens: Gnosi) (in Greek).

Mouzelis, N. & Pagoulatos, G. (2002) 'Civil society and citizenship in postwar Greece', in F. Birtek, N. Diamantouros, T. Dragona, A. Frangoudaki & F. Keyder (eds.), *Citizenship and Nation State in Greece and Turkey* (London: Frank Cass).

Nikolakopoulos, I. (1990) 'The impact of political forces on the elections', in C. Lyrintzis & I. Nikolakopoulos (eds.), *Elections and Parties in the Decade of 1980: Developments and Prospects of the Political System* (Athens: Themelio) (in Greek).

Ortiz, D. G., Myers, D. J., Walls, N. E. & Diaz, M. E. D. (2005) 'Where do we stand with newspaper data?' *Mobilization* 10(3): 397–420.

Panagiotopoulou, R. (2003) 'Voluntary and non-governmental organizations in Greece and Olympic Games voluntarism', in Ch. Vernardakis (ed.), *V-PRC Institute, Public Opinion in Greece: Research-Surveys* (Athens: Ant. Livanis) (in Greek).

Rootes, C. (1995) 'Environmental consciousness, institutional structures and political competition in the formation and development of Green parties', in D. Richardson & C. Rootes (eds.), *The Green Challenge*, pp. 232–52 (London: Routledge).

Rootes, C. (ed.) (2003) *Environmental Protest in Western Europe* (Oxford: Oxford University Press).

Rootes, C. (2006) 'Explaining the outcomes of campaigns against waste incinerators in England: community, ecology, political opportunities and policy contexts', *Community and Ecology*, special issue of *Research in Urban Policy* 10: 183–203.

Rucht, D. (1995) 'Parties, associations and movements as systems of political interest mediation', in J. Thesing & W. Hofmeister (eds.), *Political Parties in Democracy. Role and Functions of Political Parties in the Political System of the Federal Republic of Germany* (St. Augustin: Konrad-Adenauer-Stiftung).

Rucht, D., Koopmans, R. & Neidhardt, F. (eds.) (1998) *Acts of Dissent: New Developments in the Study of Protest* (Berlin: Sigma).
Sotiropoulos, D. (1996) 'Ventriloquist power: civil society and central state in the third Hellenic democracy', in C. Lyrintsis, I. Nikolakopoulos & D. Sotiropoulos (eds.), *Society and Politics: Facets of the Third Hellenic Democracy* (Athens: Themelio) (in Greek).
Sotiropoulos, D. (2004) 'Civil society in Greece: atrophic or invisible?' in D. Sotiropoulos (ed.), *The Unknown Civil Society* (Athens: Potamos) (in Greek).
Spourdalakis, M. (1988) 'Greece 2000: reaping the fruits of the a-political hyper-politicization', in Katsoulis *et al.* (eds.), *Greece towards 2000* (Athens: Papazisis) (in Greek).
Stearns, L. B. & Almeida, P. (1998) 'The formation of state actor–social movement coalitions and favorable policy outcomes', *Social Problems* 51(4): 478–504.
Szasz, A. (1994) *Ecopopulism: Toxic Waste and the Movement of Environmental Justice* (Minneapolis: University of Minnesota Press).
Tarrow, S. (1990) 'The phantom at the opera: political parties and social movements of the 1960s and 1970s in Italy', in R. Dalton & M. Kuechler (eds.), *Challenging the Political Order: New Social and Political Movements in Western Democracies* (Oxford: Polity).
Tilly, C. (1978) *From Mobilization to Revolution* (Reading, MA: Addison-Wesley).
Tilly, C. (1994) 'Social movements as historically specific clusters of political performances', *Berkeley Journal of Sociology* 38: 1–30.
Tilly, C. (2004) 'Contentious choices', *Theory and Society* 33: 473–81.
Tsoukalas, K. (1977) 'The problem of the Greek clientele in Greece of the 19th century', in G. Kontoyiorgis (ed.), *Social and Political Forces in Greece* (Athens: Greek Political Science Association & Exantas) (in Greek).
van der Heijden, H.-A. (1999) 'Environmental movements, ecological modernization and political opportunity structures', *Environmental Politics* 8(1): 199–221.
van der Heijden, H.-A. (2002) 'Political parties and NGOs in global environmental politics', *International Political Science Review* 23(2): 187–201.
Zambarloukou, S. (1996) 'Labor movement and state interventionism in post-authoritarian Greece: a comparative approach', in C. Lyrintsis, I. Nikolakopoulos & D. Sotiropoulos (eds.), *Society and Politics: Facets of the Third Hellenic Democracy* (Athens: Themelio) (in Greek).

Environmental Direct Action in Manchester, Oxford and North Wales: A Protest Event Analysis

BRIAN DOHERTY, ALEXANDRA PLOWS & DEREK WALL

The Environmental Direct Action Movement

A network of environmental direct action groups first emerged in the UK at the beginning of the 1990s, in protest against road building, the importation of tropical hardwoods and the colonisation of public space by motor vehicles. This was in marked contrast to what had seemed to be a domesticated UK environmental movement, focused on lobbying (Doherty, 1999a; Wall, 1999;

Research for this paper was funded by the UK Economic and Social Research Council (L215252034) as part of the Democracy and Participation Programme. Acknowledgements are due to Clare Saunders for her work on preparing the data and for comments on drafts to Chris Rootes and Graeme Hayes.

Rootes, 2000). In part, their emergence was a reaction against the limited opportunities for participation offered by mainstream environmental movement organisations such as Greenpeace and Friends of the Earth. Most activists in the new environmental direct action (EDA) groups were young, middle-class, university-educated, and new to political activism (Wall, 1999). Although the local groups adopted their own names, the network was loosely linked at the national level as 'Earth First!' from 1992 onwards, and national Earth First! 'gatherings' provided local EDA groups with opportunities to discuss strategy and common perspectives (Seel & Plows, 2000).

Earth First! began in the USA in 1980 as a network of activists prepared to use sabotage to defend wilderness areas against development (Lee, 1995). Other wilderness defence groups using direct action also existed in Australia from the late 1970s (Doyle, 1994). While the British groups that emerged in the 1990s took tactics and inspiration from their New World counterparts, with little wilderness to defend, they focused on other, often urban, targets. They were also less biocentric in their philosophy and were more influenced by British traditions of non-violent direct action that had preceded the turn to environmental issues in the 1990s.

Although environmental direct action groups in the UK gained much attention during the 1990s, little is known about their actions away from the high profile campaigns against new roads and GM crops, or whether the nature of their protest varied significantly by locality. Our investigation, carried out between 2000 and 2002, is of British EDA groups in Bangor (North Wales), Manchester and Oxford. We use the term environmental direct action (EDA) groups because this was a term that activists used themselves and signifies the emphasis given within these groups to direct action forms of protest. The use of the term 'group' does not signify that they had formal organisations. There were no office holders in any of these groups. Also, while most Manchester and Bangor activists organised under the Earth First! banner, in Oxford there was sometimes a group called Earth First! and at other times unnamed and *ad hoc* collections of the same EDA activists.

These locations were selected because of their different environments, and their different roles in the EDA network. Manchester is at the centre of a major conurbation of over two million people with high levels of poverty; Oxford is a more affluent, small city of 140,000 people in southern England, and Bangor is a small town of 14,000 people in mainly rural northwest Wales, where levels of income are below the UK average. Oxford and Manchester EDA groups played important roles in coordinating national EDA campaigns during the 1990s and, along with Brighton, Bristol, Cardiff, Leeds, London, Newcastle, Norwich and Nottingham, were regarded as among the strongest activist communities. North Wales was among a second group of locations in which there was fairly consistent activity by a smaller group of activists.[1] We defined activists as those who attended Earth First! or equivalent EDA group meetings and regularly took part in direct action protests.

In Manchester this was between 25 and 40 people. The largest EDA actions in Manchester, such as the May Day protests in 2000, mobilised up to 500 participants, but most of them did not attend Earth First! meetings regularly and so were not classified by us as EDA activists. Most activists lived in 'hard to let' apartments owned by the city council in a few streets in Hulme, close to Manchester city centre, within a countercultural scene of alternative arts and politics, a smaller-scale version of the alternative scenes in Kreuzberg, Berlin and other German cities in the 1980s and 1990s (Haunss & Leach, 2004).

Oxford had a smaller number of core EDA activists, usually around 20, but, as in Manchester, a wider green community of several hundred would support major EDA protests such as the Halloween Reclaim the Streets party in 1998. In periods when there was no Earth First! group in Oxford, other EDA projects filled the gap. *Corporate Watch* was an independent group that carried out research on corporations least beloved of environmental and other social movement groups. Its suite of offices in East Oxford was shared with other office projects such as *Undercurrents*, a radical newsvideo production group, and was the base for much of Oxford's EDA networking.

Gwynedd and Mon Earth First! (GMEF) based in Bangor, North Wales was a much smaller group with usually fewer than 10 regular activists. The Bangor area had seen a countercultural influx in the 1970s but there were few ties with local Welsh nationalists who had their own traditions of direct action in defence of Welsh language and culture. The establishment of a new resource centre with offices for campaign groups in the early 1980s and a shared commitment to peace movement and anti-nuclear campaigns led to stronger ties between Welsh speakers and mainly English incomers. The young Earth Firsters!, several of whom were students at Bangor University in the early 1990s, did not have close links with either group initially. However, an Earth First! campaign against a new housing project on green-field land after 1994 led to new alliances. By the end of the decade, the Earth First! group in Bangor had stronger links with other local campaigners than did the larger EDA groups in Manchester and Oxford.

The three areas we studied all had legacies from the left-wing counterculture of the 1970s and 1980s: alternative projects of various kinds, such as cafes, radical bookshops, campaign offices and resource centres that served as meeting places. There was also a history of earlier direct action on anti-military, anti-nuclear, anti-fascist, housing and community issues. All three had strong local peace groups in the 1980s, including women's groups supportive of the Greenham Common Women's Peace camp. Activists from these 1970s and 1980s groups were still present in a variety of local campaigns that brought them into contact with the new environmental activists of the 1990s.[2]

The constellation of local politics was less significant. Differences in the political characters of the local authority in each area had no discernable impact on the nature of local EDA protest. Manchester City Council was Labour-dominated but while older activists talked of the Labour Party in the

1980s as having been responsive to their concerns, by the 1990s the party in Manchester, like Labour nationally, was moving away from support for social movement agendas and favoured development schemes, such as the expansion of the airport, that were opposed by local greens. The Labour-led Council therefore became a target of regular protests. In Bangor, Plaid Cymru, the Welsh nationalist party, led the local council. Although Plaid had a record of support for environmentalism, its local support for development projects led EDA activists to see it as mostly part of the opposition. In Oxford, the strongest local Green Party in the UK controlled the City Council for a time as the minority party in coalition with the Liberal Democrats, but rather than this averting protest in Oxford, Green councillors on several occasions joined protests organised by local EDA activists.

The failure of patterns of local politics to differentiate among our cases is explained by the lack of power of local authorities, which reduced their salience, and by EDA activists' lack of interest in negotiable policy impact. EDA activists saw their role as raising issues through protest or increasing the political or financial costs of their opponents; influencing policy through negotiations even at local level was not part of this strategy.

Measuring Direct Action Protest: Methodological Challenges

Analyses based upon newspaper reports have become the principal means of measuring protest (Rucht & Ohlemacher, 1992) but it is also clear that newspapers have limitations as sources (Fillieule & Jiménez, 2003). Novel and colourful or violent protests may often receive coverage when larger protests are ignored, particularly if the larger march or rally seems merely to repeat the formula of previous events on an issue that is already assumed to be familiar to readers (Downs, 1972). While the issue attention cycle may have favoured the reporting of direct action protests in the early 1990s in the UK, what had once been novel forms of protest received diminishing coverage in later years.[3]

Rather than showing the scale and frequency of protests, reports in national newspapers can be argued to record the *visibility* of protest (Rootes, 2003a:17). This in itself may be an indicator of a movement's political impact, but we cannot be sure that the protest activity of movements has declined simply because their actions are not covered by the newspapers. Furthermore, it is not necessarily the case that newspapers are always the best source of data for protest event surveys. Even when interest in environmental direct action was at its height, coverage in *The Guardian*, the national newspaper most attentive to environmental action, was not comprehensive. *The Guardian* reported 128 environmental protests by Earth First! or other EDA groups between 1992 and 1997 (Rootes, 2003b).[4] By comparison, EDA national newsletters reported 684 separate protests involving EDA groups in the same period. Even allowing that some of the non-environmental protests by EDA groups would have been excluded from the dataset of environmental protests reported in *The Guardian*, this is a significant difference.

The culture of EDA groups compounds the problems associated with relying on press sources to measure their protest. There was a widespread hostility in EDA networks to the media, which was seen as incapable of reporting their actions accurately. Activists felt there was too much interest in their lifestyle and too little in the reasons for their protest and so they often avoided contact with reporters. EDA groups thus stand outside the general assumption that good mass media coverage is seen as essential by contemporary social movements. When good media coverage happened, it was welcomed, but for the most part EDA activists neither sought nor expected it. The alternative, which they pursued with some vigour in the 1990s, was to offset their lack of coverage in mainstream media by creating their own media. In doing so, they were following a long established trend among radical groups but unlike most of the earlier radical press, *Earth First! Action Update* (EFAU), the most consistent newsletter in the EDA network, had no editorial discussion, letters or by-lines. EFAU was a monthly, free, four-page newssheet, distributed on paper or by email. It simply reported events and carried event listings and contact details for the 25–40 EDA groups, plus an occasional insert with a practical briefing on issues such as legal rights when arrested. Production of EFAU rotated among local EDA groups annually; Oxford and Manchester (twice) edited it during the period we surveyed. A Brighton direct action collective also produced *Schnews*, a weekly national newssheet, distributed on paper, by email and on the web. *Schnews* carried analysis but also reported protest events, although less comprehensively than EFAU. EDA groups in Manchester and Oxford also produced local free newsletters: *Loombreaker* (Manchester) and *Oxyacetelene* (Oxford) reported local protests and publicised upcoming events, and paper copies were distributed in activist haunts. These local EDA sources often covered events that were not reported on in national EDA newsletters.

The results reported here are based on a survey of EFAU and *Schnews*, local newsletters in Manchester and Oxford and, in the absence of a local newsletter in the case of North Wales, participant observation by one of the researchers covering the years 1995–2001. We do not claim that activist media are always and necessarily superior to newspapers, nor that they escape problems of selectivity, only that for the subject we studied they were the most comprehensive and reliable sources available. We were fortunate in that the kinds of newsletters favoured by EDA groups in the 1990s were particularly appropriate and maintained sufficient continuity for protest event analysis.[5]

Incidence of EDA Protest Nationally

To assess the national picture we counted *all* protests (environmental and non-environmental) by all UK EDA groups reported in EFAU and *Schnews*[6] over the 10 years 1992 to 2001 (see Figure 1).

The year 1999 represents the peak, when 297 separate protest events[7] took place out of a total of 1471 in the 10 years surveyed. However, the *number* of

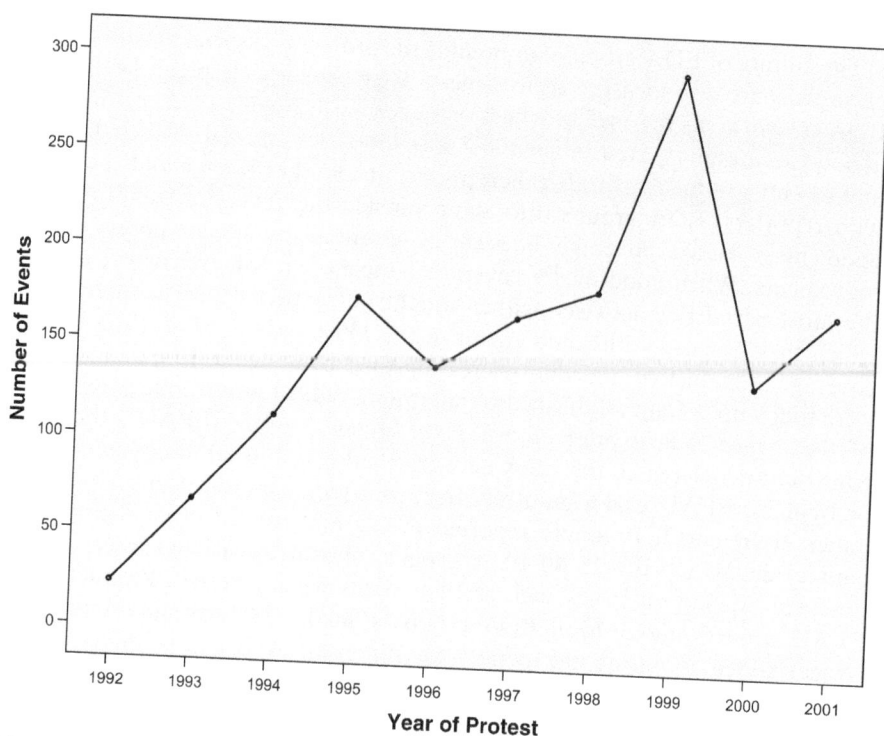

Figure 1. EDA protest events in the UK 1992–2001, reported in *Earth First! Action Update* and *Schnews*.

protests may not be equivalent to the *level* of protest activity. The rise in the number of events in 1998 and 1999 was connected to the decline in protest camps by the end of 1997. Protest camps generate few separate events,[8] but since they usually last for several months and sometimes more than a year, they are a particularly intensive form of action. They were particularly numerous during the anti-roads campaigns between 1994 and 1997 when the proposed routes of new roads were occupied in order to obstruct construction.

There was also considerable activity in 1998 and 1999 because the movement was mobilising on new issues such as global justice, which led to protests at the G8 Summit in Birmingham in 1998, followed in June 1999 by the *Carnival Against Capitalism* in London, which coincided with the G8 Summit in Cologne. Other new targets for protest in these years were the farm trial sites for genetically modified crops, which became the focus of a sabotage campaign. The decline in events in 2000 is sufficiently marked to suggest that fewer actions were occurring. While there was some stabilisation in 2001, activists we interviewed said that the number of actions was declining in the new millennium. This was confirmed by the petering out of local newsletters and the *Earth First! Action Update* around this time. EDA did not end in 2001.

Earth First! gatherings continued as did direct action, but it was undoubtedly on a smaller scale than in the 1990s.

The Incidence of Local EDA Protest

We turn now to examine the evidence on local protest. Local EDA newsletters often reported events missing from national activist sources. Sometimes these were protests in which local EDA groups worked in coalition with residents or other less radical groups, which might have seemed less interesting to other EDA groups. One example was a site occupation, reported only in *Oxyacetelyne* (November 1998), to protest at the felling of chestnut trees so that a road could be built in Oxford. Because local newsletters and participant observation only covered the period 1995–2000, we were able to examine only six of the 10 years for which we also had national sources. Figure 2 includes all protest reported in one or more of the national and/or the local sources that took place in the three areas during those six years.

It is notable that local patterns of action do not correspond neatly to the national patterns. Local factors clearly influence the level of activity that EDA groups are able to sustain. The first notable peak of activity in Manchester in 1996 was due to local campaigns against urban pollution by an EDA-led group, Fresh Air Now, and protests against the construction of a new orbital motorway in the east of the city. The decline in 1997 and 1998 reflects the effect of the anti-airport protest camp in the first half of 1997, which, despite

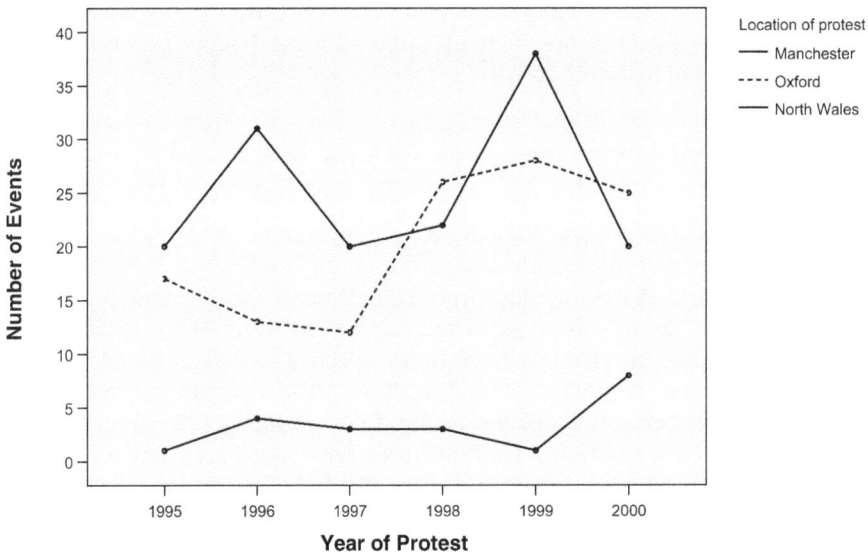

Figure 2. EDA protests in Manchester, Oxford and North Wales 1995–2000, reported in national and local sources.

increasing the intensity of activity in Manchester, reduced the number of reported events. Around 150 activists were evicted from treehouses and tunnels on the site of the planned second runway over three weeks in April and May 1997. Thereafter, activists were, according to one interviewee, 'burned out'. A second factor was the withdrawal from confrontation of several key activists in 1997, in order to establish a new environmental resources centre with charitable and public funds. Further protest camps at the airport site in 1998 and 1999 were much smaller and had little active support from most EDA activists in Manchester.

In Oxford, the lower levels of action in 1996 and 1997, compared with the previous years and also with Manchester, reflected the role of Oxford activists in the Newbury bypass campaign in 1995–6. Oxford is close to Newbury and activists from the city were more heavily involved with the campaign than those from Manchester or North Wales. Many mentioned Newbury as a turning point, following which many of those involved since the early 1990s felt exhausted and either retired or took a break from activism. The dramatic rise in activity in Oxford in 1998 was due to the emergence of local 'issue opportunities' – specific instances that facilitate mobilisation for groups already predisposed to act on that issue – including the demolition of a prized old cinema, which was squatted by EDA activists and used as an alternative arts venue for a time.[9]

The smaller group in North Wales carried out fewer local protests. The pattern of action is similar to Oxford up to 1998, when GMEF established a protest camp against a new housing project in Bangor. Following the partial success of the campaign, which reduced the number of houses to be built, activists were too tired to relaunch actions until later in 1999. In 2000 GMEF initiated a new direct action network that improved links between Welsh groups and stimulated new activity.

Travelling to Protest: Comparing Local and Extra-local Protest Activity

Analysis of local sources allows for more accurate identification of the involvement of groups from Manchester, Oxford and North Wales in events outside their areas. Figure 3 includes protests that took place in Manchester, Oxford and North Wales and also protests in other places where activists from the three local groups were reported to be involved. This is the most comprehensive record that we have of the protest activity of these groups covering the six years 1995–2000 and it allows us to compare the balance of local and extra-local activity of each group. Figure 3 shows 1996 to be the peak year of activity when activists from all three areas went regularly to join the protest camps at Newbury.[10] Nevertheless, there was also considerable local protest action in 1996 in addition to this (see Figure 2). The combination of significant local and protest camp action is consistent with the accounts given by activists in interviews, for whom 1996 was the highpoint of EDA action.[11] It is worth noting that the larger groups in Manchester and Oxford carried out

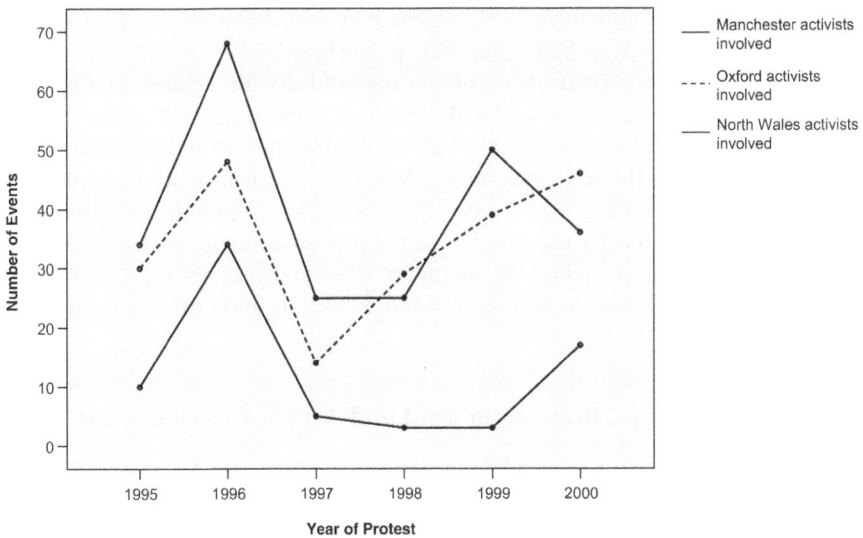

Figure 3. EDA protests in all locations by activists from Manchester, Oxford and North Wales 1995–2000, reported in national and local sources.

more local protests than protests outside their area, whereas the North Wales activists took part in more events that involved travelling than local actions.

In the patterns of action reported in Figure 3 there is evidence for a cyclical effect similar to that which McAdam (1983) identified in the US civil rights movement during the years when protest was at its height: in that case, moments of tactical innovation, such as the sit-ins at lunch counters in the spring of 1960, produced an increase in all forms of protest action by the civil rights movement. There were tactical innovations by UK EDA groups such as the creation of tunnels to extend site occupations (first used successfully at Fairmile in Devon in 1997; Doherty, 1999b), but, in the three areas that we studied, increased protest was most evident in periods when the movement was at the top of the news agenda rather than following moments of tactical innovation. Notwithstanding EDA activists' ambivalence about the media, it seems likely that being covered on the nightly news, as the movement often was in the months leading up to and in the course of the Newbury evictions in 1996 and at certain moments in 1999–2000 (anti-GMO protests in 1999–2000; the 18 June Carnival Against Capitalism in London; by proxy in the case of their allies at the Seattle protests in November 1999; the May 2000 London Guerrilla Gardening action in London; and the Prague protests of September 2000), encouraged all those involved to believe that their action was having an effect. It may also have encouraged an increase in reporting of events by activists in the national EDA newsletters. If so, this would be consistent with the pattern noted in reports of environmental protests in *The Guardian* (Rootes, 2003b). Nevertheless, in the case of EDA groups the effects of such major reinforcing events have to be weighed against the after-effects of waging a big campaign locally, which often led to 'burnout'.

Burnout can also explain some of the ups and downs evident in Figure 3. While there was an increase in local action in Oxford in 1998, this was less evident in Manchester and North Wales. In Manchester activists were tired after the eviction of the protest camps at Manchester Airport, which took place over several weeks in April and May 1997, and the same pattern followed in North Wales in 1999 after the eviction of the protest camp against new housing in 1998. While action picked up again in 1999 in Manchester, and 2000 in North Wales, there was a decline in Manchester in 2000 after another very active year in 1999.

Personal Relationships, Recruitment and Local Activist Community Cycles

As well as the effects of local cycles and national campaigns, the movement of a few key individuals in or out of a local activist community also affects the level of activity. At the micro-level, events such as the end of a relationship between two activists or personality clashes can have a significant effect on the whole group.

> These things are cyclical and the Oxford scene went into decline for various reasons, partly it was personality clashes actually. I remember it being very optimistic when it started, 'we don't do ego', . . . 'this is just for the cause', . . . this kind of stuff. And you actually genuinely believed this for quite a while and then people's egos start to take over, and people start having massive disagreements, and there was a big split within *Corporate Watch*, which really fucked things up quite badly and never really recovered. Also people went off in different directions; some people went off doing national campaigns, people went to squatting stuff, some people went to be artists, people got interested in other things. (Interview with 'Luke',[12] Oxford, 2000)

After the first few years of activism in the 1990s relatively little effort was made to recruit new activists into EDA groups. This is a common pattern for direct action groups since they are usually small groups linked by strong bonds of trust, shared experience and friendship. While there are no formal barriers to new members, anyone joining would find it hard to break into such friendship networks, a point made by several interviewees (cf. Polletta, 2002, on these processes in US social movements, and La Rocca, 2004, on Australian environmental activists). As a result, in contrast to movements with more impersonal forms of organisation, the numbers involved in EDA did not expand greatly in the UK even when its protests appeared to be having some political impact. The hidden structure of small groups of friends within local EDA networks also helps to explain some of the cyclical patterns of action locally. When activists retired or the group was 'burned out' it was not possible to increase the level of activism because there were no new activists to take up the challenge. On the other hand, even if it is in certain senses closed to outsiders, sustained direct action is a very durable form of mobilisation and many activists remained involved for more than five years. Strong ties forged over years of demanding activism still bound previous generations of activists in these localities from the 1970s and 1980s to their activist-friends and continued EDA protests in the mid-2000s suggest it is likely that this will remain the case for those from the 1990s. But this hidden structure also acts as an obstacle to the transmission of mobilisation over time because the next generation have to make their own networks anew.

The Issues of Protest

One measure of the localness of EDA groups is their ability to respond to issues that are distinctly local in scope. Figure 4 shows the balance between protests that were classified as about local, national or international issues.[13]

Although there were more events of national and international scope combined, issues of local scope were the single largest category. The majority of protests in Manchester and Oxford were carried out locally; travel to international events was rare in all three areas. The two larger groups were therefore principally local actors, even though it is as national and transnational actors that EDA groups receive most attention.

The data in Table 1[14] provide evidence about the specific claims made in protests that occurred in each of the three localities.[15] It is clear that the same issues arose in each area, even if in different proportions.

Such differences were not due to differences between the identities of the local groups; rather they were a result of the availability of targets locally. The higher proportion of defence of landscape, forestry and ecosystems in North

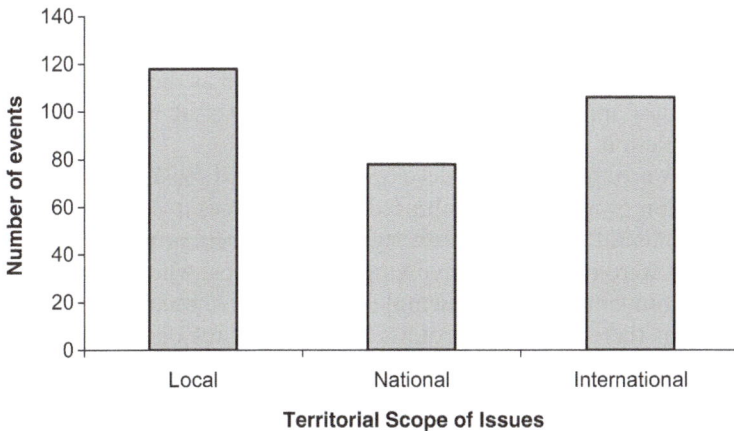

Figure 4. Scope of issue at stake (all three areas combined 1992–2001).

Table 1. Protest issues in Manchester, Oxford and North Wales 1992–2001, reported in national sources (excludes protests which activists from these locations took part in elsewhere; % for columns)

Claim	Manchester ($n = 115$)	Oxford ($n = 62$)	North Wales ($n = 22$)
Landscape, ecosystems, forestry, resource extraction	35	27	45
Opposing construction, transport and communication systems	44	39	50
Pollution and energy	11	10	5
Democracy, human rights and anti-military[a]	31	29	23
Pariah companies	23	21	36
Animal rights	0	16	0

Note: Column totals are more than 100% because of the possibility to list two claims per event.
[a]This figure excludes those pariah companies targeted for their involvement with military production (e.g. British Aerospace) when not mentioned in tandem with a more general anti-military claim.

Wales in comparison to Manchester and Oxford reflects the former's rural environment and specifically opposition to quarries in that area. Yet, even though the number of protests in North Wales was small, the pattern of issues is sufficiently similar to Manchester and Oxford to support the view that EDA groups in each area pursued a similar agenda.

The other two categories of environmental issue – pollution and energy, and opposition to construction – are relatively consistent across the three cases. In North Wales opposition to a new road in Anglesey and a housing scheme in Bangor were especially significant. This was also the only locality with a nuclear power station and so GMEF was the only group that took action against nuclear energy. In Manchester (*Fresh Air Now*) and Oxford (*Oxford is Choking*) there were specific EDA-led anti-pollution campaigns focusing on motor vehicles in the cities. Around a third of total claims relate to opposition to construction, but these protests declined after 1998 as the government's road building programme was cut and the second runway at Manchester Airport neared completion.

Since EDA groups in the UK developed from an established British tradition of direct action groups which embraced multiple issues it is not surprising that non-environmental issues were also significant in their protests. We coded all protests that were reported as involving EDA groups, whether environmental or non-environmental. Environmental issues may have been the principal focus of action, but there were also protests by EDA groups on every core issue of the 1970s' and 1980s' new social movements: feminism, gay and lesbian rights, anti-racism, asylum and immigration, state surveillance, solidarity with the third world, nuclear weapons, opposition to wars, military recruitment and the arms trade, and action in support of the rights of minority groups. Given the commitment of EDA groups to global justice issues it is also hardly surprising to find them active against controversial companies involved in global business. Three stood out as particularly significant targets: Shell, McDonalds and British Aerospace, but banks, other oil companies and supermarkets also featured prominently.

On some larger-scale protests such as those at arms fairs the local EDA groups were part of broader coalitions of anti-arms trade groups, and locally they sometimes worked with other campaigners, for instance, in regular protests at the Campsfield asylum-seekers detention centre near Oxford. For the most part, however, they initiated their own protests and campaigns on issues that might be seen as part of 'other' movement domains. The degree of involvement in these by local EDA activists varied, for instance, there were some women-only actions, such as one in Manchester to protest against a sexist advert in a chocolate shop in 2000. Since there were no centrally authorised campaigns, any particular protest or campaign whether on environmental or other issues was a project of particular groups of activists within the EDA community, and depended for its success on the ability to mobilise fellow activists through persuasion. There was no sense, therefore, in which non-environmental campaigns could be defined as marginal or non-essential to the movement. There were also, however, protests that might be thought to be cognate, but which many activists avoided taking part in.

For instance, Oxford alone had a significant number of animal rights-related protests.[16] A national campaign against Hillgrove farm, near Oxford, where cats were bred for use in vivisection, pulled in a small minority of Oxford EDA activists. However, the animal rights movement is largely separate from the environmental movement and perceived as such by activists. In interviews, EDA activists tended to argue that, although they were sympathetic to some of the arguments of animal rights and animal liberation activists, they thought them too single-issue and most rejected the violence used by a small minority of animal liberation activists. Particularly revealing was an incident, observed by one of the authors, in the Manchester Earth First! office in 2001: an EF! activist found a box with animal rights material and decided to throw it all away 'because that's got nothing to do with Earth First!'. Thus, while animal rights activists were sometimes also involved in EDA groups and part of the same social scene, most EDA activists regarded animal rights as a separate movement.

The Forms of Protest

The EDA repertoire is based primarily upon confrontational and often illegal forms of direct action. Table 2 is based on data for 1995–2000 (which includes the local sources) as this allows more accurate identification of the differences between actions carried out in the three locations and 'on the road' and shows that all three groups used the same challenging and often illegal repertoire. Occupations, blockades, protest camps and property damage make up more

Table 2. Forms of action by location 1995–2000, reported in local and national sources; % for columns

	Actions in each location			All actions that activists from these locations took part in			Actions involving activists from all three locations (n = 51)
	Manchester (n = 151)	Oxford (n = 121)	North Wales (n = 20)	Manchester (n = 238)	Oxford (n = 206)	North Wales (n = 72)	
Signatures/leaflets/judicial	17	15	15	13	12	8	4
Public demonstrations	23	25	30	23	25	21	18
Gatherings/meetings	5	5	5	4	4	3	2
Occupations/blockades	33	26	11	35	29	27	33
Protest camp events	10	4	21	13	11	27	29
Property damage/shoplifting	7	14	11	9	13	13	14
Other	9	12	11	7	9	7	6

Note: Column totals are more than 100% because of the possibility to list up to four forms of action per event.

than half the reported forms of action. Moreover, less confrontational forms of action such as leafleting were often used alongside confrontational and disruptive forms during the same event. For instance, office occupations, Reclaim the Streets parties, or disruption of shareholders' meetings usually also involved leafleting of passers-by.[17]

The main difference between the three areas was the lower proportion of occupations and blockades and the higher proportion of demonstrations in North Wales.[18] GMEF made considerable effort to construct alliances with local NGOs and campaign groups from 1999 onwards, playing a central role in organising a rally in Bangor in November against the WTO to coincide with the Seattle meeting, in which Oxfam, Plaid Cymru and Christian Aid took part. They also co-organised a protest at the Welsh Assembly in Cardiff against the Terrorism Act in 2000, at which a supportive message from Rowan Williams, the future Archbishop of Canterbury, was read out. Unlike their larger counterparts based in cities with a stronger radical subculture, GMEF put more effort into maintaining good relations with conventional campaign groups, a necessity if significant numbers were to be attracted to a rally or demonstration. Nevertheless, GMEF were in practice no less militant than the groups in other areas, as evidenced in their willingness to undertake actions involving damage to property and their reluctance to compromise their usual repertoire, even if it undermined relations with their allies.

This was illustrated when a networking coalition, Cynefin y Werin (Common Ground), was established in North Wales in January 2000 to bring together groups with a common interest in peace and nonviolence and global justice. Many members were NGOs, charities and church groups campaigning for human rights and on aid and development. GMEF was an active member but upset others when its activists prevented Clare Short, the Minister for Overseas Development, from speaking at a public meeting at Bangor University in 2001 by pelting her with a custard pie. Although all the groups in Cynefin y Werin opposed Short's support for the globalisation of trade, other groups were angry that GMEF's action denied them the opportunity to debate the issue in a public meeting, and it took some time for relations to mend.

The evidence shows that EDA is based on confrontational, disruptive and often illegal action, but minimal violence (cf. also Rootes, 2003b). The vast majority of actions in the property damage category fell into the category of minor damage to property, such as damage to GM crops and 'ethical shoplifting' that involved taking goods such as illegally imported tropical hardwoods from a shop to the local police station and reporting them as stolen goods. While our qualitative research revealed that some covert minor property damage against construction companies or McDonalds restaurants went unreported in EDA newsletters, most of what activists called 'pixieing' was on an opportunistic basis and very small-scale. In contrast to parts of US Earth First! in the 1980s (Lee, 1995), covert sabotage was not a principal strategy of the EDA networks in the UK (cf. Plows *et al.*, 2004). More extensive use of sabotage would probably have led to a more repressive response from the police and courts, as happened to animal liberation activists, and would have threatened the open public mobilisation that was the main strategy of EDA groups.

There were no cases of serious injury or death recorded in the reports we analysed. Force was used by EDA activists in only 14 of the 414 protests we coded in the 1995–2000 period. Although there were instances of major property damage, such as burning of excavators and diggers and breaking of windows, these were relatively few and mostly took place in the larger and more open rallies, such as the Newbury Reunion Rampage in 1997 or the Carnival Against Capitalism in London in June 1999, with many from outside the EDA networks taking part in the latter. Most EDA activists continued to adhere to the commitment to non-violence, a strong norm in the UK direct action networks since the 1970s.

Given the nature of direct action-type protest, it is unsurprising that most protest actions were carried out by small groups of Earth Firsters! Seventy-six percent of events reported involved only one group. Of 192 protests involving these three groups between 1992 and 2001 where numbers were reported, only 63 involved more than 500 people, 35 between 100 and 500, and the rest fewer than 100. Most actions that we observed involved 10–20 activists, and it is safe to assume that the 136 events where numbers were not reported mostly involved small groups.

The contentious politics school of social movements studies tends to see public protest as based on a claim made to authorities (Tarrow, 1998; Tilly, 2004). In certain respects this is a truism in that, as regulators of public space, the authorities are likely to be participants in the relations generated by protest but in the case of EDA it would be misleading to see their actions as generally claims for the authorities to take action. The most common targets of EDA protest were companies and trade associations rather than the government (just over 51% of the total for 1992–2001). The state made up the only other significant target (45%), divided between public institutions (27.6%) and government and Ministers (17.3%). MPs, parties, and trade unions barely figured. This reflected the view of power predominant in EDA discourse, in which business and the state were viewed as engaged in defending an ecologically unsustainable and socially unjust global capitalist system. Accordingly, it was political and business institutions that needed to be challenged and exposed rather than individuals or other political organisations that needed to be persuaded. For most EDA protestors that we interviewed, this set of targets was reflective of a politics of resistance in which the main appeal was to a potentially mobilisable public rather than to decision-makers. Few had any expectation of being able to leverage concessions from government, gain a seat at the policy-making table, or persuade allies in the political system to take up their cause.

Environmental Direct Action: The Data Summarised

This is the first systematic analysis of the protest activity of environmental direct action groups in the UK. Perhaps the most important finding concerns the sheer number of protest actions undertaken. In the six years from 1995 to 2000, these three local groups were involved in 414 separate recorded protests, which, if representative of other EDA groups in the UK, would mean significant numbers of protests, albeit small-scale, that were mostly unreported in the local or national media.

EDA groups developed a culture and repertoire of their own that they were able to sustain for more than a decade. They were not part of the mainstream, but were an important part of the local environmental and activist scenes in many of the major cities in the UK. Direct action was the preferred strategic option for these groups, irrespective of the response they gained from those in power or whether they were well received by the media. Yet being noticed and provoking a response from opponents still mattered. The evidence suggests that the impact of protests against road building, genetic modification, for global justice and later, on climate change, encouraged participants to renew their efforts at various points from 1992 onwards, even if in each instance their impact was also dependent on other political factors and actors. The multiplicity of issues raised in their protests demonstrates that EDA groups were more than simply environmental in their concerns and drew on the frames established by a range of precursor direct action groups in the 1970s and 1980s. The forms of action they used were also part of an inherited repertoire in which confrontation, disruption and illegal action were constrained by a predominant commitment to non-violence.

Protest on local issues constitutes a significant proportion of EDA action. It is precisely this kind of protest that is often missed when we look only at evidence from national sources. All three groups were engaged in similar forms of action on similar issues at national level, but in comparing their local actions some differences were apparent. The group in rural North Wales showed greater orientation towards alliance building because it lacked a critical mass of activists to sustain continuous mobilisation. Bangor also lacked the same range of targets as in the two larger cities, so extra-local actions represented a higher proportion of protests. In this sense the historic association of movements with urbanisation (Tilly, 2004) still influences even geographically mobile and globally connected activists (Chesters & Welsh, 2005). Cities still draw radical activists and provide them with more opportunities to mobilise. However, the North Wales group was just as willing to engage in more militant action even when this undermined relationships with less radical allies. In Manchester and Oxford there was very little joint protest action with other groups. Only in the non-protest campaigns of activists did they work with other groups, for instance, in the management of local resource centres.

Sustaining Direct Action: Beyond Opportunities and Cycles

EDA protest is resistant to the standard explanations of mobilisation in terms of political opportunities or protest cycles (Tarrow, 1998). Political opportunity explanations emphasise the actions of states or other opponents of social movements in providing incentives for protesters to bear the costs of action. It is when new allies become available, opponents seem vulnerable, or the state lowers the cost of repression that action seems most worthwhile (Tarrow, 1998: 71). We have already questioned the applicability of this theory to explain the emergence of EDA in the early 1990s (though without rejecting the more general relevance of changes in the political context; Doherty, 1999a; Wall, 1999) and now also question its use to explain how such groups sustained their protest. Rather than calculated attempts to influence state policy, EDA is based on the aim of developing a resistance culture, in which a way of life is challenged through protest. Activists' anarchistic commitments preclude large-scale organisations, their lifestyle and closed friendship groups inhibit recruitment and strategic alliances, so despite sustained direct action EDA did not become a mass movement. EDA is a foray from an alternative culture in which the aim is to disrupt norms, challenge acquiescence and suggest that alternatives are possible.

It is hard to identify either national or international opportunities or constraints that explain the patterns of EDA protest over these 10 years. There were changes such as the shift from road protests to GM crops and to global justice protests but these were in reaction to the imposition of a new grievance in the case of GM or, in the case of global justice, had roots in the international Zapatista solidarity networks in the mid-1990s, in which UK EDA activists from groups such as Reclaim the Streets played a part (Chesters & Welsh, 2005; Olesen, 2005; Wood, 2005). Nor was there any significant new repression of EDA protests by the state (difficult against non-violent protesters who had significant levels of public support).[19]

In the three groups that we studied it was not repression, institutionalisation or polarisation between radicals and reformers that explained the eventual reduction of protest after 2001. Rather, exhaustion (another factor that Tarrow, 1998: 147, identifies as a possible explanation of decline) was decisive. But exhaustion requires more detailed explanation, since many activists sustained intense activity for 10 years, begging the question why exhaustion did not set in earlier. Exhaustion needs to be considered alongside other factors such as interpersonal tensions within activist communities and the material costs of sustained activism. When activity began to decline in the early 2000s, one reason given in interviews was material pressures. Some now had children, and many found it too hard to sustain the low-income lifestyle of the most committed activists. But, importantly, the EDA network did not disappear altogether and was able to reconstitute itself for national protest camp actions on climate change in 2006 and 2007. The solidarity built up between groups of friends over many years of intense political action allowed such networks to re-emerge, even when they seemed to have disappeared.

Notes

1. Others in this category included Cambridge, Totnes (Devon), South Somerset, Lancaster, York, Guilford, Exeter, Warwick and Swansea. There is also a third group of major cities that had intermittent EDA groups in the 1990s–2000s: Sheffield, Glasgow, Edinburgh, Birmingham, Bradford and Liverpool.
2. The influence of previous generations of activists on the EDA generation of the 1990s in Manchester, Oxford and North Wales is examined in Doherty (2003).
3. One example is the building of tunnels in which protesters could barricade themselves to prevent the destruction of a wood for road building. Although this tactic continued it received much less attention after the first major instances at Fairmile in Devon and Manchester Airport in 1997. By 2006 there was apparently no coverage in the national press of protest camps using these tactics, such as that at Southend.
4. There were 44 attributable to Earth First! but taking into account other named EDA groups takes to the total to 110. We are grateful to Chris Rootes for providing the organisational frequencies chart from the TEA database, which allowed us to make this calculation.
5. To carry out a similar survey in 2007, local activist email lists and Indymedia websites would be the principal available sources.
6. *Action Update* reports protests by all EDA groups, not only those that use the name Earth First!
7. In our coding we followed the definition of an event given by Fillieule and Jiménez (2003: 273–4). This meant that even large-scale protests such as the Carnival Against Capitalism on 18 June 1999, which included tens of separate actions at different locations, were recorded as a single event on the basis that the protests were carried out by a network who had worked together to plan the protest, and took place close to each other in time (within a few hours) and space (within the City of London).
8. We did not code a protest camp as a form of action in itself but we did code specific events separately when they were reported, such as occupying a site and building defences, or an eviction. Following Rootes (2003b: 55, note 22), we coded only specific reported events even when a protest camp lasted for months.
9. After 1998 there were far fewer Oxford EDA actions reported to *Action Update*, but this seems to be an anomaly since the local Oxford newsletter reported a continuing high level of protest activity in 1999 and 2000 (see Figure 2). It seems that after 1998 no one in Oxford was passing on reports to the EFAU in the ways that they had done in previous years. The reason for this was that the old Earth First! group had broken up and while EDA action continued, and was mostly carried out by the same people who had been in Oxford Earth First!, the local EDA scene lacked the umbrella identity that Earth First! had provided. This is the main example of the limitations of EDA sources that we encountered.
10. When activists from each area took part in a particular protest action at Newbury that single event was counted separately for each area.
11. The analysis of environmental protest reported in *The Guardian* showed that 1995 was the peak year for environmental and animal welfare protest in the 1988–97 period, but 1996 had a higher level of protest on transport issues (Rootes, 2003b: 31) which seems to fit the pattern from EDA sources.
12. All interviewee names are pseudonyms. We interviewed 59 activists across the three locations between 2000 and 2002 (for more use of this material, see Doherty, 2003; Doherty *et al.*, 2003; Plows *et al.*, 2004).
13. A single event was only classified in one category. For instance, in Manchester activists took part in protests against the closure of a school and the destruction of a pond in the part of the city where most activists lived, events that were clearly local in scope. Events of national scope included demonstrations organised to disrupt the Manchester visit of the Home Secretary,

Jack Straw, in protest against national government legislation. An example of an event in Manchester of international scope was a blockade to disrupt an international conference of government ministers and business leaders to discuss sustainable development in September 1993.

14. We have not presented separate data based on the local sources here mainly for reasons of space but also because there were no major differences between the two sets of data. Overall the main effect of including local sources was that the numbers of non-environmental claims were increased slightly, by around 10–15% relative to the environmental claims. This is not surprising, since protests on issues such as the Kosovo and Afghanistan wars, legislation such as the Terrorism Act 2000, or seeking to prevent deportation of asylum-seekers often involved the EDA groups in local coalitions, whose actions were more likely to be reported in a local newsletter.

15. The figures exclude protests in other areas in which groups from the three areas took part because doing so allows for a clearer analysis of the effect of local context on the type of issues raised in protests.

16. Comparison with the local newsletter and participant observation data for 1995–2001 showed no animal rights EDA activity in North Wales, a slightly smaller proportion in Oxford and a small amount of activity by the Manchester Animal Protection (MAP) and hunt saboteurs groups (4% of claims).

17. The low proportion of leafleting reported in national events involving groups from all three locations was very likely due to lack of space in reports of major protests.

18. In Manchester there was a high proportion of occupations and blockades because of the central role played by Manchester activists in campaigns against the loans made by Lloyds and Midland banks to oppressive countries in the global South and a campaign against arms exports by British Aerospace, which centred upon occupying workplaces, as well as the higher number of offices of other pariah companies in Manchester.

19. Surveys of opinion on protests in 2000 showed significant support for some EDA protests, including destruction of GM crops and the anti-capitalist street demonstrations in London (Dunleavy *et al.*, 2005: 150–3).

References

Chesters, G. & Welsh, I. (2005) *Complexity, Multitudes and Movements: Acting on the Edge of Chaos* (London: Routledge).

Doherty, B. (1999a) 'Paving the way: the rise of direct action and the changing character of British environmentalism', *Political Studies* 47(2): 275–91.

Doherty, B. (1999b) 'Manufactured vulnerability', *Mobilization* 4(1): 75–89.

Doherty, B. (2003) 'Studying local activist communities over time: direct action in Manchester, Oxford and North Wales 1970–2001', European Sociological Association, Murcia, September.

Doherty, B., Plows, A. & Wall, D. (2003) 'The preferred way of doing things: the UK direct action movement', *Parliamentary Affairs* 56(4): 669–86.

Downs, A. (1972) 'Up and down with ecology: the issue attention cycle', *The Public Interest* 28: 38–50.

Doyle, T. (1994) 'Direct action in environmental conflict in Australia: a re-examination of non-violent action', *Regional Journal of Social Issues* 28: 1–13.

Dunleavy, P., Margetts, H., Smith, T. & Weir, S. (2005) *Voices of the People: Popular Attitudes to Democratic Renewal in Britain* (London: Politico's).

Fillieule, O. & Jiménez, M. (2003) 'Appendix A: the methodology of protest event analysis and the media politics of reporting environmental protest events', in C. Rootes (ed.), *Environmental Protest in Western Europe*, pp. 258–79 (Oxford: Oxford University Press).

Haunss, S. & Leach, D. K. (2004) 'Scenes and social movements', European Consortium for Political Research, Uppsala, April.

La Rocca, S. (2004) 'Making a difference: factors that influence participation in grassroots environmental activism in Australia', unpublished dissertation, Australian School of Environmental Studies, Griffith University.

Lee, M. (1995) *Earth First! Environmental Apocalypse* (New York: Syracuse University Press).

McAdam, D. (1983) 'Tactical innovation and the pace of insurgency', *American Sociological Review* 48: 735–54.

Olesen, T. (2005) *International Zapatismo: The Construction of Solidarity in the Age of Globalization* (London: Zed Books).

Plows, A., Wall, D. & Doherty, B. (2004) 'Covert repertoires: ecotage in the UK', *Social Movement Studies* 3(2): 199–220.

Polletta, F. (2002) *Freedom is an Endless Meeting: Democracy in American Social Movement* (Chicago: University of Chicago Press).

Rootes, C. (2000) 'Environmental protest in Britain', in B. Seel, M. Paterson & B. Doherty (eds.), *Direct Action in British Environmentalism*, pp. 25–61 (London: Routledge).

Rootes, C. (2003a) 'The transformation of environmental activism', in C. Rootes (ed.), *Environmental Protest in Western Europe*, pp. 1–19 (Oxford: Oxford University Press).

Rootes, C. (2003b) 'Britain', in C. Rootes (ed.), *Environmental Protest in Western Europe*, pp. 20–58 (Oxford: Oxford University Press).

Rucht, D. & Ohlemacher, T. (1992) 'Protest event data: collection, uses and perspectives', in M. Diani & R. Eyerman (eds.), *Studying Collective Action*, pp. 76–106 (London: Sage).

Seel, B. & Plows, A. (2000) 'Coming live and direct: strategies of Earth First!', in B. Seel, M. Paterson & B. Doherty (eds.), *Direct Action in British Environmentalism*, pp. 112–32 (London: Routledge).

Tarrow, S. (1998) *Power in Movement* (Cambridge: Cambridge University Press).

Tilly, C. (2004) *Social Movements, 1768–2004* (Boulder, CO: Paradigm).

Wall, D. (1999) *Earth First! and the Anti-Roads Movement* (London: Routledge).

Wood, L. J. (2005) 'Bridging the chasms: the case of people's global action', in J. Bandy & J. Smith (eds.), *Coalitions Across Borders*, pp. 95–117 (Oxford: Rowman and Littlefield).

From Larzac to the Altermondialist Mobilisation: Space in Environmental Movements

GAËL FRANQUEMAGNE

Introduction

The literature on environmental mobilisation provides many case studies, but one aspect remains little considered: the question of place. Most studies treat space as mere background and not as a constituent element of collective action, when by definition environmental mobilisations activate a local configuration of actors on territorial issues, such as the defence of a particular area of land or protection of a natural area. We want here to give voice to the spatial dimension of environmental mobilisation in order to answer the problem of space in contentious movements. The scientific literature dealing with environmental mobilisation provides many studies based on individual properties of actors linked to the notion of activist trajectory (Sawicki, 2003), on institutional opportunities (Kitschelt, 1986; Sainteny, 2000), and on organisational structures (Fréour, 2004; Martin, 2005). Inspired by Goffman (1991), framing theory also invested the field of environmental movements

(Ollitrault, 2004), and more recently attempts have been made to reconcile the individualist and the collective approaches of collective action through the concept of the 'activist career' (Ollitrault, 2001). Others have highlighted interactions involving the media in environmental mobilisations (Derville, 1997). But the literature remains quite silent on the analysis and the conceptualisation of space as a constituent element of these mobilisations. This 'silence' (Aminzade *et al.*, 2001) is all the more 'deafening' in France where a specific place (the Larzac) has a long history of contention and is perceived as the centre of the altermondialist[1] protest. Our goal here is to remedy this surprising lack.

Drawing on a case study of the Larzac mobilisations, we aim to build on the theoretical work of Sewell (2001), who tries to theorise the concept of space in contentious mobilisations and 'to provide a rudimentary theoretical vocabulary for thinking about space in contentious politics and to begin putting such a vocabulary to work' (2001: 52). Sewell's is an interesting partial synthesis about contentious politics which lays out a number of new research agendas, and especially invites empirical case studies. In accepting that invitation, we shall show how a geographic and physical place can be transformed into a rhetorical argument of mobilisation. More precisely, our concern is the understanding of what allows the actors of an environmental movement to use the argumentative resources provided by the geographic place for mobilisation purposes. This case is all the more interesting since Larzac has for more than 30 years experienced various types of mobilisation: anti-militarist, pacifist and anti-nuclear action, but also peasants' protests and finally altermondialist contention. Thus the Larzac can be considered a realisation of the ideal type of the 'iterative site' (McAdam *et al.*, 2001: 30) where contention is a constituent of social reality. Our object of study is neither continuity nor rupture in contention, but successive actualisations of contention. Contention in the Larzac is at the same time episodic, continuous and recurrent. From the struggle against the enlargement of the military camp from 1972 to 1981 to the dismantling of the McDonalds fast-food restaurant in Millau in 1999, the Larzac territory has been established as a sacred and emblematic place of contention. A symbol of the anti-militarist and pacifist movement in the 1970s, the Larzac has kept its place in the landscape of protest, to such a point that this almost deserted place can be considered today as the hotbed of French altermondialist protest. This is so true that the toponym 'Larzac' comes to mean 'the Larzac contention'.

Considering space as the key point of our study implies our forging a theoretical tool likely to give an account of this constituent dimension. That is why we talk about the Larzac case as a socio-territorial mobilisation. By 'socio-territorial mobilisation', we mean the combined discursive productions embedded in a site which aim at creating or increasing the visibility of a localised cause. This general definition must be more tightly clarified in three directions.

First, this kind of mobilisation is *situated*, that is to say, rooted in a specific site. It usually confers on the socio-territorial mobilisation a defensive, indeed corporative, dimension. We want here to stress the fact that space must not be considered as mere background, and this involves treating all the geographic data not simply as contextual ones but as deeply constitutive elements of the mobilisation. Rooted in this place of reference, a loose network develops and engages in collective action (Rootes, 2006) in order to make its claims recognised.

Second, we mean by discursive productions the *collective* acts directly related to the site. Discursive productions can be either individual (books, interviews) or collective (demonstrations), and they can take place in the site of reference (Larzac meetings, 2000 and 2003) or away from this site (European and World Social Forums).

Finally, we deal with *social* mobilisations because discursive practices are not exclusively directed towards the defence or the promotion of a specific place, but also aim at generalising claims or denunciations in a social and in a global direction.

In order to explain why local environmental mobilisations such as the Larzac and broadly contentious movements succeed in their 'struggle for recognition' (Honneth, 2000), our working assumption is that this kind of movement has two faces: they are rooted in a specific place, and at the same time they carry various issues which do not directly concern that place. But in order to be able and above all to be authorised to deal with more general issues, local actors need to base their discursive practices on a semantic bridge and on a collective grammar. They find it in environmental discourse, which can bring forth the defence of a specific site as well as a green criticism of productivism.

Drawing on a longitudinal analysis of the Larzac mobilisation, we seek to explain how the Larzac has been established as a sacred and emblematic place of contention. This study is particularly based on the discursive production of the Larzac community for 30 years (books written by major actors of the movement, media reports, meetings) and on an ethnographic survey of Larzac protest events.[2] We keep this case study within the general pattern of the constructivist analysis, insofar as place cannot be considered as a mere background or as a container within which the mobilisation process is constrained to occur. We would rather speak about place as it offers resources for people who speak in its name and about Larzac as a mobilising site and as a fund or 'repertoire' of argumentation. As Moles and Rohmer (1998: 111) put it, 'space is not neutral, it is not an empty frame to fill with behaviours, it is a source of behaviours'.

One of the major features of contemporary protest movements is to be centred on specific concerns and at the same time to be closely linked to one another. For instance, the *Confédération paysanne* (CP) represents small farmers' interests and is a strong critic of productivism, and at the same time is a founding member of ATTAC and is part of the *Sortir du nucléaire* network. This paradoxical aspect of contentious politics is part of environmental mobilisations. They can act locally, in order to defend local peasants against the extension of a military camp for instance, and they also act globally, treating space as a global good. Despite being often presented as a constraint by analysts, this paradoxical dimension of contention is in fact a resource for activists. Environmentalist rhetoric acts as a triple bridge. It might first be considered as *a temporal bridge* which relates the 1970s struggle against the military camp to the current altermondialist contention. It is also *a geographic bridge* which connects Larzac to the rest of the world and thus allows connections among various kinds of contention. It is finally and subsequently a *(common) place of contention*, that is to say, a seedbed for contentious actions such as civil disobedience, and a hotbed from which various protest and environmental movements can draw experience, know-how and legitimacy.

The Constitution of a Sacred Place of Contention

First, we should specify what we mean by 'environment'. We stress the three main aspects of this notion, insofar as each points out one of the constituent elements of the establishment of Larzac as a sacred place of contention. Thus we will successively consider environment and its defensive and reactive dimension, then environment as promotion of a specific place and soil, and finally environment as a common and global good.

The Struggle against the Extension of the Military Camp: A Heterogeneous Mobilisation

The starting point of contentious Larzac was the precipitate announcement on 28 October 1971 by Michel Debré, the then Defence Minister, that the Larzac military camp, which was created in 1902, was to be enlarged. More than a hundred properties would be affected by the project.

The Larzac is a limestone plateau in the south of the French Massif Central. It is part of the *Grands Causses*, a raised (between 600 and more than 900 metres) and arid zone located mainly in the Aveyron department (but also partly in Lozère and Hérault). It is a rural, agricultural place where sheep are bred for their meat but above all to produce milk for the well-known Roquefort cheese. Because of its semi-deserted character, the government did not envisage any opposition to its project. However, resistance was quickly organised. After an almost unanimous protest in Aveyron and the mobilisation of local notables, the 103 'peasants' (as they describe themselves) affected by the project vowed never to yield to government pressure; we call this moment the *Serment des 103* (the oath of the 103). They were supported by trade unions, by leftwing political parties and by other protest and pacifist movements. Our concern is not to report the whole story of this conflict; let us simply say that in 1981, the new President, François Mitterrand, decided to abandon the enlargement project. We underline here that it is the contention organised around various heterogeneous 'hearths [*foyers*] of mobilization'

(Dobry, 1990) that we again find in the current altermondialist contention. We can distinguish five major poles of mobilisation.

Political Contention

In the post-1968 context, the Larzac federated many leftist or radical groups such as Maoist or anarchist activists. Larzac was for them a new place of contention, and an emblematic one. If Paris was the centre of contention in 1968, the Larzac had to be the new one. This was a radical and extra-parliamentary form of contention, whose presence in the Larzac induced tensions among opponents, especially with local peasants. A specific agricultural form of political contention invested the conflict as well, such as the Working and Peasants Left (GOP, *Gauche ouvrière et paysanne*), the radical fringe of the PSU (United Socialist Party).[3]

Trade Unionist Action

Two kinds of trade unions were involved in Larzac contention. The first, especially involved in local problems, was the *Fédération départementale des syndicats d'exploitants agricoles* (FDSEA) which quickly reacted and called for a demonstration in Millau on 6 November 1971. Furthermore, FDSEA peasants supported those of the Larzac when they walked the whole distance to Paris. It is finally interesting to notice that before the conflict, the FDSEA acted as a socialising place, and that the quasi-monopoly of this main trade union would be contested and shaken by a second and more radical trade union led by Bernard Lambert. He was the founder of the working peasants' movement which worked to bring closer peasants and workers' trade unions. This movement came from an internal opposition in the CNJA (Centre national des jeunes agriculteurs) and the FNSEA between a minor trend influenced by the ideas of May 1968 and the leaders of the majority trade union and its strategy of cooperation with rightwing governments. The working peasants' movement was born from this conflict. In 1987, the CNSTP (Confédération nationale des syndicats de travailleurs paysans), that is to say, the independent leftwing agricultural trade union, and the FNSP (Fédération nationale des syndicats paysans), close to the Socialist Party, united and created the Confederation Paysan (CP).

Religious and Spiritual Commitment

We must distinguish between two faces of this kind of engagement. First, the Larzac contention quickly gained the support of the local clergy. Then this support extended beyond Larzac and was staged, symbolically and physically, when the Larzac peasants marched to Paris in 1973 and, with the agreement of the local bishop, took from Orléans Cathedral a stone which would be used for the building of the illegal farm of *la Blaquière*. We can, therefore, say that religious commitment built the Larzac territory. Second, the commitment of Lanza del Vasto contributed to diffuse protest practises such as civil disobedience. Referring to non-violence principles, this disciple of Gandhi was the founder of the first Arche community in 1948. As early as 1972 he supported Larzac peasants and installed an Arche community on the plateau by squatting a farm bought by the army. He actively took part in the Larzac contention by fasting for 15 days. The echo of this action was all the more resounding in the Catholic Aveyron countryside because it involved the bishops of Montpellier and Rodez and some peasants. The main consequence of this spiritual commitment was the adoption by Larzac peasants of civil disobedience as the major form of resistance against the army.

Ecologist Mobilisation

This form of mobilisation materialised in two directions. First, it was directly linked to the protection of a specific environment which was under the threat from the army. It is not by chance that the Larzac contention developed close links to local anti-nuclear struggles such as those of Plogoff in Brittany and Braud et Saint-Louis near Bordeaux where mobilisations opposed the building of nuclear power stations. Second, we must remember here that the 1960s contention encouraged a 'back to the earth' ideology. Indeed, since May 1968, a small fringe of urban youth was in search of rural roots, in line with the utopian ideas of the end of the 1960s. They sought a kind of communal life and the Larzac seemed to them what names a 'utopian community' (Lacroix, 1981). Even if many hippies or *baba-cool* went to the Larzac during the struggle, especially for big meetings and parties, urban people who really took part in the conflict and above all who settled permanently in the Larzac must not be compared with hippies. We would rather call them 'new rural people' (*néo-ruraux*). The promotion of green tourism, of biological agriculture and of rural handicrafts gives evidence of the major influence of the ecologist mobilisation.

The Constitution of a Regionalist Front

The 1970s was propitious for the spread of local movements who denounced central power and aimed at promoting regionalist issues. So Larzac was quickly invested by the Occitanist movement, according to the ideology of *internal colonialism*. Larzac constituted a political and ideological stake for two main reasons. First, this investment in the conflict aimed at influencing the global social contention via the peasants' movement. Second, they hoped this conflict, and consequently the place, would become symbolic and emblematic of their regionalist concerns. The commitment of the Occitan regionalist movement to the conflict left its imprint especially in the naming of place (the *Rajal del Gorp*, the Spring of the Raven in English, which is the natural site where most of the big gatherings took place) and slogans such as *Viure al pais* (live in native land) or *Gardarem lo Larzac* (we want to keep Larzac).

Besides these five major sources of mobilisation we can make another heuristic distinction between two kinds of activists. On the one hand, local peasants who had been working in the Larzac for a long time mobilised as a reaction against the project of extension of the camp, especially because they are directly concerned. They called themselves the *pur-porc*, that is to say, the pure-pigs, or *four-quarters peasants* to mark their difference from new rural people. On the other hand, there were people who did not live in the Larzac at the beginning of the 1970s but who went and settled permanently on the plateau. José Bové has an emblematic trajectory of the latter kind: when the Larzac conflict started, he was a draft-dodger; he settled with his family in the Larzac in 1976 by squatting a farm bought by the army. From this point he became a peasant and bred sheep.

The Larzac contention constituted a heterogeneous front. Each component was motivated by specific concerns. Yet that did not prevent the Larzac campaign from achieving victory; better, it gave birth to a mixed identity based on the Larzac place and, above all, on the protest values it was conveying. Two major mediums helped first to create and then to maintain unity among the various strands of the mobilisation. The first are the Larzac committees, which were created all over France in order to support and to popularise the Larzac cause – local coordinations of activist organisations (trade unions, political parties, and regionalist movements, Christians involved in social movements, anti-militarist activists, and so on). The second is *Gardarem lo Larzac*, a monthly newspaper founded in 1975 in the heart of the conflict. It aimed at the same time to counterbalance what Larzac peasants considered to be the one-sided and pro-government reporting of Larzac events by the major newspapers, and to create a forum and a link among all the Larzac committees. We must however bear in mind that it is above all participation in the same struggle which helps to maintain unity; better, the Larzac conflict set a precedent by generating shared and collective references among the different components mobilised.

It is the protection and the defence of environment as a specific space which mobilised people, but, as we shall see, the environment is not only a given fact but something built and promoted by activists. If the army is a strong landscape marker, as the Larzac camp testifies, Larzac peasants devoted all their energy to limit this influence and to build a landscape that was concurrent – and contentious.

The Semiotisation of Larzac: The Appropriation of Place

We have seen that Larzac peasants first mobilised against a governmental project. What we now want to show is what their action has built, symbolically and above all physically. Following Raffestin (1986), we assume that Larzac is a rearrangement of space. Then it is essential to analyse the various coding processes of the Larzac place by people engaged in the Larzac mobilisation, and the way they symbolically mark the land. In 1972 the 103 peasants (*les 103*) planted 103 trees on the banks of the RN 9 trunk road. It is a meaningful example, but talking about the constitution of a mythic place of contention and studying symbolic action of space appropriation is not enough to demonstrate what we really mean by the process of space building. That is why we concretely analyse how Larzac activists have shaped their environment as a contentious landscape.

Against the government strategy, which aimed at buying the landed estates affected by the army project, the Larzac peasants' strategy adapted to their opponents and began to hold the ring, in two ways. The first was a legal strategy. At that time the concern was to buy lands in the area affected by the proposed extension of the military camp, and to do it, to collect the necessary funds. It is for this purpose that the Agricultural Estate Groups (GFA, *Groupements fonciers agricoles*) were funded. The first, GFA Larzac 1, was created in 1973. Its goal was to buy the strategic lands and those 'at risk', that is to say, the zones essential for the army. The first priority was to buy isolated parcels, whatever their agricultural value, so that the land bought by the army should not constitute a continuous zone that it would find it easy to use; then the GFA focused on entire farming estates in order to maintain their activities. This strategy has been confirmed since because the lands bought by the state have been divided up and because private sales prior to expropriation were limited. Other and complementary actions have been worked out in order to facilitate the settlement of new peasants or inhabitants: repairing ruins, building farm paths, water supplies. Simultaneously, illegal actions were taken to hold the land. They contributed as well to shape the landscape: the ploughing of land belonging to the army or to presumed speculators, the digging of trenches through the RN 9 to channel water into the extension area. But the most structuring factor concerning the building of space is the construction of illegal sheepfolds and the squatting by activists who would become new peasants of farms bought by the army. Two main places illustrate these illegal actions. Concerning the building of illegal farms (for instance, sheepfolds in Cavaliès and Potensac), *la Blaquière* is an emblematic case. Planning permission had previously been refused because it was placed in the heart of the previous military extension area. So, in the first concrete action of the Larzac committees, it was illegally built between 1973 and 1975 with the help of funds set up by anti-militarists who refused, as a direct act of civil disobedience, to pay the three percent of taxes that they estimated to be the share of overall taxation attributable to the national defence budget. Three thousand people participated in the building, most of them conscientious objectors. So we can speak here of an anti-militarist coding. Two other kinds of coding can be observed. First, a religious one: *la Blaquière* is called 'the Larzac cathedral' because its first stone came from the Orléans cathedral. Moreover, a Franciscan who had previously worked on a Romanesque church took part in the building. This nickname also comes from its huge dimensions (69 × 21 metres). Besides this religious coding, we can observe an internationalist one. At the time of the setting of the first stone, it was declared: 'We don't want to destroy but to build. This is not our sheepfold. It belongs to all Larzac peasants, to people from France and from the world, people who hold their heads up high and want to stand up' (APAL, 2000). For all these reasons *la Blaquière* became emblematic of Larzac contention. Some of its stones are used as stands for writing messages in several languages. It even withstood an attack in 1975. In 1982, after the presidential elections and François Mitterrand's victory, the Plan Minister, Michel Rocard, with both region and department prefects, officially inaugurated the illegal sheepfold.

Concerning the squatting of farms, Montredon is illustrative. This Larzac hamlet located on the edge of the military camp, which had been progressively abandoned since the First World War, had begun to live again thanks to the conflict. Owned by the army during the conflict, it was squatted by protesters and restored. This new settlement went hand in hand with new agricultural production: a sheep-meat flock and cheese-making. Montredon has become a central contentious place for two main reasons. First, it is the place where Bové settled in 1976. Though not a movement leader during the campaign, Bové was nonetheless centrally involved in its direct actions, and has become increasingly influential locally, nationally and internationally since the campaign ended. The second reason is that Montredon hamlet progressively became the head office of some of the major structures of the struggle such as *Gardarem lo Larzac* and the GFA. Today Montredon remains this important place for the same reasons. As well as a well-known farmers' market, there is a rest-house which was formerly a people's university for ecologists.

The last example of the shaping of space by protest is the *Rajal del Gorp*, a dolomitic cirque to the northwest of La Cavalerie. It is an emblematic place of the Larzac contention insofar as most of the big gatherings took place on this site. In 1973, the first great meeting was organised by the working peasants' movement. Almost 100,000 people took part. The second gathering took place in 1974 (more than 100,000 people), and the third in 1977 (50,000). Finally in 1981, victory was celebrated at the *Rajal del Gorp*. Participation in the *Rajals* is experienced as a contentious pilgrimage. We can observe in this case and in that of the Larzac the same metonymical process: the conflict is associated with the place to such a point that it takes its name. The Larzac toponym means at the same time a localised place and a social-cum-territorial mobilisation. In the same way, the *Rajal del Gorp* is a *lieu-dit* and also means contentious gatherings (the *rajals*). There is a close overlap between the conflict and the geographical and geological environment. For instance, a booklet published by the Larzac eco-museum remarks: 'In the geological era, in a prophetic gesture, Larzac already stood up! Yes, stood up, 800 metres high' (Baillon, 1982: 2). Following the analysis of Deleuze and Guattari (1980: 386), natural elements such as the *Rajal del Gorp*, while becoming expressive, have been turned into 'markers' or 'placards' which delimit the place and its borders.

This protest landscape had to be managed, during and above all after the conflict. The concern is the conception of environment as something to promote. What is interesting here is that promotion of environment is always closely linked to the Larzac contentious experience. The best example is the place called *la Jasse*. Close to the RN 9, this old Caussenard sheepfold shelters the *Maison du Larzac*, a small museum of Larzac history. It is considered the window of Larzac in its dual contentious and geographical aspects. We can find there farm products, local craftsmen and tourist information. It also sells books especially dedicated to the peasants' struggle. The place is managed by the Association for the Development of the Larzac (APAL), created in 1973 as the Association for Promotion of Larzac Agriculture to collect and to manage the funds raised by anti-militarists' withholding of taxes. Then the APAL became a development instrument intended to coordinate and help young farmers to settle on the plateau, to think about new energies and to promote Larzac to the outside world. Today its activity especially focuses on social activities (local information, debates, and exhibitions) and on the promotion of innovative projects for Larzac development.

Finally, we can consider Roquefort cheese as a good example of the contentious coding of environment. Partly produced with Larzac ewes' milk, it has become emblematic of this contentious soil and of the *malbouffe* problem (see below). At Seattle in 1999, at the Citizen Forum against the WTO, the then national spokesman of the CP, Bové, spoke in English in front of 300 people gathered by American NGOs and trade unions to denounce the consequences of WTO projects for agriculture. In order to support his statement, he held up a Roquefort cheese to illustrate the linkage between Larzac peasants and altermondialist networks, and as a symbol of Larzac and beyond altermondialist contention.

Environment as a Global Good: International Solidarity and De-sectorialisation of the Conflict

Larzac contention first meant a defensive and reactive protest against an attempted intrusion by outsiders. But the contentious repertoire of activists quickly moved in two directions in an attempt to make the conflict less corporatist. The first direction of these discursive actions is what can be called international solidarity actions. According to the conception of environment as a global good, we notice three cases of commitment in the field of international solidarity that refer to various constituent dimensions of the Larzac conflict. The first is directed towards peasants in Southern countries. This kind of support is expressively staged by Larzac activists: for instance, in 1974 the *Harvest for the Third World* was organised during a meeting in the Larzac in which 50,000 people took part. The money collected was sent to the peasants of the Sahel. Interdependence between both situations was underlined: the slogan of the demonstration was 'wheat keeps people alive, arms kill'. The second concerns opposition to state power. Here support was extended to opponents of the construction of Narita airport in Japan in 1982, and to Polynesian people, stressing both the pro-independence and regionalist dimensions of the conflict and anti-militarist concerns. Finally, links between Larzac peasants and the Kanak cause were tight. As Bové notes in an interview given to the newspaper *L'Humanité*, 'thanks to our lawyer, we made contact with people from New Caledonia, Jean-Marie Tjibaou and the FLNKS (National Kanak Socialist Liberation Front). Some Kanak people came to Larzac, and delegations from Larzac went there. In 1985 or 1986, members from the FLNKS introduced us to the Tahitian pro-independence leader, Oscar Temaru. For peasants, for Melanesian or Polynesian people, the central point is land. The fact of being despoiled of it and being excluded from the future of this land brings us together and makes us stick together' (*L'Humanité*, 1995). This support was strengthened by the French policy of conducting nuclear weapons tests in Polynesia. During the whole period of the conflict, Larzac peasants increased this kind of international support and connections: for instance, in May 1973 a delegation from the American Indian Movement and Irish people close to the IRA went to the Larzac to join a meeting concerning minorities protesting against state powers. Larzac contention took benefit from the peasants' lawyer's international network: François Roux, counsel for the Larzac peasants, is also the counsel for Kanak leaders and Polynesians campaigning for independence. Out of his non-violent and spiritual commitment to anti-militarist, pro-independence and pacifist movements, he wove contacts all around the world. This experience helped to link heterogeneous struggles by defining shared concerns (environment) and a repertoire of collective action focused on non-violence and civil disobedience.

The second point concerns the will of activists to de-sectorialise their cause, and so to link it with other types of conflicts. The emblematic case is the mutual support between two of the most famous French social conflicts of the 1970s: Lip and Larzac. Lip was a French company near Besançon that produced watches. Its 1973 takeover and restructuring produced significant job losses and provoked strong protests. The workers barricaded themselves in their factory, started machines again, and sold their production. It was then considered an emblematic case of self-management (Piaget, 1973; Lourau, 1974), and delegations were sent everywhere to present and to popularise their struggle. Lip workers went to the Larzac at the very beginning of their conflict. In 1973 many Lip workers joined the *Rajal del Gorp* gathering where the bringing together of workers and peasants was pleaded. This kind of link was all the more easy to establish in that it answered the shared desire to broaden the struggle. Besides this national case of solidarity, local connections were made between factory workers and Larzac peasants, such as the solidarity strikes by Millau workers. These connections as a whole were staged in the Larzac and so contributed to build the Larzac territory as a contentious landscape. For instance, Larzac peasants sold the Lip workers a parcel of land. As well, in September 1985 they symbolically offered the Kanak community, represented by the FLNKS leader Jean-Marie Tjibaou, land and a *cazelle* (a hut built of dry stones). *Le Canard Enchaîné*, a French political and satirical paper that has supported the Larzac cause from the beginning and helped in the creation of *Gardarem lo Larzac*, was given a pond by the Larzac peasants.

Since the 1970s, people involved in the Larzac conflict have been building a contentious place both symbolically and physically. Larzac has been shaped as an 'obligatory passage point' (Callon, 1986: 205), in other words a contentious melting-pot for many protest movements commuted into altermondialist struggle. Gaining strength from their victory, and according to an enlarged conception of environment, Larzac peasants provided necessary arguments in the construction of public problems concerning the environment and placed a contentious address book at their partners' disposal. That is what we shall now show through the construction of the public problem of genetically modified organisms (GMOs).

The Local Construction of Global and Environmental Public Problems: '*Malbouffe*' and GMOs

The French word '*malbouffe*' originally meant unhealthy or 'junkfood' (de Rosnay & de Rosnay, 1979). But its current meaning, popularised by Bové and Dufour (2000), enlarged it to three more general concerns. Its first dimension is cultural; this reactive component of *malbouffe* aims to promote local products (Roquefort) against standardised food such as Coca-Cola and McDonalds. The second meaning stresses a political and economic dimension, by fighting for food sovereignty and defending sustainable or fairtrade food. Finally, the *malbouffe* arose from the fear of food contamination, from beef injected with hormones through to GMOs. We must make it clear that the word '*malbouffe*' has been used after the event; it did not appear on tracts calling the meeting at which the momentous decision was made to attack the McDonalds restaurant in Millau.

The mobilisation of various protest actors about a cause such as the *malbouffe* implies a minimal agreement about the analysis of the situation, the available repertoire of collective action and the aim of the struggle. Goffman's *Frame Analysis* (1991) turned attention to the question of the participation of people in collective action. The concept of 'frame' aims to overcome the inadequacies of the theory of resource mobilisation. Snow *et al.* (1986) show that support and enrolment of people in a collective movement has been made possible through a 'frame alignment' – strategic work done by the movement itself in order to match up its mobilisation frame with potential activists' expectations. This theoretical approach faces three major difficulties. Very briefly, frame analysis tends first to mean simply any social movement's cultural dimension. Second, McAdam *et al.* (2001) already criticised the excessively strategic vision of Snow's work. Finally, this kind of approach is heuristic at a macro-sociological level, because it can stress important movements of frames, but struggles with the micro-sociological question of the concrete motives of people who commit to a collective action. That is why we proceed to a sociology of a contentious event (the dismantling of the McDonalds in Millau) and highlight the most concrete and tangible elements of the construction of GMOs as a public problem. Narratives of the dismantling and the diverse appropriations of this event gave various protest groups the possibility to join a contentious configuration centred on the GMO problem.

The Dismantling of McDonalds: A Localised Transformative Event

Since the dismantling of the Millau restaurant, Larzac has been renewed not with protest but with media-centred contention. More, this event constitutes a turning point for Larzac contention. On 12 August 1999, 300 people 'ransacked' or 'dismantled' (the choice between the two terms has been the subject of a robust semantic controversy between opponents and protagonists of the event) a McDonalds restaurant under construction in Millau, a town on the edge of the Larzac plateau, to protest against the United States' taxation of Roquefort. Five activists received short prison terms as a result.

We first have to explain what we specifically mean by *event*. Indeed, we face here a specific temporality which is not reducible to a mere spatial and territorial occurrence. We consider, following Paul Ricoeur (1983), that an event is more than a singular occurrence and that it gets its meaning from the development of its narration, i.e. its meaning derives from its place within a developing narrative. Studying the event itself is essential because an analysis based on the outcomes of the action does not account for what really happened that day. Moreover, the meaning people gave to the action when it occurred was not the same as that they later gave to the same event. This implies that we should not focus exclusively on the construction of the event through its media coverage, nor should we adopt too strategic an approach. Indeed, if analyses such as that of Molotch and Lester (1996) must be credited with stressing the intentional strategies of the actors in mobilisations, they undervalue the fact that it is not the event itself but the meaning that will later be assigned to it which confers importance upon the event. There is no event without the meaning that is given to it when it is received. An event does not have an *a priori* meaning. To borrow Boudon's words (2003), the 'good reasons' people had to act when they dismantled the McDonalds are not the 'good reasons' they used later to justify their action.

Second, we would underline the *localistic* dimension of the McDonalds action. Indeed, the local context and local concerns are not merely a backdrop but are really part of the event (Sawicki, 1988; Briquet & Sawicki, 1989). This aspect is interesting for three main reasons. First, it took place in Millau, below the Larzac plateau. In the eyes of the general public, this action was renewing the 1970s contention. We can also notice that some of the Millau co-accused (such as Léon Maillé and Christian Roqueirol) were already part of the Larzac contention against the military camp. The dismantling had been decided upon some days before in Saint-Affrique, a town at the western border of the Larzac plateau. Second, this indicates that the decision had been made mainly by Larzac activists (in fact members of the Aveyron CP) and not by the trade union officials. François Dufour, the spokesman at this time, knew about the dismantling but did not take the decision. He recognises that 'the Aveyron *CP* moves a lot and often aims straight' (Bové & Dufour, 2000: 40). The dismantling was decided not by the departmental Committee of Aveyron CP but by the ewes' milk producers' trade union (SPLB), led by activists from the CP who produce milk in the Roquefort area, which was the true instigator of the action. Third, the action was the product of an analysis of the local situation. Indeed, the event must be linked to the American retaliatory measures against the European refusal to import meat injected with hormones. Roquefort cheese, the market for which is the main outlet for Larzac producers, was among the European products subjected to a 100% customs surtax to enter the American market. Despite its localistic dimension, the McDonalds event gave Larzac activists the opportunity to activate their international networks and particularly to emphasise American support.

Finally, we deal here with a *transformative* event. In Sewell's (2001: 110) view, 'the key feature of transformative events is that they come to be interpreted as significantly disrupting, altering, or violating the taken-for-granted assumptions governing routine political and social relations'. In other words, following French institutional analysis and especially Lourau's work, we can say that transformative events are *instituting events* insofar as they constitute a disrupting of temporality and a rupture of intelligibility. These 'moments of collective effervescence' evoked by Durkheim can be considered as 'instituting disorder' (Lourau, 1974). An event is not intrinsically transformative; further events and accounts of them can make an event transformative or not. As Sewell (2001: 112) notes, 'it is not the event itself, but the importance that comes to be assigned to it in the immediate aftermath of the event that determines its transformative potential'. The dismantling of the Millau restaurant can be seen as a transformative event because it is first a spatially concentrated event, and second, it introduced a new and potent template for French altermondialist movements. Our objective is not to underestimate the true relationship between the 1970s conflict and this event. On the contrary, the McDonalds episode ushered in a new epoch of Larzac gatherings (2000, 2003). But we want specifically to insist on the event as a 'concentrated moment of social creativity' (Sewell, 2001: 102) and on the changes it raised. Briefly, the McDonalds event introduced five elements that can be considered as resources for the altermondialist contention. It gave it first a new date of reference which symbolises resistance against economic globalisation. Furthermore, the anniversary of the event is celebrated in the Larzac and gives the opportunity to mobilise, according to a sort of virtuous circle. The post-McDonalds period inaugurates a new contentious calendar given rhythm by anniversary celebrations and commemorations (for instance, the anniversary of the first great Larzac gathering in 1973 was celebrated in 2003 in the same place) and by major altermondialist dates such as social forums. Second, it offers altermondialist movements a fixing point, when until this moment their claims were often disembodied. Then it took to the forefront new actors able to give social conflict their voice. On an individual level, Bové has been playing the role of the leader, and on the collective level the CP henceforth became the leading organisation (with ATTAC) of French altermondialist contention. This strategic and central position of the peasants' trade union helped to constitute a new public problem shared by most of the altermondialist movements which takes into account their specific concerns. Finally, this event provided a repertoire of discursive actions which is not really new but that Larzac activists are trying to make more legitimate.

The Constitution of a Discursive Cause: The Malbouffe

From the Larzac conflict of the 1970s, and especially from the 1981 victory to the dismantling of McDonalds, some specific topics have been progressively put in the shade, or 'virtualised' (Lupasco, 1973), such as the Occitanist concerns or the religious component. They have not really been abandoned, but they are no longer the driving force of Larzac contention. The new template of altermondialism has been activated, and the question of the *'malbouffe'* and beyond that, of GMOs, is becoming the new leading actualisation of Larzac contention. The connectionist aspect of the *malbouffe* cause refers to the complex and above all polysemic meaning of environment as it is defined by Larzac peasants. The relationship to nature is the heart of this global ideology, which involves the whole world. This conception goes beyond the problem of the environment as we traditionally conceive it. It centrally embraces social concerns: community living is valorised and industrial and technical mediations are criticised. It gives rise to social movements whose concerns are differentiated: GMOs, nuclear and so on. More precisely, we stress here the main components of the *malbouffe* cause's construction, and especially its environmental dimension. According to Gusfield (1981: 9), 'to describe the structure of public problems is to describe the ordered way in which ideas and activities emerge in the public arena'. Three major processes can be distinguished. They are not mutually exclusive, but we separate them analytically to aid comprehension.

The first component of the construction of this discursive cause is its economic dimension. What is mainly denounced here is the role of multinational companies in the commercialisation of transgenic seeds, especially in Southern countries, and the risks of dependence it generates for peasants. This criticism of 'commercialisation' integrates the cause and people who support it into the anti-globalisation contention. It also gives the opportunity for alliances between quite heterogeneous groups such as the CP and ATTAC.

The second feature is the international process of discourse construction. We consider the June 2000 Millau trial about the dismantling of the McDonalds restaurant as a good example of this strategy of internationalisation. Seventeen people, including Lori Wallach (the spokeswoman of *Public Citizen*) and

Rafael Alegria (the coordinator of *Via Campesina*), intervened during the trial to legitimate the action and to de-singularise it, and to turn the trial into a trial of the WTO.

The third component of this construction process concerns environmental problems more directly. The rhetoric of environmental denunciation of GMOs balances according to a local/global dialectic. From a local point of view, GMOs are accused of endangering soils and products attached to local soils. GMOs' opponents especially focus on the dissemination problem. On a global level, the concern is food sovereignty as it is defended by the CP and *Via Campesina*. It is the rhetoric of risk that allows linkage between the two levels. Analysis, criticism and actions from the opponents of GMOs are undertaken in the name of the precautionary principle. The *malbouffe* problem, and especially that of hormone-injected meat, has been translated into the denunciation of GMOs.

Conclusion

The spatial dimension of social facts in general and of environmental concerns in particular has been occluded for a long time. We have tried here to consider space as a constituent of environmental mobilisations and to analyse it through the prism of the Larzac experience. The Larzac territory and its identity are inventions that have been progressively built by the semiotisation of the place, by the construction of markers that have impregnated the mythology of contention in France. To quote Halbwachs (1939: 822), 'All phenomena occur as though the thought of the group could not be born, survive, and become aware of itself without relying on certain visible forms in space'. On such symbolic bases, space becomes a strong instrument of social mobilisation. Larzac has been invested with its own contentious values that also are proper to other local environmental mobilisations. We have here explored the way environmental discourse is mobilised to denounce global problems from a local place, and above all how a particular place is turned into a think tank of general arguments available for local environmental mobilisations. Larzac operated as a matrix for environmental mobilisations and, beyond that, for other contentious movements.

Notes

1. 'Altermondialist' – literally 'other worldist' – is a term used in France to describe what in the English-speaking world is sometimes, misleadingly, labelled the 'anti-globalisation' movement, and sometimes 'the global justice movement'. It has the advantage of signalling that 'another world is possible' – the slogan of the World Social Forum – without being specific about the contents of the alternatives desired.
2. Particularly the mass gatherings in Millau in 2000 and in 2003, and by the European Social Forums in Florence and Saint-Denis, and more precisely by the way Larzac was represented there.
3. The PSU was the 'New Leftist' ally of the much larger Socialist Party, led by Mitterand.

References

Aminzade, R. R., Goldstone, J. A., McAdam, D., Perry, E. J., Sewell, W. H., Tarrow, S. & Tilly, C. (2001) *Silence and Voice in the Study of Contentious Politics* (Cambridge: Cambridge University Press).

APAL (2000) *Larzac 1971–1981*. Videotape, Gardarem lo Larzac.

Baillon, E. (1982) *Le Larzac terre en marche. Histoire de la lutte du Larzac de 1971 à 1981* (Paris: Éditions écomusée du Larzac).

Boudon, R. (2003) *Raison, bonnes raisons* (Paris: Presses Universitaires de France).

Bové, J. & Dufour, F. (2000) *Le Monde n'est pas une marchandise. Des paysans contre la malbouffe* (Paris: La découverte).

Briquet, J.-L. & Sawicki, F. (1989) 'L'analyse localisée du politique. Lieux de recherche ou recherche de lieux?', *Politix* 7–8: 6–16.

Callon, M. (1986) 'Some elements of a sociology of translation', in J. Law (ed.), *Power, Action and Belief: A New Sociology of Knowledge?* pp. 196–229 (London: Routledge).

Deleuze, G. & Guattari, F. (1980) *Capitalisme et schizophrénie, tome 2: Mille plateaux* (Paris: éditions de Minuit).

Derville, G. (1997) 'Le combat singulier Greenpeace – SIRPA. La compétition pour l'accès aux médias lors de la reprise des essais nucléaires français', *Revue française de science politique* 47(5): 589–629.

Dobry, M. (1990) 'Calcul, concurrence et gestion du sens', in P. Favre (ed.), *La manifestation* (Paris: Presses de la fondation nationale des sciences politiques).

Fréour, N. (2004) 'Le positionnement de Greenpeace', *Revue française de science politique* 54(3): 421–42.

Goffman, E. (1991) *Les cadres de l'expérience* (Paris: Gallimard).

Gusfield, J. R. (1981) *The Culture of Public Problems: Drinking-Driving and the Symbolic Order* (Chicago: University of Chicago Press).

Halbwachs, M. (1939) 'Individual consciousness and collective mind', *American Journal of Sociology* 44(6): 812–22.

Honneth, A. (2000) *La lutte pour la reconnaissance. Grammaire morale des conflits sociaux* (Paris: Cerf).

L'Humanité (1995) 'José: du plateau du Larzac à l'atoll de Mururoa', 28 août.

Kitschelt, H. (1986) 'Political opportunity structures and political protest: anti-nuclear movements in four democracies', *British Journal of Political Science* 16(1): 57–85.

Lacroix, B. (1981) *L'utopie communautaire* (Paris: Presses universitaires de France).

Lourau, R. (1974) *L'analyseur Lip* (Paris: Union générale d'édition).

Lupasco, S. (1973) *Du devenir logique et de l'affectivité. Essai d'une nouvelle théorie de la connaissance* (Paris: Vrin).

Martin, J.-P. (2005) *Histoire de la nouvelle gauche paysanne: des contestations des années 60 à la Confédération paysanne* (Paris: La Découverte).

McAdam, D., Tarrow, S. & Tilly, C. (2001) *Dynamics of Contention* (Cambridge: Cambridge University Press).

Moles, A. & Rohmer, E. (1998) *Psychosociologie de l'espace* (Paris: L'Harmattan).

Molotch, H. & Lester, M. (1996) 'Informer: une conduite délibérée. De l'usage stratégique des événements', *Réseaux* 75: 23–41.

Ollitrault, S. (2001) 'Les écologistes français, des experts en action', *Revue française de science politique* 51(1–2): 105–30.

Ollitrault, S. (2004) 'Des plantes et des hommes. De la défense de la biodiversité à l'altermondialisme', *Revue française de science politique* 54(3): 443–63.

Piaget, C. (1973) *Les Lip* (Paris: Stock).

Raffestin, C. (1986) 'Écogenèse territoriale et territorialité', in F. Auriac & R. Brunet (eds.), *Espaces, jeux et enjeux*, pp. 175–85 (Paris: Fayard).

Ricoeur, P. (1983) *Temps et récit* (Paris: Seuil).

Rootes, C. (2006) 'Facing South? British environmental movement organisations and the challenge of globalisation', *Environmental Politics* 15(5): 768–86.

de Rosnay, J. & de Rosnay, S. (1979) *La Malbouffe. Comment se nourir pour mieux vivre* (Paris: Olivier Orban).

Sainteny, G. (2000) *L'introuvable écologisme français?* (Paris: PUF).

Sawicki, F. (1988) 'Questions de recherches. Pour une analyse locale des partis politiques', *Politix* 2: 13–28.

Sawicki, F. (2003) 'Les temps de l'engagement. À propos de l'institutionnalisation d'une association de défense de l'environnement', in J. Lagroye (ed.), *La politisation*, pp. 123–46 (Paris: Belin).

Sewell, W. H. (2001) 'Space in contentious politics', in R. R. Aminzade, J. A. Goldstone, D. McAdam, E. J. Perry, W. H. Sewell, S. Tarrow & C. Tilly (eds.), *Silence and Voice in the Study of Contentious Politics*, pp. 51–88 (Cambridge: Cambridge University Press).

Snow, D. A., Rochford, B., Worden, S. & Benford, R. (1986) 'Frame alignement processes, micromobilization and movement participation', *American Sociological Review* 51(4): 464–81.

Resisting the Costs of 'Development': Local Environmental Activism in Ireland

MARK GARAVAN

Attempting to examine a national environmental movement raises difficult preliminary questions of sense and reference. What do we mean by environmentalism in contemporary Ireland, given that it encompasses a broad, multifaceted set of beliefs, claims and actions that manifest themselves in the diverse domains of health, food, religion, philosophy, agriculture, art and, of course, politics? What are its boundaries so that we can identify who is in it and who is out? Is there really, as a recent study suggests (Leonard, 2006), a simple progression and continuity from one protest mobilisation to another so that we can speak of a clearly demarcated environmental social movement? In particular, how are we to categorise local mobilisations that raise, either centrally or marginally, environmental claims? Are they part of an integrated environmental movement?

In the Irish case these are important questions because of the extent to which environmental activism is, at least in its political and protest manifestations, predominantly a local phenomenon. Protest event data from 1988 to 2002 (Garavan, 2004) show that protest is far more likely to be employed by local actors in prosecuting local disputes. During this period, reported environmental protest mobilisation occurred exclusively at a local level in two-thirds of cases. Three-quarters of all reported grievances were sub-national in scope.[1]

That Irish environmentalism is so profoundly local in its protest mode has given rise to the implication that it is defective in some way as a social movement by comparison to the northern European norm (Baker, 1990; Yearley, 1995; Tovey & Share, 2001). Localism seems to imply a narrow, 'NIMBY'-style focus on immediate issues and grievances with a concomitant failure to address wider social and political matters. Given that social movements are meant to be about structural transformation, this raises the possibility that actors with a local horizon are not the real thing. Thus Burstein *et al.* (1995) identify the challenging, outsider dimension of social movements (cf. Tilly, 1984) as their most characteristic aspect.

> Virtually everyone writing about social movements agrees that they have two defining characteristics: they demand social and political change, and they are outside political institutions...Thus, we define social movements as organized, collective efforts to achieve social change that use noninstitutionalised tactics at least part of the time. (Burstein *et al.*, 1995: 277–8)

But how true is this characterisation of social movements? Many empirical studies (Landmann, 1999; Rootes, 2003) have shown that collective actors generally recognised as representative of, or as emanating from, the environmental movement are, in fact, less oriented around protest and conflict than might have been expected, and more inclined towards political exchange. Yet, drawing on a theoretical tradition from Weber and Michels, these features have often been interpreted as evidence of institutionalisation (van der Heijden, 1997) and are generally cited as a sign of decline in which movements depart from their original purity as an oppositional force to become co-opted into the conventional political process.

Much of this expectation of how social movements behave arises from their historical emergence in mass protest movements such as the labour and agrarian mobilisations of the 19th century and the anti-nuclear, anti-war and civil rights mobilisations of the 1960s and 1970s. Similarly, the environmental movement too is frequently perceived as having arisen from the protests of these decades. The empirical validity of this claim is uncertain; contemporary environmentalism may originate as much in popular scientific writings such as those of Rachel Carson, Jane Goodall, James Lovelock and the various 'countercultural' projects of these decades. Nevertheless, the narrative account of an origin in protest has set a standard against which the contemporary movement is measured. It therefore follows that, by comparison with the foundation myth of disruption and rule-breaking, the contemporary movement may appear sedate and conventional and, at least in part, pacified (Blühdorn, 2000).

The assertion that a social movement, by definition, does not orientate itself around political exchanges with the state has been described as a 'fetishisation of autonomy' (Hellman, 1992, cited in Gledhill, 2000: 189). It seems much more reasonable, and much more consistent with the evidence, to postulate not so much an 'institutionalisation' of an ontologically complex and variegated 'movement' but rather a continual evolution in forms of activism in response to new knowledge, new opportunities (personal, political and technical), and new shifts in the configuration of political power. It is necessary to recognise that activism, environmental activism perhaps especially, occurs within a variety of social locations and contexts and that each of these contexts presents its own logic and constraints.

The organisations that carry the environmental claim into social and political spaces are perhaps better understood as providers of opportunities for particular forms of activism within the public sphere. Grounding an under-standing of the movement within personal domains and 'submerged networks' (Melucci, 1988) allows one to understand the inherent heterogeneity of Irish environmental activism which, since the late 1990s, has become increasingly characterised by flexible *ad hoc* networks of activists who cooperate and act in ways that increasingly criss-cross and transcend formal organisations. Technological changes, such as the Internet, email and discussion lists, have become crucial catalysts for these new types of mobilisation. It follows that the Irish environmental movement is a highly variegated social phenomenon in which particular organisations and actions are but the most visible expression.

If this characterisation is correct then local-level activism can be seen as simply another dimension of the complex and variegated modes of environ-mental activism. Here we will make two arguments.

First, a preponderance of protest occurring at a local level is not surprising given the specific constraints and opportunities of the Irish political system; it is not necessarily a sign of a defective or deficient social movement. National-level groups are more likely to direct their activities toward achieving policy objectives through a repertoire of lobbying and awareness-raising. It is equally likely that the concentration of a specific grievance in space and time makes that issue more visible and therefore more easily translatable into a problematic capable of mobilising collective action. It is surely to be expected that those most directly affected by an issue are those most likely to protest and hence we should expect to see a preponderance of protest actions occurring among local-level collective actors.

Second, local-level protest is not always or merely a 'NIMBY' phenomenon or something limited and partial. Instead, this paper will argue that local-level protest often implicitly, and sometimes explicitly, raises fundamental claims regarding the nature of modern society. Frequently buried in disputes ostensibly about specific grievances are claims regarding the good life, the nature of modernity and the costs of maintaining the industrial system. This possibility makes local protest far more socially and politically potent and challenging than might otherwise appear to be the case.

In advancing this argument, we will first undertake a brief overview of Irish environmentalism, then outline some key protest event findings, and finally reflect on some features of the protracted conflict between Shell Oil and local residents in North-West Ireland regarding the location of a gas refinery and pipelines.

The Irish Environmental Movement: History and Contextual Constraints

It has been suggested that the Irish environmental movement has been shaped by three outstanding historical features (Yearley, 1995: 660). First, it emerged in response to specific threats such as fears of industrial pollution arising from the pharmaceutical and mining industries. Second, the main targets of its activities were foreign firms. Third, it was initially composed of largely local, usually community-based organisations. Thus, localism is proposed as a defining feature of environmentalism in Ireland.

This characterisation of the Irish movement as largely reactive and divided between the national and local (cf. Tovey & Share, 2001: 514–20) draws heavily on an earlier study of the movement (Baker, 1990). Baker places the origin of the Irish environmental movement largely within the same time-frame as that of most other western European movements and attributes it largely to the same type of issue – nuclear power. The proposal to construct a nuclear power plant in the 1970s mobilised an extraordinarily diverse range of protest groups, many of them politically radical.

A number of the activists mobilised in the apparently successful campaign against nuclear power (no nuclear plant was constructed in Ireland) went on to involvement in a series of campaigns in the 1980s against the chemical industry. These campaigns were particularly concentrated in county Cork, especially around Cork harbour which the Industrial Development Agency (IDA) had designated as a growth zone for the international pharmaceutical industry. The 1980s were also characterised by a series of anti-mining disputes. What these diverse conflicts seemed to have in common was their reactive nature and their local domain of contention. Therefore, they appear to be as much protests over community rights as environmental protests *per se*. Indeed, it has been observed that many of these protest actors rarely invoked a discourse of the environment at all, and if they did, it was only as subservient to the dominant paradigmatic protest discourse offered by nationalism or republicanism.

> ...in 1981 many of the local groups opposed to [the] toxic industry united under the umbrella of the Alliance for Safety and Health. The Alliance, like many of the more radical anti-nuclear groups previously in existence, framed their analysis in terms of nationalist ideology. They argued that the presence of such a high degree of penetration of foreign

direct investment into the Irish economy was a result of its colonial legacy. Furthermore, they argued that the solution to Ireland's toxic and nuclear problems lay not in regulation and monitoring but in the resolution of the national question, that is, the unification of Ireland and the re-appropriation of its natural resources by the Irish people. (Baker, 1990: 63)

Thus, right from the beginning, Irish environmental activists and their organisations struggled, unsuccessfully, to open up a new cleavage in the Irish political system. The environmental problematic, in its protest and political articulation, was either indelibly shaped, or drowned out, by the dominant political frame of nationalism. This, combined with the largely local domain of environmental action, imposed a certain constraint on environmental groups whereby many new activists could only be mobilised by the use of a traditional discourse of community rights over 'our' land and resources, which frequently invoked values of family and community (Tovey, 1992a: 285). This had the effect of placing 'environmental' protest in a continuum of anti-state protest activism stretching back into the 19th century.

The local and reactive character of 1970s and 1980s environmentalism resulted in considerable organisational turnover. It is in contrast to this historical background of multiple local group formations and disbandments that Baker suggested the occurrence of a qualitative change in the Irish movement from the mid to late 1980s with the arrival of 'European-style Green politics'. The groups conveying this new style were qualitatively different because 'they address a wider range of issues than typically found among the other groups we have examined'; they 'address issues across a broad spectrum of ecologism' (Baker, 1990: 71).

In 1990, Baker could identify only three national-level groups that were carriers of this new politics: Earthwatch, the Green Party and Greenpeace. She excluded the traditional conservation groups active at the time, such as An Taisce or the Irish Society for the Protection of Birds, on the grounds 'that they do not present a political analysis of ecological problems or of conservation issues' (Baker, 1990: 79, note 15).

However, this account of the origin of Irish environmentalism appears to over-emphasise its political and protest manifestations. The genesis of the Irish movement is likely to have been far more complex and multidimensional than an origin in reactive protest. Other points of emergence must include the conservation and heritage movements, various countercultural currents, religious groupings, especially those centred on 'Celtic spirituality', and the impact of new ideas and knowledge emanating from scientists and intellectuals from the 1960s onward.

The 1990s have been characterised by a significant increase in the number of new national-level groups, with a corresponding growth in the diversity of claims and forms of activism. Yet the emergence of new national groups has not heralded an increase in protest action. Protest remains largely locally based. Why is this and what does this tell us about the Irish movement?

It is clear that environmental movements are profoundly shaped by their national settings (Rootes, 2004). A number of contextual constraints can be usefully identified to account for the nature of the movement in Ireland by comparison with many of its western European counterparts.

- Demographic constraints. There is a relatively small population from which to draw activists and supporters. This imposes a certain limit on the resource mobilisation capacity of the organisations.
- Environmental constraints. By comparison with many other western states, late industrialisation produced a low level of visible environmental degradation until the 1980s. This has resulted in a delayed awareness of an environmental 'problem' and a correspondingly small constituency for environmental claims.
- Perceptual constraints. The invisibility and technical nature of much environmental degradation has made the mobilisation of broad-based, non-issue-specific environmental groups difficult.
- Political constraints. The historically dominant political cleavage of nationalism and republicanism has resulted in a relatively weak left/labour movement. This has limited the discursive space available for radical political positions and reduced the number of potential allies for the emerging environmental problematic.
- Agricultural constraints. The economic dominance of agriculture has resulted in a conceptualisation of 'nature' as a resource to be utilised for economic benefit. This view combines with a widely held attachment to private ownership and control of land and a consequent antipathy to external regulation.
- Economic constraints. The long Irish experience of relative poverty and emigration has resulted in widespread support for policies of economic growth and industrial development.

The political weakness of the Irish environmental movement is demonstrated in its exclusion from the neo-corporatist National Agreements that the Irish state has negotiated with labour and employer representatives since the late 1980s. In the absence of a strong left, or green, political party, the political opportunities for the movement have been extremely curtailed. The consequence is that Irish environmental organisations have been obliged to operate within a very inauspicious political setting.

Applying the three aspects of institutionalisation suggested by van der Heijden (1997) – organisational growth, internal institutionalisation and external institutionalisation – the Irish movement appears institutionalised. However, this may be somewhat misleading because it may rest on a misunderstanding of the role of the nationally organised groups as pragmatic vehicles for public action and an exaggeration of their influence on the movement as a whole.

Instead, it appears that the extraordinarily low level of material resources mobilised by Irish groups, because it forces them to rely on volunteer activists, has left the organised Irish movement more exposed than other European movements to influences from underlying activist networks and local campaigners. The weakness of the organisations in material and political terms may also leave them less dominant in the configuration of the overall movement's expressions of activism. Consequently, from the perspective of the wider movement milieu, the national-level environmental organisations must be seen as vehicles for activism within the formal public sphere and thereby bearers of an instrumental purpose rather than a representative function. If this is so, then this distinction may also point to possible sources of tension between local activists whose horizon might be limited to the grievance at issue, and national-level actors whose concerns may be far broader. The difference may ultimately rest on the differing contexts within which each operates. While the two levels are certainly distinct, there is a high level of cooperative interaction between them. However, co-operation does not extend to merger. Local groups in Ireland are not inclined to form themselves into branches of national-level organisations. The precise reasons for this are not entirely clear. It may be in order to preserve their independence and decision-making capacity, or because they wish to avoid overt association with 'environmentalism' due to its perceived limited focus or poor image in certain local settings, or it may be because of a reticence to forge any link with formal political groups possessing 'wider agendas'.

Our argument is that environmental activism in Ireland is politically manifesting itself both more deeply and more radically at a local level than might be apparent from a concentration on national-level organisations. To examine this hypothesis, we first outline some relevant protest event data and, second, one such local-level campaign.

Protest Event Data

It seems that most Irish environmental protest is local, reactive and moderate (Garavan, 2004).[2] By comparison, protest-oriented networking by national Irish environmental groups is extraordinarily low. Protest event data indicate that in each year of the 15-year period 1988–2002, with the sole exception of 1995, reported local mobilisations outnumbered national. The patterns of sub-national- and national-level mobilisations closely mirror each other. This suggests that the preponderance of local mobilisations was a stable feature of Irish environmental protest. This in turn indicates that Irish environmental protest activism is essentially a local-level phenomenon. The figures clearly show that the majority of protest activism occurs outside the formally organised, national environmental organisations.

In addition, the single most identifiable social category engaged in protest was 'residents'. The reported mobilisation of residents was never less than 25%

of total protests in any one year. On average over the 15 years, residents accounted for 42% of reported protests, with an increase (to 46%) in the five years from 1998.

By contrast, the protest event data revealed that the volume of reported joint protest actions engaged in by national-level Irish environmental groups is very low. Of the 634 protest events coded for 1988–2002, there were only 27 where it was reported that two or more national-level environmental groups acted together. With aggregate actions by national-level groups making up less than 32% of total reported protest events, the figures suggest that in only one protest out of every seven or eight in which they engaged did national groups act in alliance with one another. This finding tells us more about what the national-level movement is not than what it is. And what it is not is a movement primarily oriented around joint *protest actions*. In other words, engaging in joint protest is not what binds the movement together.

The data from a survey commissioned by the Irish environmental organisations themselves and conducted by Sadhbh O'Neill confirm this characterisation of a largely conventional and moderate movement.

> ... [I]n the main, environmental organisations work through existing legal and democratic channels to achieve their goals. They rarely resort to protests or demonstrations to highlight their concerns to the general public. (O'Neill, 2001: 17)

O'Neill's survey asked groups to identify their most important area of activity. Her results (Table 1) clearly indicate how low a priority is accorded to protest action.

These various findings throw into clear relief the marginal position occupied by protest activism among the organised environmental groups. Rather than protest, the Irish groups emphasise pedagogical and policy-oriented actions. Their concern appears to be with effecting transformation through example, argumentation and knowledge rather than through confrontation targeted on the state or private corporations. It is this logic, more than simply an evolutionary decline towards co-optation or pacification, that better explains why contemporary Irish national-level environmental organisations may act as they do.

What were local actors protesting about? The most striking feature of the protest event data was the predominance of claims centring on industrial pollution and urban ecology. Only in 1993 and 1994 did these claims fail to constitute the largest single category of reported protest. Furthermore, from 1997 reported industrial pollution and urban ecology claims rose sharply. This rise coincides with the general rise in overall protest levels reported from this period. This seems to indicate that the reported rise in Irish protest can be largely explained as a response to the growth in infrastructural and development projects from the mid 1990s onwards.

This possibility is perhaps more clearly apparent if we investigate what specific issues were raised within the broad category of industrial pollution and

Table 1. Areas of activity of Irish environmental organisations

Areas of activity	No. of groups
Education & public awareness-raising	23
Lobbying & participation in policy formulation	20
Publications, information collection & dissemination	20
Networking with other NGOs & joint activities	18
Environmental projects	16
Environmental advice/EIA/planning	13
Environmental inventories, fieldwork & research	12
Practical conservation	11
Professional services	3
Property acquisition & management	3
Protest actions	1

Source: Core Funding Group Survey (2001: 16).

urban ecology. A number of key grievance types can be examined: road construction; housing and other buildings; communications systems (mobile phone masts); waste infrastructure; and pollution on lakes, rivers and seas. Taken together, these constitute virtually all the claims within this category. It seems reasonable to conclude that most of the reported industrial pollution/ urban ecology grievances arose in response to infrastructural and 'developmental' projects, and that they occurred in reaction to perceived threats or risks.

Indeed, there were identifiable differences in the categories of reported claims raised between national-level and local-level actors. National-level actors were reported as much more likely to protest about a variety of grievances – particularly over more 'pure' environmental matters such as nature protection. Those centring on industrial pollution/urban ecology constituted a majority of reported claims raised by national actors in only two of the years since 1995 (1998 and 2002). By contrast, the reported claims of local-level actors were almost entirely concentrated on industrial pollution. Only in 1992 were these claims a minority of the claims raised by local actors.

However, while these data add to the impression of a 'localisation' of Irish environmental conflict, some interpretative caution is required. A grievance concentrated in space and time is more likely to give rise to conflict than more spatially and temporally diffused issues – as Jiménez (2003) found in his investigations of Spanish protest patterns. This is because: the grievance is likely to be more identifiable and tangible; it is on balance easier to mobilise among existing communal and local networks; the resolution of the grievance is likely to be somewhat clearer; and the interlocutor or target of the protest is correspondingly more likely to be readily identifiable.

In the absence of these factors, more global and less tangible issues may not lend themselves as easily to resolution by protest. Indeed, it can be reasonably anticipated that the majority of national-level environmental organisations are orientated in their activities towards these larger, global issues rather than locally occurring grievances. Bigger issues require bigger solutions involving mixtures of policy changes, legislative reforms and inter-governmental agreement. This type of resolution suggests a strategy of long-term lobbying rather than protest events. It may follow that a higher level of protest among local actors involved in local-level disputes is simply what one would expect to find.

It should also be noted that many 'global' problems manifest themselves locally. Therefore, even though the specific grievance may be locally incarnated, the issue raised may form part of a wider national, or even global-level, problem. This is apparent in issues such as waste management or water pollution. For this reason too the data on this point may not be pointing to a simple localisation of Irish environmental protest. Local protesters may be well aware that their grievance is a manifestation of a larger environmental problem but, without the inclination or resources to fight the larger battle, they confine themselves, not unreasonably, to the symptom on their doorstep.

In any event, it is clear from the data that protests by local actors – the majority of all reported environmental protests – occurred largely in response to the incidence of development projects. This in turn suggests the possibility of a dialectic between levels of development and levels of protest. The increase in development projects consequent upon the 'Celtic Tiger' period of national economic growth seems to have given rise to a reactive series of conflicts with local actors who were determined either to mitigate, or prevent entirely, perceived negative consequences for local areas arising from those projects. Thus, reported environmental claims seemed to be issue-dependant and therefore largely confined to the redress of particular matters rather than addressing wider environmental problematics.

However, this is not always the case. If the dispute is prolonged over time the possibility arises that far deeper issues emerge that render what may appear mere 'local' protest far more challenging to the contemporary social and political order than may otherwise seem to be the case. One such is the protest against a gas refinery in North Mayo.

Contesting a Natural Gas Refinery in North Mayo

The campaign of protest mounted by a group of residents in North Mayo in the west of Ireland against the siting of a natural gas processing refinery in their rural and ecologically sensitive area reveals the presence of potentially more significant meanings underlying local protest. The collective action undertaken by these local activists, as it emerged and was reflected on over time, was regarded by them as motivated by a desire to defend their 'place' from a mode of development imposed by outside actors. The concept of place constructed by the activists combined concerns about human well-being with that of the physical environment. While 'place' included conceptions of the 'environment', the latter was not always invoked in overt or usual terms. This feature points to the complexity of the environmental problematic as it is shaped by its various settings of articulation.

As noted above, protest event data have shown that a significant proportion of Irish environmental protest is conducted by local actors apparently concerned to defend local place against external threats. This, indeed, may be one reason why nationalist or anti-colonial discourses figure so prominently in Irish environmental protests. If this is so, then the question arises as to how specifically does environmentalism, as a practice and a discourse, fit into discourses of place and community? The evidence of the North Mayo campaign suggests that environmentalism, as discursively invoked by local activists in protest settings, is integrally bound up with complementary discourses of family, community, health and physical locality to produce a hybrid discourse of dissent and opposition to dominant 'official' versions of progress and development. The different components of this hybrid become prioritised or publicly articulated according to opportunity and criteria of efficacy.

The dispute in North Mayo centred on the proposal by a consortium of oil and gas companies led by Shell, and including Statoil and Marathon, to construct a gas refinery and production pipelines nine kilometres inland on Ireland's northwest coast. The first application made by the consortium was in 2000. A significant number of the local community mobilised almost immediately to oppose it. Their campaign of opposition went through a number of distinct phases. The initial focus of the campaign was activists' attempt to stop the project by contesting the planning application to construct the refinery. This took four years to resolve until, after three separate planning applications and two appeal processes to An Bord Pleanála (the Irish Planning Appeals Board), the refinery finally got permission.

The campaign's attention then turned to the high-pressure pipeline proposed to service the refinery. This pipeline was to carry unprocessed gas within 70 metres of some residences in the small village of Rossport. A number of local landowners refused permission to the consortium to access their lands for the purpose of laying the pipeline. Previously, the Irish government, which fully supported the project, had granted compulsory acquisition powers to the companies over the lands that the pipeline was to cross. The refusal by the local landowners culminated in their breaching a High Court order directing them to permit access. Shell then sought and was granted a committal order against five local men, three of whom were landowners, which caused the men to be imprisoned indefinitely in June 2005. They subsequently spent 94 days in Cloverhill prison in Dublin.

The imprisonment of the men transformed the campaign. What had been largely perceived as a local issue now became a matter of national prominence. A concerted campaign to free the men developed, mobilising thousands of people in rallies throughout Ireland. Local residents picketed the refinery work-site, causing all activities there to cease. Eventually, under the intense pressure of the mounting campaign, Shell was forced to vacate its court order, and the men were released.

By autumn 2006, with local pickets continuing on a daily basis, Shell agreed to re-route the pipeline away from people's houses. However, the conflict took a serious turn in October 2006 when a large force of police escorted Shell workers back onto the refinery site to recommence construction work that had been suspended in July 2005. Local residents were forcibly removed from the entrance to the site. A contingent of police has been deployed each day since October 2006 in order to maintain access to the site and the conflict has become more intense and charged. A number of violent incidents have occurred between protesters and police, an occurrence highly unusual in the Irish setting.

What is of interest in this campaign is how a 'local' issue contained within it matters which raised significant cultural and political challenges to the status quo. This campaign, though perhaps novel in its intensity and duration, nevertheless reveals that ostensibly local protest may contain buried issues that expose the often pejorative inaccuracy of the 'NIMBY' categorisation.

In examining the community reaction to the natural gas proposal, three important points need to be recognised. First, there was no one, fixed community response; second, the community's public framing of the dispute continually shifted in the light of new knowledge and with the advent of new interlocutors; and, third, community opposition rested primarily on a visceral and intuitive sense of the project being somehow 'inappropriate' and dangerous.

In effect, the proposal forced the community to reflect on the nature of their cultural identity and the value of place. In time, as the campaign progressed, general community opposition to the specific gas refinery proposal consolidated.

> The opposition has remained consistent all the time. You had a small number of people with a vested interest who thought they would make immediate money on it. A small number of them obviously favoured the project from the start. You had a small number of people like us who would be directly affected by the project and who had read up about it, knew what the dangers were and who were opposed to it. And then you had the mass of the people of Erris[3] who were very worried about it, who didn't like the idea but who wouldn't make a fuss about opposing it. The vast majority were concerned. (O'Seighin [one of the imprisoned men] in Garavan, 2006: 74)

The key to the mobilisation of these actors was the perception that their locality was under threat from the company proposal. Hence, this group drew most of its activists from the Ballanaboy area, where the refinery was to be built, and from Rossport, where most of the pipeline was to be laid. The group was supported by other residents from the immediate area. Other important actors among this group were the local fishermen who feared the threat to their livelihoods arising from possible pollution from the proposed discharge pipe from the refinery. A number of the leading opponents to the refinery were schoolteachers – both primary and post-primary. Some of these held traditional Republican political positions. Their role as teachers provided them with a measure of intellectual confidence and local authority. Republicanism seemed to instil a critical perspective and confidence in informing their assessments of the state's role in supporting a foreign multinational corporation.[4]

An assortment of distinct discourses can be identified among opponents of the refinery. Significantly, the 'environment' was merely one discourse used, and was by no means the most important or regularly employed. From the beginning of the conflict in autumn 2000, health was the most significant concern voiced. There were also concerns regarding the potential threats the refinery posed to the indigenous economic activities of fishing, farming and tourism. Discourses invoking the physical character of the area were in frequent use. As used by residents, the concept of beauty referred not just to aesthetic qualities of the area, but also seemed to encapsulate a way of life that was regarded as valuable and unique. There was a cluster of concerns that could be categorised within a discourse of marginalisation. This discourse came particularly to the fore as local perceptions of the refinery as a pollutant with little real benefit, combined with the failure of the consortium and the state to engage directly with them, caused the project to be framed as emblematic of the age-old marginalisation of the local area by outside forces.

Environmental discourses were employed but usually as an explanatory background to the risk to health. Abstract concepts of 'the environment' did not appear to carry any mobilising potential among the community. The more visceral reactions centred on evocations of the character of the local place and community.

> I was born and reared on this farm. It's memories that are making us do what we are doing. My father came here in 1947. The place then was pure bog with a fallen-down house. The memories we have are of the way we were brought up. Hard times. They're the memories you have and the memories you have to keep.

> To see someone coming in now and trying to destroy it, as Shell is doing, it kills you. Our footsteps are around the place since we were able to walk. (Corduff [one of the imprisoned men] in Garavan, 2006: 15)

> My ancestors have lived here in Rossport for many generations, at least six generations, in the same spot along the shore on the northern side of Sruth Fada Conn, that is the estuary of the Glenamoy River that flows into Broadhaven Bay. The home place down by the shore is called Rinn na Rón, where the seals used to congregate and sometimes come ashore. That's where I was born and reared. So we've been here a long time and as you'd expect we have a strong attachment to the land and a deep sense of belonging to the place has been built up over many generations. (V. McGrath [one of the imprisoned men] in Garavan, 2006: 157)

If you think back on all we had when we were young. All the freedom we had. I could play anywhere within this whole area on either side of the estuary. That included the Ballanaboy site. We used play in there half the time. And I thought it was grand. It was like fairyland. It will never be again if this project got in. Think of this area gone forever. (M. McGrath [wife of one of the imprisoned men] in Garavan, 2006: 171)

Among those in the community who opposed the refinery and pipeline, or who had concerns about it, an early decision was made not to establish any formal organisation or structure. Instead, opponents agreed that individuals, or small groups, would pursue their opposition in their own way and that there would be occasional meetings only to compare notes and exchange information. This was a conscious decision to remain as a 'loose network' (fieldnotes, Ceathrú Taidgh, March 2001), a decision which was not fundamentally changed through the course of the conflict. There were a number of reasons for this important decision. First and most importantly, it was in keeping with a general desire to avoid creating visible division within the wider community. Second, choosing not to create an organisation allowed those opposing the project to avoid questions of leadership and organisational roles. This would have been both potentially divisive and time consuming. Finally, this flexibility of function allowed activists to vary their levels of involvement. Thus, *participation* became the standard of belonging, not *membership*, and at a level to be set by the individual him- or herself.

What does this campaign tell us about the nature of contemporary Irish environmental activism? Indeed, where can environmentalism be located in the gas refinery conflict?

Community activists in North Mayo suggested that their action was a reflex response to a perceived threat from an outside agent.

It is as if we were attacked by a virus. We reacted like a body to defend ourselves and destroy the threat. It was instinctive, natural. (fieldnotes, local resident, Ballina, December 2002)

This explanation of their protest appears to tally with the macro-perspective on protest offered by the protest event data, which indicated that much Irish environmental protest appears to arise in response to an immediately apprehensible threat or to the perception of a threat. The temporal-spatial concentration of threats suggests how it is that 'defence of place' appears to figure so significantly as a mobilisation factor in Irish environmental conflicts and hence why nationalist and anti-colonial discourses may feature so prominently. But place must not just be understood as merely designating physical, geographical and biological characteristics. Drawing on the findings of the North Mayo campaign,[5] the meaning of place also appears to incorporate conceptions of culture, local forms of life and human physical and psychological health. In short, place seems to act as shorthand for notions of holistic human well-being, in which health and environment become part of a wider concern with 'all that surrounds'. That conceptions of place in local environmental protest may include features of the physical and the cultural indicates that references to place, if narrowly or literally interpreted by researchers or interlocutors of such protest actions (as in crude designations of such protests as nimbyism), may obscure the presence of much deeper concerns with the character and quality of the social and 'natural' worlds.

Indeed, local activists themselves consciously repudiated 'NIMBY' characterisations of their campaign.

> There was a core group of us who were opposed from the beginning on very good grounds because we had done the research and we were not being fooled. We weren't the usual suspects. We hadn't campaigned against any project in the past. They couldn't label us in that way. We weren't NIMBYs either. We knew the project as planned was wrong and dangerous and we didn't want it anywhere else either. Our opponents tried to make out that we were against development. I don't know of anyone around here, or any other place in Ireland for that matter, who is against development. It depends on what you mean by 'development'.
> (V. McGrath [one of the men imprisoned] in Garavan, 2006: 176)

Of course, in acknowledging the essentially reactive character of the gas refinery protest, as with much Irish environmental protest generally, one must exercise, in seeking to interpret such protest, due caution in moving from the particular to the universal. While it may not quite be safe to suggest that these conflicts call into question 'development' in a general sense – most people still presumably favouring 'growth' and material accumulation – nonetheless, *particular* conflicts do call into question *particular* instances of development. The implications of these localised conflicts are that, *in certain cases*, communities are unwilling to pay the environmental and social costs associated with furthering economic growth and 'progress'.

The wider implications of these localised refusals are apparent if one examines the consequences of protest actions for the viability of particular infrastructural/development projects. These consequences may take two forms. First, what might initially be a localised protest may give rise to a national protest, or, second, in what may have the same effect, a local protest regarding a specific project may stimulate a series of such reactive local protests, thus rendering particular projects unrealisable in any location. For example, the specific proposal to construct a nuclear power station in Carnsore Point in the late 1970s gave rise to a national-level campaign against nuclear power. The level of protests against waste incinerators in Ireland at present illustrate the second possibility and indicate that there is no known community willing to accept their construction in their area.

The arrival of the gas refinery proposal obliged the community in North Mayo to enter into an unusually deep reflection on the nature and values of their 'place' and community. It was in the light of this that many of them commenced a critical reflection on the refinery and became mobilised to resist it. While initially it appeared as if the company's and the state's presentation of the project as heralding 'development' may have been rhetorically effective, it is also clear that this ceased to have significant effect for a number of local residents once they began to investigate the claims being made.

That the problematisation of the gas project implied a rejection of a *version* of development and modernisation being forced upon the community was most clearly expressed in the community activists' argumentation before the An Bord Pleanála oral hearing.

> Real cumulative change is evolutionary: 20 or 30 years is an Asahi-type aberration [a reference to a previous industry nearby which had caused much visual and other pollution]... My problem with [the company's CEO] and more so with the guardians of our democracy, elected or appointed or just doing a job, is a cultural one of incomprehension.... When asked what would be the position of local workers who may have got employment before the proposed terminal ended its tour of duty, [a consultant] answered that by that time they would have enough skills to move on. The whole point of community is not moving on: community is rooted and so builds up strategies and implementations for survival; fish spawn that is free moving has a tiny survival rate. In the round, [he] has made our case – there is no evident interface where these two attitudes can merge... [I do not] see any chance of a narrowing of the cultural gap between this civilised community and the flotsam and jetsam that wallow in the wake of the ship of Marathon, Statoil and Enterprise Oil. (O'Seighin submission, An Bord Pleanála Oral Hearing, Ballina, February 2002)

This submission rhetorically contrasts two forms of life: the transient, exploitative one represented by the oil and gas consortium, versus the rooted, sustainable one forged by the local community. Clearly then, two versions of being-in-the-world, two versions of development, are placed side by side and judged in the light of each other. Even more clearly, not only is the specific proposal of the consortium rejected, but so too is the *principle* of the type of development that the proposal represents.

It is therefore possible to discern in this campaign a cognitive progression among the protest actors from an initial *reaction* to the terminal proposal, towards an *affirmation* of a particular set of values, as exemplified in the local community. It is this interesting dimension to the North Mayo activists – their slow excavation and affirmation of a view of the good life – that connects what might otherwise be categorised as a local, NIMBY-style protest to a wider environmental praxis. Environmental protest in Ireland largely arises when threats emerge to places and forms of life regarded as being of value. In this sense, threats can be regarded as, to employ Paulo Freire's rich phrase, a 'cultural invasion' (1972: 129) and are resisted accordingly. In doing so, environmentalists and local communities can be regarded as sharing the desire to uphold certain conceptions of the 'good life'.

It is in this sense that local protest actions can be understood as not only defensive and reactive. They are also necessarily assertions by protest actors of autonomy, participation, and democratic rights – in short, of being subjects who possess a legitimate view of their own and a possibly distinct version of what constitutes development and modernisation.

Local protest activism is therefore, even if only in part, a refusal to accept versions of 'reality' (reinterpreted as 'threats'), as well as an effort to intentionally transcend political and discursive limits in order to create new possibilities. The North Mayo campaign evidence, together with the evidence from the protest event data, indicates that environmental collective action does occur on quite a wide scale in Ireland, and that some of the costs, and versions, of development are, in practice, continually contested. Implied here is a dynamic and positive account of human agency.

Conclusion

We have argued here that a preponderance of local-level protest is, first, what one might expect to find in an environmental movement, but that, second, such protest may be far more significant in its political and cultural implications than it might otherwise appear. The contention is that what we are witnessing is not a simple institutionalisation of the movement but an evolution towards a greater complexity in the construction of the environmental problematic. Rather than the 'environment' having become a resolved and domesticated issue, it appears more likely that it will remain centre-stage in various local and 'cultural' battles, though perhaps it will do so increasingly under the guise of 'place' or 'development' conflicts (cf. Curtin & Varley, 1995; Goldman, 1998).

The consequence of this is that battles for control of place may not necessarily invoke discourses of the environment, or, even in the cases where they do, activists may not necessarily be committed to a broad environmental problematic. Indeed, the discourses of many anti-pollution protests in Ireland in the 1980s were of the family and community rather than of modern environmentalism (Tovey, 1992a, 1992b). The pluralism among Irish environmental activists, to such an extent that they may even resist being labelled as 'environmentalists', was also noted by Tovey in her study of organic farmers. She reports that a 'discourse of "environmental protection"' hardly appears at all in what participants in the organic movement say about their motivations for engaging in this form of farming (Tovey, 1997: 27). All of these findings substantiate the view that 'environmental' protesters are heterogeneous and that 'different environmental campaigns do not comprise a movement in any centrally co-ordinated sense' (Curtin & Varley, 1995: 394).

Contributing to this impression of discursive diversity is Tovey's (1992b) suggestion that environmentalism is employed in two different senses in

Ireland: a populist and an official sense. Official environmentalism, she suggests, is mainly led by academic 'experts' who usually work through state bodies and established environmental organisations. Populist environmentalism can be understood as reflecting local communities' experiences of development struggles.

> ...[P]opulist environmentalism...represents a relatively independent movement of dissent, by ordinary people working at the local level, from the dominant ideologies of modernisation, development and growth. Populist environmentalism reflects the activities of a different set of organisations, such as the community development movement in rural Ireland, and its activists may not see themselves as environmentalists (though they are increasingly likely to claim this label as it becomes more politically legitimate). (Tovey & Share, 2001: 461)

What appears to be particularly distinctive about local environmental protest in Ireland is that the lines of conflict are frequently drawn over control and defence of place. The categorisation of much of this protest as 'NIMBY' fails to recognise the significance of this growing social phenomenon of resisting the physical costs of maintaining the industrial system. However, similarly, categorising such protest actions as 'environmental' (in accordance with a semiotic convention) may obscure the wider pluralistic issues involved in protests over place. Particularly in Ireland, environmental discourses are blended with discourses of community, of nationalism and of health to produce a hybrid discursive construct. The balance of emphases within this hybrid differs from case to case, and is often the product of contextual features such as the structure of discursive opportunities open to protesters.[6] Thus, environmentalism must take its place as one voice in the choir of resistance. Frequently, what harmonises these different voices, apart from their grounding in complementary visions of the 'good life', is the identification of a common adversary. The extent to which this is the case demonstrates how outside 'elites', perceived as threatening a place, can unintentionally forge reactive alliances and thereby create new social networks of resistance. If this can occur on a local and national scale, it is not unlikely that we are at present witnessing the beginnings of a global network of resistance corresponding to (and unintentionally created by) the contemporary global configuration of power.

Notes

1. In the seven EU states covered by the TEA project (Rootes, 2003), this degree of localism was exceeded only in Greece.
2. The protest event research was conducted as part of a broader investigation into the patterns of Irish environmental activism employing similar methodologies to the Transformation of Environmental Activism project coordinated by Christopher Rootes, University of Kent, Canterbury. The Irish research was carried out under the aegis of the Environmental Change Institute, NUI Galway (Human Impact Cluster).

3. Erris is the barony name of the local region.
4. As noted above, the presence of republican and nationalist views among Irish environmental protesters is one frequently reported in the literature on Irish environmentalism. See, for example, Allen and Jones (1990).
5. The author undertook close study of this campaign from its inception in 2000 to 2003. From then on the author has had a close involvement in the campaign including acting as a spokesperson since 2005.
6. The concept of discursive opportunity structure can be defined as the extent to which, in the course of conflict, actors are permitted by various institutional and political structures not only to produce discourses which allow them address what they regard as the causes of conflict but also the extent to which these discourses are recognised as legitimate by their interlocutors and, therefore, are permitted to have an effect on policies and decisions. Much of the extent of this opportunity structure depends on the openness or closedness of the institutional rules which govern the decision-making process (or the grievance resolution process), particularly the levels of genuine participation permitted to 'informal' interlocutors. Implied in the concept is the contention that discourse is shaped by various rhetorical considerations. In short, actors have their interlocutors in mind when speaking (cf. Edmondson, 2007).

References

Allen, R. & Jones, T. (1990) *Guests of the Nation: People of Ireland versus the Multinationals* (London: Earthscan).

Baker, S. (1990) 'The evolution of the Irish ecology movement', in W. Rüdig (ed.), *Green Politics One* (Edinburgh: Edinburgh University Press).

Blühdorn, I. (2000) *Post-Ecologist Politics: Social Theory and the Abdication of the Ecologist Paradigm* (London and New York: Routledge).

Burstein, P., Einwohner, R. & Hollander, J. (1995) 'The success of social movements: a bargaining perspective', in J. C. Jenkins & B. Klandermans (eds.), *The Politics of Social Protest: Comparative Perspectives on States and Social Movements* (Minneapolis: University of Minnesota Press; London: UCL Press).

Curtin, C. & Varley, T. (1995) 'Community action and the state', in P. Clancy *et al.* (eds.), *Irish Society: Sociological Perspectives* (Dublin: Institute of Public Administration).

Edmondson, R. (2007) 'Rhetorics of social science: sociality in writing and inquiry', in S. Turner & W. Outhwaite (eds.), *Sage Handbook of Social Science Methodology*, pp. 959–1007 (London: Sage).

Freire, P. (1972) *Pedagogy of the Oppressed* (Harmondsworth: Penguin).

Garavan, M. (2004) 'The patterns of Irish environmental activism', PhD thesis, NUI Galway.

Garavan, M. (ed.) (2006) *The Rossport Five: Our Story* (Dublin: Small World Media).

Gledhill, J. (2000) *Power and its Disguises: Anthropological Perspectives on Politics* (London: Pluto Press).

Goldman, M. (ed.) (1998) *Privatizing Nature – Political Struggles for the Global Commons* (London: Pluto Press).

Hellman, J. A. (1992) 'The study of new social movements in Latin America and the question of autonomy', in A. Escobar & S. E. Alvarez (eds.), *The Making of Social Movements in Latin America: Identity, Strategy and Democracy* (Boulder, CO: Westview Press).

Jiménez, M. (2003) 'Spain', in C. Rootes (ed.), *Environmental Protest in Western Europe* (Oxford: Oxford University Press).

Landmann, T. (1999) 'Organization and impact: the Green movement in comparative perspective', paper presented at the ECPR Joint Sessions, Mannheim, March.

Leonard, L. (2006) *Green Nation* (Galway: Greenhouse Press in cooperation with Choice Publishing).

Melucci, A. (1988) 'Social movements and the democratisation of everyday life', in J. Keane (ed.), *Civil Society and the State: New European Perspectives* (London: Verso Press).

O'Neill, S. (2001) Results of questionnaire: Environmental NGOs Core Funding Project.

Rootes, C. (ed.) (2003) *Environmental Protest in Western Europe* (Oxford: Oxford University Press).

Rootes, C. (2004) 'Environmental movements', in D. A. Snow, S. A. Soule & H. Kriesi (eds.), *The Blackwell Companion to Social Movements*, pp. 608–40 (Oxford and Malden, MA: Blackwell).

Tilly, C. (1984) 'Social movements and national politics', in C. Bright & S. Harding (eds.), *Statemaking and Social Movements* (Ann Arbor: University of Michigan Press).

Tovey, H. (1992a) 'Environmentalism in Ireland: modernisation and identity', in P. Clancy, M. Kelly, J. Wiatr & R. Zoltaniecki (eds.), *Ireland and Poland, Comparative Perspectives* (Dublin: University College Dublin Press).

Tovey, H. (1992b) 'Rural sociology in Ireland: a review', *Irish Journal of Sociology* 2: 96–121.

Tovey, H. (1997) 'Food, environmentalism, & rural sociology: on the organic farming movement in Ireland', *Sociologia Ruralis* 37(1): 21–37.

Tovey, H. & Share, P. (2001) *A Sociology of Ireland* (Dublin: Gill and MacMillan).

Van der Heijden, H.-A. (1997) 'Political opportunity structure and the institutionalisation of the environmental movement', *Environmental Politics* 6(4): 25–50.

Yearley, S. (1995) 'The social shaping of the environmental movement in Ireland', in P. Clancy, S. Drury, K. Lynch & L. O'Dowd (eds.), *Irish Society: Sociological Perspectives* (Dublin: Institute of Public Administration).

Local Contention, Global Framing: The Protest Campaigns against the TAV in Val di Susa and the Bridge on the Messina Straits

DONATELLA DELLA PORTA & GIANNI PIAZZA

For a Twinning of NO TAV – NO BRIDGE

For the sovereignty of inhabitants in places from the North to the South of Italy, there emerges a single struggle...The peaceful revolt of the inhabitants and the mayors of Val di Susa has placed the question of democracy and justice at the centre of political debate in Italy. That which has been frequently defined as a particularistic interest – whether of the community of Val di Susa or those that live within the area of the Messina Straits – is instead the expression of the sovereignty of

The interviews in Val di Susa were conducted by Massimiliano Andretta and Eugenio Pizzimenti, who also helped with the collection of newspaper articles and written documents. The interviews in the area of the Messina Straits were conducted by Gianni Piazza. This article has been translated by Alex Wilson.

populations that reside within that territory, who are re-claiming their legitimacy to decide their own future and that of their children... The struggle in Val di Susa is the same as the struggle against the Bridge on the Messina Straits, against incinerators, against nuclear plant... (DME17)

Local Conflict between Interest and Identity: A Definition

The leaflet that promotes the alliance between the far North and the far South of Italy is signed by the *Rete No Ponte* ('No Bridge Network'), which unites various associations and committees from the area of the Messina Straits that are opposed to the construction of a bridge between Calabria and Sicily, and the *Rete Meridionale del Nuovo Municipio* ('Southern Network for a New Municipalism'), which seeks to involve both local politicians and citizens in the practices of participatory democracy. The twinning is proposed above all with the 'No Tav' committees in Val di Susa (close to the border with France), who oppose the building of a new high-speed railway.

The No Tav protest began in 1990, with initiatives to inform the affected population supported by the mayors of the lower Val di Susa and the *Comunità Montana* (mountainous community). Mass mobilisation has developed since 2000, with the emergence of local committees of residents, peaking after 2003 in long-lasting site occupations and occasional clashes with the police. Especially since 2000, actors mobilised on different themes (squatted youth centre, unions, social forum), and actors from outside the valley joined the campaign, providing national and transnational references and resonance. In this period, networking intensified with the activists of the No Bridge campaign that had started in the second half of the 1990s, with counter-information organised especially by environmental organisations. Mass protest developed especially since the spring of 2002, with the mobilisation of citizens committees, social forums, squatted youth centres, environmental organisations and local parties opposed to the bridge. The battle against the bridge became very quickly connected to the campaigns against large-scale public works in Italy and inserted into the framework of a more general struggle against neo-liberal globalisation. As in the Val di Susa, in the Messina Straits the local committees and No Bridge activists see different people and their political experiences intertwined in various organisational initiatives and campaigning practices.

We will analyse the framing processes of these two conflicts relating to Locally Unwanted Land Use (LULU), discussing also the principal hypotheses from the sociological literature on local conflict, but also on global movements, within which these mobilisations can be located.

The aggregation of needs and interests within a territory is certainly not a new phenomenon, but in the early 1990s scholars' attention has focused on new forms of local protest. Studies of environmental movements have confirmed that while environmental organisations at national level have become institutionalised (to a greater or lesser degree), protests at local level have certainly not diminished (della Porta & Diani, 2004). In them, a principal role is played by citizens committees: organised but weakly structured groups formed by citizens aggregated on a territorial basis and which mostly use protest to oppose interventions which they consider will damage the quality of life within their territory, or otherwise to demand improvements in their environments (della Porta, 2004: 7).

The presence of these localised conflicts has frequently been perceived with alarm – above all when, in the beginning of the 1990s, there was an increase in protests against the installation of incinerators or mobile telephone masts, which were seen as obstacles to the realisation of collective goods and a potential source of economic damage. With the demand for a 'disinterested' action, normally not applied to other collective actors, citizens reunited in committees have often been accused of being solely interested in their 'own back yard', and of masking this by an avowed preoccupation with natural or artistic heritage.

In the sociological literature, LULU conflicts have been regarded primarily as NIMBY ('not in my back yard') protests, associated with conservative attitudes and motivated primarily by selfish resistance to social change. Above all in analyses on the production and implementation of public policy protests against the local level have been perceived as perfect illustrations of 'free riderism', that is, the refusal to pay the necessary costs for attaining collective goods. Citizens' committees at local level have been described as a 'specific organizational form which accompanies the NIMBY syndrome' (Bobbio, 1999: 196), characterised by the 'limited range of their requests and claims. They do not fight in favour of the "great causes" in society, but to defend material interests that are very specific and restricted' (Buso, 1996: 197). Concern over these types of 'egotistical' protests is accentuated by the fact that they are sometimes successful in their aims. Concentrating on the threat (real or perceived) can favour the aggregation of those who feel unfairly targeted and those who feel a strong sense of injustice and, when this is combined with a material threat, can even push some towards radical forms of protest. Above all, given the territorial structure of representation, these protests may gain the support of local politicians who fear a loss of electoral support, and are then willing and able to press for a relocation of the 'public bad', pushing elsewhere the troubled question of allocation.

On a different note, passing from the focus on 'output' to a focus on 'input', LULU conflicts can be seen as expressions of different types of social movements (della Porta, 2003). As Sebastiani (2001: 111) has observed, the citizens committees which act at local level have a 'hybrid character, half-way between interest groups and social movements, oscillating between lobbying activities and participatory actions'. From this point of view, such local mobilisations have been perceived as the exercise of active citizenship, expressions of resistance to projects which seek to mask their own particularistic interests as broader causes for the 'common good'. In fact, 'their horizon is not always particularistic' (Bobbio, 1999: 198), and they often appeal to universal values (William & Matheny, 1995: 183).

Also in the literature on social movements, local conflicts can be perceived as a threat, but also as a resource for democracy. On the one hand, it is argued that in cases where parties no longer function as mediators of consensus, or as intermediaries between the population and the government, there now emerges a tendency for citizens to organise themselves and campaign directly. Not forming part of more elaborate ideological discourses, this local mobilisation of interests is often presented as particularistic and fragmented. However, these mobilisations do not express individual egotism but rather the action of 'citizen-workers', who by exercising their rights as citizens defend the quality of life within their community (Gould *et al.*, 1996).

The transformation of forms of environmental movements can be derived from changes in the social structure. In particular, it has been theorised that there is now an emerging conflict between 'urban regimes' (or growth machines), that is, informal/formal networks between public and private actors, that are primarily interested in economic development (Stone, 1993: 3), and weakly structured coalitions of various types of groups that seek to resist change. In the US as in Europe, the crisis of the welfare state has accentuated the territorial competition for economic resources, above private sources of investment (Thomas & Savitch, 1991: 7). Coalitions of local politicians (interested in further electoral success), local business (interested in profit), public bureaucrats (interested in expanding their own autonomy), unite to attract economic investment within the territory (Elkin, 1987: 36). These 'urban machines for economic development' (Logan & Molotch, 1987) tend to be controlled by business elites, in alliance with land and property owners, bankers, financiers, businessmen, local press, professionals, and are often supported by universities and cultural associations. They tend to find most opposition in voluntary associations, which may see funds for social assistance to marginalised groups cut, or by organisations of local residents, who may perceive projects of urban transformation as damaging. The increase in control over public decision-making by economic interests is thus contrasted by social movements that propose alternative models of development (Levine, 1989). In such a perspective, social science research underlined the weak capacity for mobilisation of diffuse interests which defend the rights and use of their respective territory against the strength of economic interest which privilege the value of exchange. Comparative analysis of different forms of local conflict in the US concluded that 'all of these citizen-workers found themselves locked out of processes, outmatched by other participants and unable to gain legitimacy for their concerns' (Gould *et al.*, 1996: 164).

A characteristic of both these strands of literature is to consider interests as exogenous. In our research we concentrate instead on definitions which the actors themselves give of the conflict, thus reconstructing the identity of the challengers. Previous research on territorial conflict has underlined that those who protest are able to overcome the NIMBY syndrome. The local committees which oppose the undesired use of their land in fact seek to adopt a rhetoric which distances them from accusations of particularism, shifting wherever possible from a local discourse to a global one. They respond to authorities that accuse them of opposing the common good for particularistic reasons by developing a 'NOPE' (Not On Planet Earth) discourse (Trom, 1999). Often the generality of the conflict is affirmed by the use of a rhetorical procedure that defines their own activity as an opposition to the abuse of powers or the lack of transparency in the public decision-making process, in addition to attacking the collusive alliance between government and business (Gordon & Jasper, 1996). The sense of community, increased through the action, then offers to the activists a basis for belonging, facilitating solidarity and construction of an identity (Lichterman, 1996).

In our research, we concentrated on the transformations of local conflicts into instances of global protests. As we shall see, the definition of the protest emerges through cognitive conflicts about the definition of what is at stake. We have reconstructed the 'frames' (or interpretative schemes) which 'place the individual in a position to localise, perceive, identify and label events that occur in their daily life and more generally in the world', allowing them to give meaning to their actions (Snow & Benford, 1986: 464). These frames permit them to attribute significant meanings to distant phenomena, to identify social problems, but also to 'propose solutions, hypotheses on new social assets, new forms of regulations and relations between groups, new procedures to develop consensus and exercise power' (della Porta & Diani, 1997: 87). One of the accusations against the urban growth machine is that it considers economic growth as the primary objective, to which environmental concerns are subordinated. Against such conceptions of development, in these local conflicts there emerge frames on the defence of the environment, but also on the right to oppose large-scale public works presented by the promoters as economic launch-pads, but which are perceived by residents as immediately pernicious to their quality of life. We will observe that the evolution of frames on local conflict occurs through a process of networking that allows them to overcome the discourse of risk for the community. This creates a process of contamination in action, through mechanisms of multiplying individual belonging and organisational networking, which facilitates the transformation of identity, frame bridging, and creation of trust (della Porta & Mosca, 2006).

Our research is based on the comparison of two cases of mobilisation against public works, both developed with a similar time-frame, which coincides with the development of the global justice movement. However, the two cases differ significantly in terms of the context of mobilisation, particularly with regard to social structure (the industrial North of the Val di Susa protest; the 'backward' South for the Messina Straits protest) and political culture (strong leftist subculture in Val di Susa; weak traditions of associationalism and protest in the Messina Straits). The juxtaposition of these different contexts will be primarily oriented towards highlighting common dynamics. The reconstruction of these two cases is based on three principal sources: systematic scrutiny, printed press, analysis of documents and websites of the organisations which participate in the protests, and semi-structured interviews with activists.

In the following pages, we will look at the effects of mobilisation on the emergence and evolution of frames relating to the definition of the identity of the actor, the diagnosis and prognosis of the problem, and finally the motivation of the action.

Framing Identity: Between Localism and Community

> The community of human beings is not a natural product, it is a work ... half the *Valsusini* work outside the valley and half of those who work in the valley are not *Valsusini*: you are *Valsusino* because you accept certain values, you share a path, nothing ethnic here. The history of the valley is that of a passing valley, a history which belongs to everybody ... there is the idea of a common destiny ... (IVS2)

As in the words of this unionist, fundamental to mobilisation is the definition of the identity of those who protest, sharing values and interests: the 'us' and the 'them' (Gamson, 1988). The definition of identity comes prior to the definition of interest, insofar as preferences are constructed by a symbolic process. Only if I define my own identity, am I able to name my long-term interest (Pizzorno, 1993). In local conflicts, there is often a tension between increasing solidarity at the level of the local community (the history of a 'valley of transiting') and the appeal to universal values (a 'common destiny') that is necessary for mobilisation of external allies.

A central theme in the discourse of local opposition to large-scale public works concerns the territorial extent of the contention. The local dimension is stigmatised by supporters of large-scale public works as egotistical. Thus, referring to the opposition to the Tav, the centre–right ex-minister for the Environment, Matteoli, spoke of the 'egotism of an instrumentalised protest' (*la Repubblica*, 4 November 2005) and the centre–left president of the Piedmont regional government, Bresso, repeated that 'the interest of the few cannot prevail over those of the many' (*la Repubblica*, 27 November 2005). Similarly, of the protests against the bridge, Matteoli declared that 'everybody needs the bridge ... the protest is brought by sectoral interests, such as environmentalists or strictly localised groups' (*la Gazzetta del Sud*, 23 January 2006).

Defined as localist, those who contest large-scale public works frequently emphasise a communitarian aspect to their defence of territory suffering from external aggression. In the No Tav protests, the first objective of the mobilisation is to 'save the valley' (*la Repubblica*, 30 January 2000). This communitarian dimension is presented as an identification with the territory above classes or ideologies; 'All united, without educational, economic or political barriers, or municipal divisions' (Margaira, 2005: 37). As in Val di

Susa, in the Messina Straits there is a communitarian dimension to the defence of territory under attack; in fact, since the first appeal of the Committee '*Tra Scilla e Cariddi*', in June 1998, UNESCO was asked 'to assume under its protection the area of the Messina Straits, insofar as it is an intangible good and the heritage of humanity' (DME1). The final appeal of the large demonstration in Messina (22 January 2006) ended with: 'Everyone in Messina to defend the Straits', a place 'unique in the history and the culture of the Mediterranean sea' (DME18).

The appeal to community leads to a redefinition of the activists' identity. In the Tav protests, during the course of the action, it was 'as if an always denied Val di Susa identity is emerging ... the valley is rediscovering its soul' (*la Repubblica*, 14 July 2005). During the protest campaigns, there emerges a positive definition of community, which has historical, political and cultural specificities (della Porta, 2004). Significant in the definition of local identity are references to the anti-Nazi Resistance history of Val di Susa: the president of the mountainous community talks of a 'valley with a history. Here were the partisans' (*la Repubblica*, 9 December 2005). The partisan past is often evoked by testimonies of the will to 'resist' of the inhabitants of Val di Susa. One local mayor remembered: 'I was a member of the 42nd Garibaldi Brigade. My motto is "resist now and for always". Yesterday against the Nazi occupation, today against the diggers.' The activists remember 8 December 1943 in the valley where the partisan Resistance was born (*la Repubblica*, 9 December 2005). The partisans are recalled in the logo within the No Tav banner; in particular 'the old man with the closed fist has been invented by the committee of Bussoleno and remembers the grandfather who fought in the Resistance and who shouted "You will not pass here"' (IVS4). The identity of the community is also present in the area of the Messina Straits. Not only are frequent appeals and references made to the Italian *Mezzogiorno* (South), to the notion of being southern, but the activists also talk of the 'fighting character of the people of the Straits', making reference to past battles against the coal-fired power plant in Calabria (DME21).

As for the symbolic construction of the community, the activists stress that identity is formed in action: 'the traditions, the identity counted, but they were elements that were acquired, rather than starting points' (IVS1).

The reference to a community presents the risk of isolation, if community is conceived in an exclusive sense. In the course of mobilisation, however, the search for alliances with external actors brings about a process of 'bridging' between local and global identities. The opponents of the Tav emphasise a change in the frames during the evolution of the protest, with a progressive widening of the horizon beyond the valley: 'it is true that the initial opposition to the Tav was at times simplistic and even egotistical: "they will throw me out of my house, they will make me leave the valley, how much value will my house lose?" ...', but later the belief spread that 'this is not a party question, nor only an environmental one, it has become an ethical and moral question, but we at first did not realize that' (Margaira, 2005: 118). In fact, instrumental frames lead the way to ethical ones. During the campaign, 'we automatically realized that at risk was not only our territory... [but] the death of a countryside and the foundation of collectivity: ethics, reciprocal respect' (2005: 123). Thus, latterly, the campaigns developed a global dimension. The campaign against the Tav is considered 'the first, concrete no-global struggle, not only in Italy but at European level. We do not say it, we do not like labels, but this is a no-global struggle, because we oppose an international project which overrides the rights of local communities' (IVS11). Similarly, 'an important component of the No Bridge movement is linked to the larger movement against neo-liberal globalisation' (IME4).

Diagnostic and Prognostic: What Progress?

> In contrast with the liberalist enunciations on the centrality of the market, it is public money (subtracted from public services) which is used to realise these large-scale public works (bridges, highways, tunnels, dams, power plants) which are then given, through privatisation, to economic groups that are collateral to the political class, whose essential contribution is to store away the profits. So then we have a repeat of the traditional passage from public money to private profit. On this level is evident the convergence of interests of powerful financiers, businessmen, politicians and Mafiosi, whose intertwining is now no longer a crime or even a scandal. (DME3)

Thus No Bridge activists recall another central feature of the symbolic construction of the conflict: the definition (not only in a negative sense) of the stakes. Snow and Benford (1988) talked of diagnostic frames, oriented to develop a new image of what is wrong, and prognostic frames, which suggest solutions for the identified problems. Opponents of LULUs have been said to privilege the value of their environment (use value) against 'growth machines' that instead stress the importance of economic development (exchange value). In this image, residents have a vested interest in defending their quality of life (health, cultural heritage), while economic investors (and often local politicians) push for their economic (and political) interests. The strength of the growth machines has been seen in their capacity to convince residents that economic development would have a positive spillover onto their lives as well. However, the definition of the interest of the citizen remains open to a symbolic struggle. The very conception of the public interest emerges in fact as central for Tav and bridge opponents, as well as their supporters.

In these two cases, as in other similar conflicts, opposition to large-scale public works is characterised by their supporters as maintaining 'archaic prejudices and cultural backwardness or instrumentalisation and political bad faith' (e.g. Borelli, 1999: 39). One of the frames used against those who protest is their assumed opposition to progress. In the anti-Tav struggle, on the centre–right Confalonieri (Forza Italia) speaks of a 'retrograde opposition to a work that is fundamental for the progress of the country' (*la Repubblica*, 30 November 2005), and the national secretary of DS (Left Democrats), Fassino, repeats that 'there is a cultural problem: we must fight against anti-scientific thinking, the irrationality of which generates fear' (*la Repubblica*, 7 February 2005). Similarly, Quilici, a famous documentarist of marine fauna and supporter of the bridge, called the struggle against it 'obscurantist: we cannot imagine the world will progress without constructions of this type. Rome was a village of brigands before the *Campidoglio* was realised or the bridge on the Tiber' (*la Gazzetta del Sud*, 23 January 2006).

The central theme of the supporters of large-scale public works is that economic development requires large strategic projects. At the local level, large-scale works are presented – in Piedmont, as in Calabria and Sicily – as necessary to break out of isolation. The regional minister Borioli insists that 'the infrastructure is indispensable for getting Piedmont out of the cul-de-sac in which it currently finds itself' (*la Repubblica*, 25 June 2005). At the national level, in a bipartisan manner, the minister of the centre–left government, Bersani, affirms that 'without a Turin-Lyon [link], the loss would be above all for the West of Italy', given that the Tav 'is a European choice which responds to a grand design' (*la Repubblica*, 3 November 2005). Also those who support the project of the bridge on the Messina Straits define it as being essential not only for the economic development of the immediate area, but of all the Italian South. The centre–right national government of that time strongly supported the bridge, Minister Lunardi defining it as 'a fundamental project for our South and strategic for communication links with Northern Europe and the Mediterranean' (*il Messaggero*, 13 March 2004), 'an epoch-making work. The largest of the 21st century ... thanks to which the South will return to the centre of the Mediterranean' (*Corriere della Sera*, 22 April 2004). The President of the Province of Catania, Raffaele Lombardo (leader of the centre–right 'Movement for Autonomy'), declared that we need 'to quickly build the bridge, which is the mother of all infrastructures, which will then make indispensable other infrastructural projects ...' (*Corriere della Sera*, 8 December 2005).

In light of these appraisals of the project, those who protest against the Tav and the bridge risk stigmatisation as opponents of progress. Rejecting this accusation, the activists affirm the necessity to privilege well-being (use value) above economic development (exchange value). The defence of public health is often invoked by citing doctors from Val di Susa who assert that 'there is the real possibility of severe damage to public health' (DVS2), highlighting the risks of tumours tied to asbestos (mesothelioma) and uranium (lymphoma), both of which are found in the ground which is to be excavated.

The image of living in the past and opposing progress is also contested through the elaboration of an alternative model of economic development. Quality of life is defended against works that are defined, in both North and South, as pharaonic, *anti-economic* and *useless*, as well as damaging for the territory. The anti-economic aspect of the work is supported by underlining its *incompatibility* with the characteristics of local development from tourism tied to agriculture and fishing. In an appeal for a general strike in Val di Susa we read: 'if the ecosystem is destroyed so will the economic structure of the area. The damage would be incalculable. The pollution caused by the asbestos dust would place in crisis the agricultural small and medium-sized industries of the area' (DVS5). Moreover, the protestors, citing data on the current use of the railway network and projections for future demand, emphasise the uselessness of building another line, and instead propose a much cheaper reconstruction of the existing line. Similarly, the No Bridge activists speak of a

> useless work, anti-economic and devastating, from a wrong era and in the wrong place. It could have been a good idea 40, 30 or 20 years ago, because it was a work that for better or worse had a certain 'image', but currently there is a situation that pushes not only Europe, but the whole world to rely on transport via sea, reducing the consumption of petrol, of car traffic, privileging forms of transport much less damaging than cars...they pretend that the city should have to adapt to the bridge rather than the bridge to the city. (IME1)

Moreover, protesters denounce the damage it would do to local economic activity, without bringing the lasting increases in employment claimed by those in favour of the project.

The promise of jobs is contrasted with the menace of unemployment. An activist of the 'CariddiScilla' coordination declared that 'the people of Messina, of the Straits, have discovered that the bridge barely interests them and it goes against their local interests, because it can only lose jobs, and is useless from the point of view of increasing employment' (IME2). In Val di Susa, a flyer of the rank-and-file trade union, Cobas, asserts that 'in the jungle of the neo-liberal market, investment does not produce work, but profit. Unless by work we mean the exploitation of precarious workers with the hours of a slave, without rights or defences' (DVS7).

In denouncing the economic damage large-scale public works do to local development, the *alternative use* of the territory is underlined (more socially just and ecologically sustainable). In the pro-Tav and pro-bridge statements, the project is considered to have 'zero cost', because it is financed externally (by EU or private companies). Investments in the Tav or in the bridge are never balanced against possible alternatives, and the risk of losing EU funding is stressed. Protesters, on the other hand, denounce the waste of resources which could be better used in other ways. 'Why not improve the old railway, today under-utilised and badly utilised, for transporting goods and commuters? The entrepreneurs who fight for Tav are private actors, but the money spent will be public' (*la Repubblica*, 12 August 2005). In the words of a flyer calling for a demonstration, 'public money is necessary first of all to improve local transport, social and health services, for research and for all those important things which instead they are cutting' (DVS6). Similar arguments are made by opponents of the bridge. A WWF activist denounced the 'insane costs to the state, even if they say these are private funds, up till now there haven't been any. They are funds left by IRI[1] which should have gone to the Treasury but instead are going to the SdM group, so it is public money. All of this despite other more impelling needs, the basic needs necessary to live in a dignified and civil way, for which they claim not to have a euro' (IME1). No Bridge asked, in various calls to demonstrate, that six billion euros allocated for the construction of the bridge should instead be invested in 'adapting and strengthening existing infrastructure in Calabria and Sicily' (DME18), and in particular for 'improving sustainable maritime mobility and reclaiming the coasts' (DME13).

To those who define them as backward and isolationist, No Tav protesters respond with a definition of themselves as being aware of the *future*. The flyer calling for the march from Susa to Venaus on 4 June 2005 called for 'Everybody to Susa to defend the future of our territory' (DVS3). In parallel, No Bridge campaigners observed that 'they say that we are "backward" and "against the future", as if a bridge of cement and steel were the future, given that they were being built 80 years ago, when people were still thinking about the society of automobiles' (IME4).

Thus the symbolic challenge targets the very definition of progress. If pro-Tav and pro-bridge define their investments as leading to progress, their opponents propose instead a different conception of progress: a *human* progress, against inhuman economic progress. The anarchists of FAI propose 'a more livable environment for a civilisation founded on people and not on profit, on the quality of life and not its speed' (DVS8). The protesters also develop a *critique of consumption*, which echoes the protest against growth, synthesised in the slogan: 'consume less, consume better', 'We cannot think of a world where economic growth continues. High-speed trains consume energy, in a world where energy is exhausting itself, destroying agricultural fields and historical panoramas' (Mercalli, activist and meteorologist, *la Repubblica*, 4 June 2005).

Thus interviews with the activists indicate a search for an alternative model of development which goes beyond 'sustainable development', calling for 'life at a low speed'. They state, 'We are in opposition to that very model, the violent way to impose their own interests, we want to live our life at a low speed, decently: we do not think that time is money. That is a principle of bosses. Time serves to live well, and also work must be a tool of well-being' (ISV10). In the struggle against the bridge, the definition of development is likewise placed under scrutiny: 'the idea of "development" which is being continuously imposed implies waste, incinerators, thermoelectric plants, large-scale public works and claims that these projects will be able to provide work for the poor unemployed in the South' (DME6). According to the metalworkers union, Fiom, 'we are the victims of an exclusive model of development. But these no longer convince us' (*la Repubblica*, 8 November 2005).

The interest in large-scale public works is framed as the interests of a few: 'money-makers', 'speculators' or even 'corrupt' and 'Mafiosi'. The supporters of the Tav are defined as 'businessmen' (DVS10), or the 'pro-Tav lobby' as 'gigantic speculators' (DVS7). It is 'a great idea for brick-layers or, as we call them, the "lobby of the reinforcing rod", who have decided that this work will certainly bring a lot of money into their business and so they developed this project and sold it to the politicians ... until we end up today with a right–left lobby in favour' (IVS5). The bridge is 'a business for a few people ... *the lobby of cement*, the club of large-scale works ... tied to political parties and accustomed to the sharing out [of public goods], to networks which nullify controls and competition, to exploiting [public] resources' (Mangano & Mazzeo, 2006: 14). Moreover, attention is drawn to 'the role of the Mafias: the infiltration of local crime which controls the territory through subcontracting and the attempt by the international Mafia to directly finance the work' (2006: 14).

Together with the notion of progress, the conception of general or national interest is here contested. An observer stated, 'We need to ask ourselves if it is not precisely the inhabitants of Val di Susa who, with their opposition to the Tav project, are carrying out the national interest' (Gallino, sociologist, *la Repubblica*, 7 November 2005). According to an activist, 'We are against those who accuse us of Nimbyism, for which our particularistic interest would be opposed to a general interest, to the common good. We need to define what is meant by common good, because here we are talking about old-fashioned speculative operations, in this case a classic show-piece construction project' (IME4).

Motivational Frames: The Rights of the Community, Mobilisation of the People

> It does not matter whether we win in the end; there is the idea that together we can do things ... It is not important that David wins, but that he has bridled Goliath for five minutes; if you bridled him for five minutes, you can bridle him for five hours and you can not be beaten. (IVS9)

The struggle between David and Goliath is often cited in the analysis of local conflicts. An important function of the framing process is that of producing motivations to act – i.e. giving people a reason to join the protest by convincing them that collective action is not only possible but also potentially successful (Snow & Benford, 1988). In this process, the stakes of the conflict expand to the meta-frames of democracy, as well as the right to protest (della Porta, 1999). As in other territorial conflicts, in our two cases the discourse extends to procedures: 'those opposing are able to transform the nature of the problem: it is no longer only the danger of the project that is in question, but also the correctness of the procedure that led to the decision about the siting of the project' (Bobbio, 1999: 189). Typically in local conflicts the rights of the local population to decide on large-scale public works is one of the main stakes. So too in our cases, when there is an open discussion about a LULU, normally the project 'is already tied to a specific site. They can discuss how, but not "where"' (Bobbio, 1999: 193) or, in our cases, 'how', but not 'whether'; a discursive strategy of the promoters of large-scale public works is that of the 'accomplished fact'.

Those who oppose these works must therefore articulate in a credible manner a discourse that points towards the action, by accentuating a sense of injustice, and by spreading the belief that an alternative *is* possible.

In the case of Val di Susa, it is above all the Piedmont and national politicians of the centre–left who seek to limit the role of the mayors, who are all against the Tav. The President of the Region, Bresso (DS), asserts that 'the decision on whether the work will be undertaken is a decision for Europe, the two states involved, and the two regions involved. The choice on how to do it, with what guarantees for the population involved, with which characteristics for the building sites, is a choice that must involve the inhabitants and the local politicians of Val di Susa' (*la Repubblica*, 15 November 2005). Similarly, the promoters of the bridge reply to the No Bridge dissidents by suggesting that their 'criticisms are based on slogans without technical, environmental, socioeconomic or financial foundations. These are in fact statements which contrast with the evidence of facts, with what is stipulated in the project, with the approval from the competent authorities, with the valuation of the Government, the Italian and European Parliaments' (*il Giornale di Sicilia*, 22 January 2006).

In reaction to this, one of the first frames used in Val di Susa by those protesting underlined the rights of local politicians to represent their territory. In the demonstration of 30 May 2002, the president of the *Comunità Montana*, Ferrentino, declared that 'they cannot ignore the views of locally elected officials' (*la Repubblica*, 1 June 2003). Brought together in Piazza Castello (Turin), 37 local councillors asked for the involvement of local bodies, protesting at not having been minimally involved (*la Repubblica*, 20 March 2005). Although local politicians on the Messina Straits are divided in their attitude towards the bridge, the inclusion of the local communities in decision-making is also an often used frame. According to the activist of the WWF, the bridge 'violates all the norms on democracy. The *Legge Obiettivo* is everything but democratic: they passed it to realise their public works more quickly, but they thus excluded local communities from the decision-making process' (IME1). The claim becomes the right to self-determination: 'the problem is to change the criteria by which choices become imposed in the territory, as if they were colonies, whereas we are firmly convinced that territories must be subject to the judgment of the people who inhabit them, and that they should decide their own programmes and their own future' (IME4).

The lack of democratic procedure in the allocation of large-scale public works is denounced by both No Tav and No Bridge but the development of a meta-discourse on democracy goes beyond the involvement of local politicians and populations. It is the very conception of democracy that is put under scrutiny. The demand for democracy is the demand for another type of democracy – more participatory and 'from below'. In the No Tav protest, the rights of the community to decide their own fate are claimed in the name of the people; it is no coincidence that the organisers choose names such as 'Committee for the Popular Struggle Against High-Speed Trains' or '*Spinta dal Bass*' (Push from Below). During the march of 15,000 against the 'militarisation' of Val di Susa, a participant declared on the megaphone: 'It is immoral to keep all these men here to guard a peaceful valley. This is not an emergency, this is participatory democracy' (*la Repubblica*, 6 November 2005). A document of the '*Rete Meridionale Nuovo Municipio*' asserts 'that which is defined as a particularistic interest – whether it be of the community of Val di Susa or the area of the Straits – is instead the expression of the sovereignty of the people who live within that territory, reclaiming their legitimacy to decide their future and that of their children' (DME16).

In this discourse, participatory democracy does not exclude representative democracy, but modifies it, disconnecting it from 'delegation'. As an anti-Tav professor put it:

> participatory democracy is not always easy. It is easier for citizens to delegate, because they no longer have to bother, and for politicians to be delegated, since they do not have to repeat the same thing three times: they aim at the common good, but only one or a few friends decide. Participatory democracy means to have ideas, but before implementing them, to discuss them with citizens in assemblies and other meeting places. (IVS9)

The theme of democracy re-emerges also in terms of the rights to protest as a form of citizens' participation, in opposition to the stigmatisation of the protesters as violent rioters. The violence frame was utilised in particular by the pro-Tav lobby in autumn 2005, faced with the growth of direct action. Even the theme of danger to public security echoes on both right and left. On the right, the former Prime Minister, Berlusconi, alleged that 'antagonistic extreme left groups and anarcho-insurrectionalists are trying to extend the disorder from Val di Susa to Turin, Milan, Rome, and various other cities' (*la Repubblica*, 8 December 2005). On the left, Fassino condemned the 'violent methods of the anti-Tav protesters', who are attacking 'a well-considered project that will guarantee development, growth, work and well-being' (*la Repubblica*, 7 November 2005). A symbolic conflict about the democratic right to participate emerges around the conception of legality. For pro-Tav politicians in Piedmont, the protest becomes illegitimate if opposed to the decisions of the majority. 'Democracy works like this. You discuss issues and then, without abandoning your initial views, you must accept the decision of the majority. If someone does not want to do that, and instead decides to lay bombs, they thus exclude themselves thus from civil society' (Bresso (DS), *la Repubblica*, 11 May 2005). The frame of violence and illegality has been used also by the supporters of the bridge. The daily *La Gazzetta del Sud*, one of the main supporters and sponsors of the bridge, has accused the 'eco-pacifists' opposed to the bridge of responsibility for a series of explosions, that caused no damage to people or buildings, on the coast of north Messina in February 2004. A No Bridge interviewee remembers that 'they threw mud at us, saying that it was the movement against the bridge, which had nothing to do with it; and then they found those responsible, who had nothing to do with us, but in the process they sought to portray us as terrorists' (IME1).

The theme of public security is defined by those who oppose large infrastructures as being instrumentalised to discredit an opposition which has persistently chosen peaceful means. However, given the mass participation in protest, No Tav activists consider the labelling of 'bad protestors' ineffective. An interviewee remembers: 'to the attempt at criminalising us, Grillo [a famous comic actor involved in environmental campaigns] answered when, during a demonstration, he pointed to an elderly woman shouting: "You, anarcho-insurrectionalist, what are you doing here?" The limits of the ridiculous have been overcome' (IVS3). Defending their right to protest in Turin (whose mayor had sought to ban the procession on 17 December, stating that there were not 'the conditions for a peaceful protest'), a mayor of the valley repeated that 'it was precisely the large demonstrations that allowed the possibility of mediation' (*la Repubblica*, 9 December 2005). In a similar manner, the support of local politicians has a strong legitimising value, reducing the credibility of those who describe the protesters as violent.

The right to protest is here defended not only as legitimate, but also as ethically central: 'Our force is the anger of the meek' (*la Repubblica*, 3 December 2003). The petition of the Turin Committee expressing support for Val di Susa (DVS6) invites us to find 'the famous grain of sand capable of stalling the powerful motor', praising the 'great lesson of participatory democracy' in Val di Susa. As an activist writes, 'We do not have hope, we do have certainties; we are only grains of sand but we are many, we have no secondary aims, we are not against progress and in this campaign we have made very few mistakes' (Margaira, 2005: 132).

It is precisely on the meta-frame of the right to protest that the statements of solidarity for the inhabitants of the valley multiply beyond the valley. Numerous national associations promote a petition to 'block the unacceptable violence against the protestors', defending 'their democratic right to protest in a peaceful manner' (DVS16). On the issue of a different democracy, these protests also show the alliance between Val di Susa and the Messina Straits.

Concluding Remarks

Our attention here has focused on framing processes, which we conceived not only as important strategic instruments for mobilisation, but also as mechanisms of fundamental importance in the construction of the identity of those who protest. We have suggested that the opposing portrayals of LULU conflicts either as egotistical NIMBY protests, or as expressive mobilisations of a social conflict about the relative use or exchange value of territory, both consider the values, interests and preferences of actors as exogenous, concentrating instead on the capacity of these interest representatives to mobilise organisational resources and allies.

In our analysis, we have instead focused on the emergence of these values, interests and preferences through a symbolic conflict which itself defines identity, stakes and motivations. We have analysed the tensions around three important levels of definition of the actor and the action. In the definition of the identity of the actor we observe on the one hand an elaboration of the positive identity of the community (strongest above all in Val di Susa, around the idea of a valley which currently resists a 'useless and damaging' public work, as it had in the past resisted fascism), and on the other hand, the search for universal values, finally arriving at a global definition of the conflict. Against their opponents, who accuse them of manifesting the NIMBY syndrome, the protesters respond through a symbolic construction which values the community, but without making it an object of exclusive identification.

In search of a definition of the public good, their framing of the dispute tends to supersede the dichotomy between defence of nature and economic development by constructing an alternative model of progress. While the themes of the health of citizens and the value of the natural environment are both present (as in many other local conflicts), significant attention is focused on defining the struggle as being one oriented to the future rather than to the past. To those who accuse them of wanting to block 'large-scale public works', which are 'strategic' for local and global economic development, those who protest in Val di Susa and the Messina Straits respond by presenting these works not only as damaging from the point of view of health and nature, but also from the point of view of economic progress. By opposing a single model of economic development focused on large-scale investments, they underline the value of local economies, and even propose models of 'de-development' in order to defend not only the environment, but also levels of employment and quality of life. Against projects that are frequently defined as being 'cost-free', because they are presented as externally financed, opponents underline instead the waste of public money, and suggest alternative uses for it. It is thus the conception of general interest which is at the centre of these symbolic conflicts, where activists reject accusations of egotism (typical of the NIMBY syndrome). In the discourse of the protestors, the strategic interests defended by the promoters of these 'large-scale public works' are presented as the interests of speculators (corrupt in Val di Susa, mafia in the Messina Straits), while the protesters propose themselves as the true interpreters of the general interest.

Last but not least, the motivational frames underline the possibility of changing decisions, which are often presented as being 'already taken', through the collective mobilisation of citizens. Together with the assertion of a political decentralisation which takes into account the rights of local communities to take decisions which will affect their own destiny, there is the increasingly explicit affirmation of a different conception of democracy, based on participation rather than delegation. This 'good' politics is presented as coming from below, made by citizens rather than professional politicians, and based on local knowledge rather than the 'bureaucratic expertise' of representative institutions.

Are all the frames elaborated by the protesters only instrumental? Could it be that regressive aims are masked within a discourse of alternative progress? Stressing the presence of all the mentioned elements in the narratives of the protest does not of course automatically translate into a disconfirmation of the presence of selfish interests that might be instrumentally hidden behind a more ethical discourse. The search for 'true motives' is difficult in empirical research focusing on collective frames. However, we have shown that the definition of some fundamental values as the general good, progress, future or democracy is fundamentally contested. The protest arena is indeed also (sometimes mainly) as a space for symbolic struggle over meanings, identities, interests.

In addition the evolution of the conflict, through the interaction of different actors, involves complex shifts in the symbolic scale of the protest. A growth in generality is a symbolic process which facilitates interactions between different actors. The evolution from a local to a global definition of the conflict, the elaboration of images that show an alternative future and a different conception of the general interest, the presentation of these actions of protests as the laboratory for an alternative conception of politics and a more appropriate definition of democracy, all take place in the course of these campaigns. They emerge as diverse actors join the protest (della Porta & Piazza, 2008). Committees and local politicians, social centres and trade unions, environmental associations and social forums, all meet, network and bridge their more specific frames in the course of the protest. Above all, changes in the symbolic construction of identity, the stakes and the motivations for action, appear to link the protest campaigns in Val di Susa and the Messina Straits with the mobilisation of the movement for globalisation from below or 'global justice movement'.

Note

1. IRI (Istituto di Ricostruzione Industriale) was a state-owned entity.

References

Bobbio, L. (1999) 'Un processo equo per una localizzazione equa', in L. Bobbio & A. Zeppetella (eds.), *Perché proprio qui? Grandi opere e opposizioni locali* (Milano: Franco Angeli).
Borelli, G. (1999) 'Davide contro Golia. L'inceneritore Fenice a Verrone', in L. Bobbio & A. Zeppetella (eds.), *Perché proprio qui? Grandi opere e opposizioni locali*, pp. 15–52 (Milano: Franco Angeli).
Buso, G. (1996) 'Resistenze e proteste contro le decisioni del governo locale: i comitati spontanei di cittadini', in L. Bobbio & F. Ferraresi (eds.), *Decidere in Comune, Analisi e riflessioni su cento decisioni comunali*, pp. 126–41 (Fondazione Rosselli: Torino).

della Porta, D. (1999) 'Protest, protesters and protest policing', in M. Giugni, D. McAdam & C. Tilly (eds.), *How Movements Matter*, pp. 66–96 (Minneapolis: University of Minnesota Press).

della Porta, D. (2003) 'Social movements and democracy at the turn of the millennium', in P. Ibarra (ed.), *Social Movements and Democracy*, pp. 105–36 (New York: Palgrave Macmillan).

della Porta, D. (2004) 'Comitati cittadini e democrazia urbana: una introduzione', in D. della Porta (ed.), *Comitati cittadini e democrazia urbana*, pp. 7–41 (Soveria Mannelli: Rubbettino).

della Porta, D. & Diani, M. (1997) *I movimenti sociali* (Roma: Carocci) [in English: *Social Movements: An Introduction* (Oxford: Blackwell, 1999; 2nd edn 2006)].

della Porta, D. & Diani, M. (with the collaboration of M. Andretta) (2004) *Movimenti senza protesta? L'ambientalismo in Italia* (Bologna: il Mulino).

della Porta, D. & Mosca, L. (2006) 'In movimento. Contamination in action and the Italian global justice movement', *Global Networks: A Journal of Transnational Affairs* 7(1): 1–28.

della Porta, D. & Piazza, G. (2008) *Voices of the Valley, Voices of the Strait: How Protest Create Community* (Berghahn, in press).

Elkin, S. (1987) *City and Regime* (Chicago: University of Chicago Press).

Gamson, W. A. (1988) 'Political discourse and collective action', *International Social Movement Research* 1: 219–44.

Gordon, C. & Jasper, J. M. (1996) 'Overcoming the "nimby" label: rhetorical and organizational links for local protestors', *Research in Social Movements, Conflicts and Change* 19: 159–81.

Gould, K. A., Schnaiberg, A. & Weinberg, A. S. (1996) *Local Environmental Struggles. Citizen Activism in the Treadmill of Production* (Cambridge: Cambridge University Press).

Levine, M. (1989) 'The politics of partnership. Urban redevelopment since 1945', in G. Squires (ed.), *Unequal Partnership* (New Brunswick, NJ: Rutgers University Press).

Lichtermann, P. (1996) *The Search for Political Community: American Activists Reinventing Tradition* (Cambridge: Cambridge University Press).

Logan, J. R. & Molotch, H. L. (1987) *Urban Fortunes: The Political Economy of Place* (Berkeley: University of California Press).

Mangano, A. & Mazzeo, A. (2006) *Il mostro sullo Stretto. Sette ottimi motivi per non costruire il Ponte* (Ragusa: Sicilia Punto L/terrelibere.org).

Margaira, O. (2005) *Adesso o mai più* (Borgone Susa: Edizioni del Graffio).

Pizzorno, A. (1993) *Le radici della politica assoluta* (Milano: Feltrinelli).

Sebastiani, C. (2001) 'Comitati di cittadini e spazi pubblici urbani', *Rassegna Italiana di Sociologia* 42: 77–114.

Snow, D. & Benford, R. (1988) 'Ideology, frame resonance, and participant mobilization', *International Social Movement Research* 1: 197–217.

Stone, C. (1993) 'Urban regimes and the capacity to govern', *Journal of Urban Affairs* 15: 1–28.

Thomas, J. C. & Savitch, H. (1991) 'Introduction: big city politics, then and now', in H. Savitch & J. C. Thomas (eds.), *Big City Politics in Transition* (Newbury Park, CA: Sage).

Trom, D. (1999) 'De la réfutation de l'effet NIMBY considérée comme une pratique militante: notes pour une approche pragmatique de l'activité revendicative', *Revue Française de sciences politique* 49: 31–50.

Williams, B. A. & Matheny, A. R. (1995) *Democracy, Dialogue and Environmental Disputes. The Contested Languages of Social Regulation* (New Haven: Yale University Press).

Interviews

IME1: A. Giordano, WWF – Southern Italy, Messina, 9 May 2005.

IME2: C. Pigneri, Coordination 'CariddiScilla' – Ds, Messina, 9 May 2005.

IME3: S. Visicaro, committee 'La Nostra Città' – 'Messinasenzaponte', Messina, 14 May 2005.

IME4: M. Camarata, 'Laboratorio contro il ponte' – Coordination 'Rete No Ponte', Messina, 12 December 2005.

IVS1: Chiara, Centro Sociale Askatasuna, Val di Susa, 16 February 2006.

IVS2: C. Scarinzi, secretary of CUB, Val di Susa, 16 February 2006.

IVS3: G. De Masi, Provincial Councillor of Greens, Val di Susa, 16 February 2006.

IVS4: M. Piccione, Comitato Spinta dal Bass di Avigliana, Val di Susa, 15 February 2006.

IVS5: P. Coperchio, Legambiente Piemonte, and G. Richetto, university professir, Val di Susa, 15 February 2006.

IVS6: O. Casagrande, journalist 'Il Manifesto', Val di Susa, 15 February 2006.

IVS9: M. Clerico, university professor of Environmental Security at Politecnico of Turin, Val di Susa, 17 February 2006.

IVS10: N. Dosio, Secretary of the PRC section of Bussoleno-Val di Susa, Val di Susa, 17 February 2006.

IVS11: G. Vighetti, Comitato di Lotta Popolare contro l'alta velocità di Bussoleno, Val di Susa, 16 February 2006.

Documents

DME1: *'Perché prevalga la saggezza'*. Appeal of the 'Tra Scilla e Cariddi' Committee, 16 June 1988, Calabria.

DME3: *Accoglimento Proposta del SFE di Firenze per la realizzazione del Campeggio Internazionale contro il Ponte sullo Stretto da realizzarsi a Messina-Villa S. Giovanni 28/7–2/8 2003*. MSF–RSR–Coordinamento Calabrese contro il Ponte, 1 March 2003. Available at: www.No Ponte.org

DME6: Press release, *Convocazione del 2° Campeggio Internazionale contro il Ponte sullo Stretto, 2–8/8/2004*. Area dello stretto, 18 January 2004. Available at: www.No Ponte.org

DME13: *Documento conclusivo del 4° Corteo nazionale contro il Ponte*. ReteNoPonte 2005, Messina, 6 August 2005. Available at: www.terrelibere.org

DME16: *Mozione finale dell'Assemblea della Rete Meridionale Nuovo Municipio/No Ponte*. Reggio Calabria, 10 December 2005. Available at: www.terrelibere.org

DME17: *Per il gemellaggio NO TAV – NO PONTE*. Coordinamento NoPonte – RMNM. Reggio Calabria, 29 December 2005. Available at: www.reteNo Ponte.org

DME18: *Appeal 'TUTTI A MESSINA – 22/1/2006 – PER DIFENDERE LO STRETTO'*. ReteNoPonte. Messina, 5 January 2006. Available at: www.messinasenzaponte.it

DME21: *'L'opposizione del popolo dello Stretto. Il referendum anticentrale'*, in A. D'Agostino (a cura di), *Lo Stretto di Messina. Il ponte insostenibile e le sue alternative*, in 'Quaderni del sud – quaderni calabresi', special issue, 98–99, December 2005–March 2006.

DVS1: Coordinamento dei comitati no tav valle di susa, Torino e Gronda Ovest, *Il 6 e 7 ottobre a Venaus non devono entrare*, leaflet, 29 September 2005.

DVS2: Appello medici di base valsusini, *TAV: amianto e uranio*, petition, 30 May 2004.

DVS3: Comunità montana alta Val di Susa, comunità montana bassa Val di Susa, Conferenza dei sindaci della Val di Susa e della 'Grotta Ovest' di Torino, Comitati No Tav, Ass. Col diretti, Ass. Montagna Nostra, Legambiente, WWF, Pronatura, Arci Val di Susa, Associazioni ambienta-liste, Sabato *4 giugno 2005: Tutti a Susa*, leaflet.

DVS5: Petizione dei lavoratori della Val di Susa, *Decidiamo il nostro futuro*, petition.

DVS6: Coordinamento torinese No Tav . . ., *Sabato 17 dicembre: Manifestazione No-Tav a Torino*, leaflet.

DVS7: Cobas Scuola Torino, *Contro i treni ad alta velocità, sciopero di popolo in Val di Susa*, leaflet, 16 November 2005.

DVS8: Federazione Anarchici Italiani Torino, *Fermiamo il treno della morte*, 11 April 2005, leaflet.

DVS10: No Tav. *Appello degli artisti*, press release, 4 November 2005.

DVS16: Arci *et al.*, Stop subito alla violenza in Val di Susa, s.d.

Index

Page numbers in *italics* refer to tables.

protest event analysis (PEA) 3, 9–10,
68, 69, 70–9, 125, 130–3
protest waves 71, 79
public good 155, 159
public money 153–4
public works, Val di Susa TAV and
Messina Straits Bridge 12, 144–60
Purdue, D. *et al.* 49, 53

Rajal del Gorp 111, 114, 116
Rau, N. 37, 38
recruitment to direct action group
94–5
regional organisations 16, 25, 27,
29–30, 31–2
regionalist front, constitution of
111–12
religious commitment 110–11, 113–14
research methodologies 3
resistance culture 102
resources: exchange network 50;
strategic imperatives and 22–4
Rete Meridionale del Nuovo Municipio
('Southern Network for a New
Municipalism') 145
Rete No Ponte ('No Bridge Network')
145
rights of community 155–8, 159
road campaigns 23, 37–8, 90, 91, 92,
96, 100, 102
Rootes, C. 11, 15, 16, 17, 19, 46, 65, 66,
68, 85–6, 88, 108, 125, 129; *et al.* 6
Roquefort cheese 109, 115, 117, 118,
119
Rossport natural gas refinery, County
Mayo, Ireland 11, 13–14, 15,
133–40

sabotage 99–100
sacred space of contention 109–17
Sartori, C. 34–5, 37
Schlosberg, D. 4, 19, 24
Schnews, UK 89–90
Schofield, R. 39
Sebastiani, C. 146

semiotisation: appropriation of space
112–15
Sewell, W.H. 107, 119
Shell 97, 127, 134–5, 136
Snow, D. 117; & Benford, R. 148, 151
social forums 17
social movements 45–7, 100, 125–6;
dynamics 54–60; and interest
groups 146–7; and political parties
66, 67, 70, 79, processes 48
social structure, transformation and
147
'socio-territorial mobilisation' 107–8
'soft' and 'hard' protest waves 71, 79
space *see* place/space
squatting 111, 112, 113, 114
staff 27–8, 30–1
Stearns, L.B. & Almeida, P. 65, 66,
68, 79
supportive networks 33–6, 74, 75, 78
'sustainable development' 154
sustaining direct action (EDA)
102–3
SYN (Coalition of the Left,
Movements and Ecology) 67, 71

Tarrow, S. 62, 66, 100, 102
TAV, Val di Susa and Messina Straits
Bridge, Italy 12, 144–60
taxes 115, 118, 119
Thornhill, P. 34, 37–8
Tilly, C. 46, 66, 68, 100, 101
Torrance, J. 33–4
Tovey, H. 128, 140–1; & Share, P.
127, 141
trade unions 74, 110, 118–19, 153, 154
transformation and social structure
147
transformative event 118–20
travelling to protests 92–4
triangulated research method 24–5
triple bridge of environmentalist
rhetoric 109
Twyford Down M3 extension 23,
37–8